THE RESTORATION OF ANTIQUE AND CLASSIC CARS

The Restoration of
ANTIQUE
and
CLASSIC
CARS

BY

Richard C. Wheatley
and Brian Morgan

With drawings by
R. F. Neale

ROBERT BENTLEY, Inc
872 Massachusetts Avenue
Cambridge, Massachusetts 02139

First published in the United States of America
1964

FIFTH EDITION, 1975

ISBN 0–8376–0135–5

Library of Congress Catalog Card Number 74—25850

Manufactured in the United States of America

PREFACE

THE interest in old cars has been steadily increasing for the past ten years. As cars of the Vintage period are generally used by their owners for a considerable mileage each year, it is inevitable that these remaining examples of the 1919–1930 era must gradually deteriorate. The collector who is lucky enough to find a Vintage motor-car which has lain unused for many years in a remote coach-house will also generally find that time has taken its toll. Others even less fortunate will find the motor-car of their dreams lying in a field or breaker's yard, with possibly a van or hearse body in place of the original coachwork.

It is the purpose of this book to show how an amateur may restore his car to at least as good a condition as that in which the makers sold it many years ago. Those who wish to put their car into "Show Model" condition, without in any way altering its original character, will also find guidance.

This book describes the complete overhaul and restoration of a motor-car carried out to the limit of the Authors' abilities. They must admit, however, to being fortunate enough to possess well-equipped workshops and to having access to outside help from their many friends in Birmingham. The reader will have to decide just how far he will go in the detail of his restoration depending on his own circumstances. Wherever possible, names of firms who will give help, or whose products have been found particularly suitable, are mentioned, their full particulars being given in Appendix IV.

Our description has obviously had to be general and does not apply to any specific make of car. Each make has its peculiarities and the potential restorer will be well advised to join the one-make club, or register, should such exist, specialising in his particular car. The Secretaries of such clubs can generally put members in touch with sources of information and spare parts which it would be impossible to include in a book such as this.

Anyone possessing a natural aptitude for the use of hand tools and who has a little outside help on machining and the more specialised trades, can make a presentable restoration. The first-class rebuild really does require a good workshop and considerable help from outside. The work cannot be done cheaply but, as it is bound to take a long time, the expense tends to spread itself out and the Bank Manager to get used to the overdraft.

The satisfaction of having done a good job is something which can only be understood when it is experienced, and the Authors hope that this book will help at least a few on the way to that delight.

Birmingham,   R.C.W.
July, 1957   B.M.

5

CONTENTS

CONTENTS

8

CONTENTS

LIST OF ILLUSTRATIONS

THE PLATES
Between pages 96 and 97

DRAWINGS IN THE TEXT

ACKNOWLEDGMENT

THE Authors and the Publishers wish to record their grateful thanks to the following for their permission to reproduce the photographs which appear in this book:

Mr. Charles Dunn, Woking, for Plate IX.

Messrs. Saga Services Ltd., Birmingham, for Plates IV to VIII, X and XI.

Mr. Frank Wheatley, for Plates II and III.

They are also much indebted to Mr. Ralph Buckley, of The Antique Auto Shop, Northfield, New Jersey, and to Mrs. E. Ann Klein, of Klein Kars, Elizabethtown, Pennsylvania, for kindly supplying the information from which the American Appendices have been compiled.

CHAPTER I

THE CHOICE OF A CAR TO RESTORE

CHOOSING a car to restore is a most enjoyable pastime, particularly for your friends, as it is not marred by any financial worries for them. You should not lack both cheery and helpful company when you journey forth to seek the car of your dreams.

This chapter applies particularly to novices. We do not presume to instruct experienced buyers but to provide a little guidance to those who have not bought this type of car before. Do not allow yourself to be rushed, and get as much good advice as you can. Also give the subject plenty of thought and, above all, make sure it really is the car you will like when you have spent many hours, and possibly a considerable amount of money, on its restoration.

Type of Car

The first consideration is to decide on the type of car you require. Is it to be a really stark sports car, in which performance is the only object, or will it be a tourer or limousine? Again, is it to be large or small? Your choice of size, unfortunately, will be affected by the garage space which you have available. If the car is too large for the space and you do not have enough working room, the restoration is likely to become a misery. You will also have to bear in mind the amount you will be using the car. A large car having a much more lightly stressed engine is unlikely to be so worn as a small and possibly under-engined one. All the other parts will most likely be far more robust, and, what is even more important, the larger type of car is generally of much higher quality. There are of course exceptions to this rule. A smaller type will probably be more expensive to buy, owing to its lower running costs. For instance, note the price of, say, a Bentley 3-litre and a 40/50 Rolls-Royce of the same date and condition. The former has a petrol consumption of about 20 m.p.g. and the latter about 12 m.p.g. If your annual mileage is not likely to be very great, the total buying and running costs may be about the same on either car over a considerable period. You must, of course, also take the cost of tires into consideration.

Remember that there were good and bad cars made in all periods. Do not be led astray into thinking that one built between 1919–1931 is bound to be good merely because it is Vintage. A word of warning here may be helpful. Do not expect too much performance from the Vintage touring type of car. Compared with most mass-produced modern cars it will

13

appear rather sluggish. The compensation will be in the ownership of a fine piece of machinery.

A beginner would be well advised to join the Vintage Sports-Car Club as this is a club dealing with all makes and, today, all types, not merely sports cars. There are also a number of "one-make" clubs, one of which may specialise in your particular choice. A list of these clubs will be found in Appendix II.

Having joined the club, you will meet experienced members who will be able to give you a great deal of information. You will be able to examine different makes at meetings and possibly try them on the road, which will be a great help in your ultimate choice.

When you have made up your mind on the make and model, try to ride in, or better still, drive the same type. Although possibly you have always admired this particular car, you may be very disappointed when you do drive it. It is most important that the car you have chosen does in fact suit you in every way, otherwise you will not have the necessary inspiration to carry out the complete restoration. Neither will you get the pleasure which you deserve when it is finished.

The beginner will be well advised to choose a make of car of which there are still plenty in existence. In this case, not only are spares more likely to be available, but the car must have been reliable to have lasted in quantity so long. Most important, you will meet so many more knowledgeable friends with the same make.

It is erroneously believed in some quarters that two-wheel brakes are illegal. Not only is this a misconception, but they can be quite efficient when well restored and adjusted. Care must be taken, particularly when driving on wet or icy roads, but some of the early four-wheel brakes were no better than really good two-wheel brakes.

If, however, you have had considerable experience and are determined to give yourself a really difficult job, it is most exciting to try to find an only example of a rare make, such as one of the earlier racing cars. In this case take plenty of time and give the car a very thorough examination, bearing in mind your workshop facilities and bank balance.

If you find anything very grim there will be no chance of getting even secondhand spares, and replacements will be very expensive. The 1914 Grand Prix Opel which we once owned is a good example of this. The cylinder-block required a re-bore and as there were no data available, it was impossible to know that the cylinder walls were far too thin. The result was that on test a part of the wall broke away into the water-jacket, there was an hydraulic lock and the block was smashed. The cost of a new block was about £600. Gear-wheels, particularly spiral bevels, are also very expensive and parts such as crankshafts and connecting-rods are almost impossible to make or buy. In a case such as this, do try to drive the car before buying it. Maybe the car is the only survivor because it is so poor that it is not worth having. If so, it is much better forgotten.

14

It may be, however, if the car is very rare, that the pleasure derived from the finished product may depend more on its uncommonness than on its perfection of handling.

Finding the Car

The next most important problem is how and where to find the car. This is one of the great advantages of being in the right club, as you may easily hear of it from one of the members, or read of it in the V.S.C.C. and other club circulars. If you are looking for a Vintage or Thoroughbred car, a likely place to find its whereabouts is the small advertisement section in *Motor Sport* or *The Veteran and Vintage Magazine*. You will generally only find Thoroughbreds in *The Motor* or *The Autocar*. If you have made up your mind what you require and cannot find it in any of the above sources, it is always worthwhile putting an advertisement in one of these papers for the model you want. This also applies to spare parts and even a body if the car, when you have bought it, is lacking in this respect.

Examination before Purchase

Having located the car, take with you a knowledgeable friend, preferably one who has had experience of the particular make. He will be a great help in giving it a thorough examination and a steadying influence if you are too keen. Try to drive the car if it is at all possible. This is far better than just going for a run in it, especially if you have never driven that type of car before. There is nothing more annoying than, after months of hard work, to find that although you have a car which is a thing of beauty, you hate every minute you spend driving it.

At this stage a word of warning will not be out of place from those who have suffered at least once. Do not allow your enthusiasm to be so wild that you will take on the role of salesman as well as buyer, and sell yourself an absolute heap for a large sum of money. Allow yourself plenty of time and compare the price with others advertised, if possible. We once bought a car which was in such a shocking state that we had to work on it all after-noon before it was fit for us to buy. We then had a journey home of two hundred miles during which everything went wrong, including boiling all the water away in the middle of the night, miles from anywhere. We eventually found a night watchman on a new water main, only to be told when we awakened him that he could not find us even half a pint. The journey finished at 5.30 in the morning after the last eighty miles in thick fog. This is a bright example of how not to buy a car, yet it must be admitted that we look back on it as one of the most amusing trips. In this case only parts of the chassis were actually required for a very extensive rebuild. The one who had the work in hand was so badly bitten by the bug that he could not wait to find the separate pieces.

When examining the car remember that the condition must be related to the availability of spares, either new or secondhand. A list of manufacturers who can still supply at least some spares for their older models will be found in Appendix VI. Also bear in mind your workshop equipment, and your chances and the cost of getting parts made and jobs done by an expert. For instance, if chassis work is no trouble to you but bodywork has to be done out, then a worn-out car with all the wings undented and a good hood and upholstery is better than a poor body on a recently overhauled chassis. In any case, if you propose to do a complete rebuild, you might just as well save money by buying a really rough one so long as it is complete, with no major parts broken. If, however, you have no very great facilities, and you do not wish to do much in the way of rebuilding but only cleaning, repainting and adjusting, then it will be much cheaper for you to try and find a car in really good condition and pay a greater price for it. Unless you are very lucky you will either have to pay hard or work hard.

On giving the engine an external inspection, beware of plates on the side of the engine where they are not standard, as this probably indicates that a rod has been thrown or the water-jacket cracked. Look for deep corrosion on the chassis frame, brake drums, steering-arms and other exposed surfaces, as this will be almost sure to have caused irreparable damage. A chassis which is well covered in thick black grease and oil is usually found to be in much better condition than one which is painted over rust. Check the steering-arms for symmetry and the steering-box for play, as if this is not adjustable it may be very expensive to put into good condition. Listen for unpleasant noises from the engine, examine the radiator for leaks—this is a repair which it is unlikely that you will be able to do yourself and may be very expensive. Make sure that all the gears are there and that the gear-box and back axle are not too noisy. How much play is there in the propeller-shaft? Jack up the front wheels and check the king-pins and hub bearings for wear. Note if the wheels run true, and have the car driven past you, slowly, to check this. And last of all, drive behind the car to check for chassis straightness. Ask if there is an Instruction Book.

Bringing the Car Home

Having bought the car, and if it cannot be driven and you have a long way to tow, a rigid tow-bar is an absolute joy, especially as the brakes may be very poor and the driver will be new to the car. Also, being towed a long way by a rope is very tiring. It is not too difficult to make a tow-bar, but if this cannot be managed and a rope is the only thing, then take a third person with you. He will be able to watch the towed one and, by noting the degree of petrifaction in his expression, will have knowledge in advance of impending trouble and, thereby, may be able to avert disaster. If the car is to be towed, travel a short distance in gear with the clutch out to circulate the gear box oil.

If the car is to be driven, check the oil in the engine, gear-box and back axle and see that the oil pump is working. Make sure that the radiator holds water and that the fan and water pump, if fitted, are working properly.

Examine the steering, tires and brakes and, if necessary, adjust the brakes. Should the journey be likely to finish in the dark make sure that the lights all work and that the dynamo is charging, otherwise you may have to leave the car somewhere with the journey incomplete. Regardless of whether the car is to be driven or towed, do take a set of tools. In addition to a set of spanners and the other usual tools, and unless you know for certain that the car will include this item, you should have a jack. If the car has Dunlop wheels take the correct spanner, and if Rudge wheels, a copper hammer, or a C-spanner if it has the non-eared type of locking ring. An electric torch may also be very useful. Failure to provide these very necessary tools may result in irreparable damage being done to the car if you should have a breakdown or puncture.

Listing the Work to be Done

If possible drive the car as bought, before dismantling, for at least a month and during this time give it a very careful examination. Make notes of any peculiarities which need rectifying. Look for leaks of all kinds—air, oil, petrol and water. Adjust the brakes and then test them for efficiency. After oiling the steering and inflating the tires to the correct pressure, note if the steering feels correct. If it does not, it may of course be due to the wheels being out of balance. Check if there is enough castor action. The charging rate and cutting-in speed of the dynamo should be examined, and also the reliability of the starter motor. Make notes also of any modifications you will want to carry out, not only with regard to the performance of the car but also with regard to the driver's comfort. Try out the lighting at night and decide on the type of dashboard and position of instruments to give good visibility as well as good looks. Make sure that the windscreen does not have any blind spots, that the controls are handy and the seating is comfortable. The steering-wheel position, if it does not suit you, will take all the pleasure out of driving. Unless it is adjustable, it will certainly have to be modified during the restoration. The car may have been fitted with chauffeur's rake and will have to be altered to "owner-driver".

Compare notes with, and have the car driven by, knowledgeable owners of similar cars. It is most aggravating having finished the restoration to be told, on the first time you take it to a meeting, that if you had made some small modification, one which was probably done by the makers on the model a year later than yours, the running would be improved out of all recognition. You will then have sleepless nights debating the possibility of stripping the car again, or leaving it alone and being for ever dissatisfied.

The testing and collection of "gen" should now be complete, and it is time to drive the car into the garage and get down to the real work. By this time you should have prepared your wife for many evenings to be spent alone. You may, of course, have aroused her enthusiasm to such an extent that she will be helping you with the work. So much the better, and you can now summon the demolition gang.

CHAPTER II

THE DISMANTLING

THE best advice that could possibly be given on the subject of dismantling is to do it yourself and on your own. In this way each peculiarity of design, each shortcoming in the past owner's maintenance, each part which is as good as new, can be carefully scrutinised with alternating joy and misgiving by you, the one who will have to put it all together again. We know, however, that if you have any friends at all who are even slightly interested in motor-cars, then they will be in attendance at this engrossing performance. It is difficult to analyse the reasons for this, but you have only to mention to any enthusiast that "old so-and-so" will be taking his car to pieces next Sunday morning and, come rain or shine, your enthusiast will be there to lend a hand. Whether it is some sadistic motive which secretly longs for a sight of the inner horrors which may be revealed, or whether it is a purely academic interest in adding to one's store of Vintage knowledge that brings the audience, we do not know, but we have never yet been the only onlookers to a Vintage dismantling.

Preparation

Start by siting the car in a suitable position for removing the body. Remember that it is usually easier to lift the body backwards over the chassis than in any other direction. As it is quite possible that the body will have to be lifted to some height in order to clear inside obstructions, such as the gear lever and steering wheel, it may not be possible to perform the act of body removal inside the garage at all, due to lack of sufficient headroom. In this case make your plan of action accordingly and do not, for instance, make the car immobile before the body is removed.

Before any parts are actually taken off the car, collect together as many boxes and containers as you can in order that all the small parts of each particular type can be kept together for future ease of finding. If the aforementioned unpaid help has arrived, go through the plan of action with them. Ask all members of the dismantling gang to bring to your notice any peculiarities of assembly which they come across, as it is fairly certain that they will not be there when you are putting the car together again. The object of the exercise in which you are about to indulge is to reduce the motor-car to the *minimum* number of major sub-assemblies each of which will be left in a complete state until its turn comes for dismantling, cleaning, renovation and reassembly into the growing motor-car. We would also like

18

to stress our belief that, at this stage, only the minimum amount of dirt should be removed, as greasy or oily filth is a fine rust preventative where the necessary paint has long since vanished.

The next preliminary is to drain the radiator, petrol tank and engine sump. Do not drain the gear-box or back axle, as these can easily be emptied when their turn comes for stripping and, once again, the oil will stop the likelihood of rusting. If these components are to be left for a long time, rotate the shafts occasionally to spread the oil. As none of the moving parts of the engine except the oil pump are in the sump this does not apply here. You are now ready for the dismantling proper to begin.

First Stages of Dismantling

Start by taking off the spare wheel and then the parts most likely to be damaged when the heavier portions are being removed. These are the head-lamps, side-lamps, horns, instruments and other rather delicate pieces. Put these away carefully in some place where heavier parts cannot be dropped on top of them. Next remove any coachwork frills such as the dumb-iron apron, if one is fitted, the hood, if the car is a tourer, the number plates, rear lamps, and finally the bonnet complete.

The latter is generally a most clumsy article to handle and to store, and it will be found best at this stage straightaway to knock out the bonnet hinge-pins, and to reduce the assembly to four easily-handled pieces. For some reason most bonnets are endowed with steel hinge-pins, which are usually rusted solid into one or other of the hinge sections. Penetrating oil and a certain amount of hammering on the end of the pin with a brass punch will generally start it on its way out. As soon as one end of the pin projects, it can be seized with the Mole wrench, and further twisting and pulling will remove it completely. At this point you are generally in a good mental state for making a resolution never to use anything in future but either brass or stainless steel for bonnet hinge-pins.

Next take off the radiator. Do not attempt to salvage the water hoses. They are generally vulcanised on to the inlet and outlet pipes by the action of heat. It is best to hack-saw through the centre, leaving the actual removal until it can be carefully attended to at a later stage. Put the radiator away very carefully. It is so often seen propped up against the garage wall where it can easily be knocked over, with subsequent catastrophic damage to its shell, core and to its enamelled badge. These are all expensive matters to rectify, and do remember that the radiator is the first thing that most people look at when admiring the finished car. It must therefore be in absolutely flawless condition. The best position for storage is flat on its back, wrapped up in an old blanket and, if possible, not in the workshop. Under the visitors'-room bed is not a bad place.

Another accessory that can be taken away at this stage is the battery. The storage of this is always a problem. If you are aware that the battery

19

is about on its last legs, then there is no problem. Throw it away now and be done with it. If it is new, or nearly new, then either make use of it on another car, if this is possible, or even sell it. It is possible to maintain a battery, if you have a charger, by alternately charging and discharging it at frequent intervals. In the authors' experience this generally gets forgotten and, by the time the restoration is complete, what was a valuable component has deteriorated to a fairly useless box worth only the value of the lead inside it.

If the car is a tourer, the windscreen can now be taken off complete with wiper. Following this take anything easily removable out of the body which will help its ultimate removal. The doors, for instance, can all come off. It is best to knock out the hinge pins in this case, and not to take out the wood screws which hold the hinges to the wooden frame of the body. It is quite possible that these screws will have to come out eventually, if the hinges are to be replated, but they are generally rather difficult to remove and are best left until they can receive some careful individual attention. This care cannot be given with the "let's-get-it-apart-quickly" mentality that prevails at the main dismantlement. Replace all hinge-pins in their respective hinges. All the carpets, seat cushions, bucket seats and floorboards can now come out.

The next stage in the proceedings is to detach the front mudguards, followed by the running-boards and rear mudguards. Here again dismantle into as large pieces as possible. Take the mudguard stays off at the chassis and leave the running-boards on their brackets, taking the brackets off the frame. All this is to cut down the number of small parts to be stored separately, and to aid identification at later stages in the restoration. Wherever possible replace bolts, in the holes from which they came, in the part which is being removed. The mudguards off, next take away the bonnet boards and any valances which may run along the chassis side members. There will, in all probability, be a fair amount of chisel work required here, as all the bolts holding these fittings on to the chassis are very exposed to wet and dirt.

If a bolt has to be cut through, always try to cut up against the most robust member possible. For instance, if a mudguard valance is bolted to the chassis frame with a row of immovable bolts, chisel through these on the inside of the frame, which will not suffer if care is taken. Chiselling against the valance will tear the sheet metal, which will either have to be replaced or extensively repaired. This is a simple point but one which is often overlooked. Always use a saw in preference to a chisel if it is possible to do so.

Removing the Body

We are now ready to loosen the body. Take a careful look round to see where the framework is attached to the chassis. The body frame will obviously be bolted to the chassis side members, and to the bulkhead if this

20

is part of the chassis. In all probability coach bolts will have been used and when you attempt to undo the nuts inside the chassis members, the head of the bolts will turn in the woodwork. You now have several alternatives. Either hack-saw a screwdriver slot in the mushroom head of the coach bolt, or hack-saw two flats on the head, so that it can be held with a spanner. If it is a bolt with a countersunk head, which is flush in the wood, then neither of these ideas is any good, and you will either have to chisel the nut off the bolt, or cut the bolt through. It is sometimes possible to insert a hack-saw blade in between the chassis and body member and, holding the blade in an Eclipse pad handle, to saw through the bolt. The hammer and chisel is the last resort and, if it has to be used, split the nut through at its thinnest point rather than attempt to chisel straight through the nut and bolt. With a 2-lb. hammer and a good cold chisel it is generally possible to split a ⅜-in. nut with half a dozen good blows. Immovable nuts in other parts of the chassis can often be loosened by means of a blowlamp, or penetrating oil, or both, but coach bolts in wood preclude the use of a blowlamp and, in any case, it is impossible to stop the bolt turning if a very powerful effort is required on the nut. Here make another mental note that, when the body is replaced, hexagon-headed bolts, in steel plates recessed into the woodwork, will be used.

Having got all these body-to-chassis securing bolts out, find out what else remains that ties the body to the chassis. If the dashboard is an integral part of the body then obviously all pipes, flexible drives, wiring and controls coming to the dashboard must be disconnected. The steering column will probably have a bracket on to the body. If the petrol tank is scuttle-mounted, disconnect the fuel pipe and, if the bulkhead forms an integral part of the body, make sure that it is not connected to the chassis by any pipes or controls. Should the bulkhead be separate from the body, or be easily separated from it, then leave it as part of the chassis at this stage.

We have come to the conclusion that it is a great advantage to have the bulkhead and dashboard as part of the chassis. There may be insuperable difficulties in the way of carrying out such modification on your particular car, but on many Vintage cars the bulkhead is already a separate component bolted rigidly to the chassis. To carry the dashboard off this, instead of mounting it direct in the body, is only a minor modification and in no way alters the character of the car. It has the great advantage that the chassis can be finished as a complete roadworthy vehicle, with all the wiring and instruments in working order, which can be road-tested without a body, thus greatly facilitating adjustments and minor final alterations that may be found necessary. Bearing this in mind, and before finally removing the body, make notes of any further alterations which will be necessary if this modification is to be carried out. You will already have seen if the positions of the instruments suit you and made notes accordingly, but you must now pay particular attention to any variation in the shape of the dash, to allow the body to clear it all round and to enable the body to be passed over it when replacing. Also note its exact position relative to fixed points on the chassis which will enable you to fit it without the body in place. A template of the new dashboard, if this is decided upon, can easily be made from hardboard, with wooden brackets. The instruments can be represented by paper shapes cut out and pinned on to the board. This can be put away until you are ready to make the new dashboard.

The body can now be lifted off and stored away. As it will not be needed for some time, cover it over with a dust sheet if possible. All the floorboards, seats, windscreen and other coachwork accessories can be stored inside the body to reduce the space required. Put the patient away comfortably as it may be some time before he receives his treatment. If put in a damp bed the complaints from which he is suffering will be distinctly aggravated.

Next, remove all electric wiring from the chassis. It is very seldom that this is of any use for replacement and it can therefore be cut out and thrown away. Take care, however, to keep any of the clips, terminal ends and junction boxes associated with the wiring, as these are often hard to get and were generally better made in Vintage days than are their modern counterparts. All piping can now be removed and, if this is in any way kinked or shows signs of having been bent and straightened many times, discard it, keeping only the union nuts and nipples, and other pipe fittings which may be non-standard and difficult to replace. The piping can be cut off close to any of these and the fittings left attached to their various accessories for future reference.

Methods of Identification

Before we continue with the description of the actual dismemberment of the chassis, we would like to mention some methods of marking parts for identification. It is obviously desirable that certain mating parts are marked before being taken apart, in order that they go together in exactly the same relationship to that which they originally bore to one another. A very common way of marking such parts is by the use of a centre punch. This method is both crude and unworkmanlike as, if there are sets of exactly similar parts, numbers of centre-punch dots have to be put on each. We have seen parts bearing up to sixteen dots marked in this way. A set of number and letter punches is a real investment and will allow each part to be identified with only one mark. Before putting any mark on to a component make absolutely sure that it is necessary, as it may already be marked. Again, many sets of components are made so that they will only go together in the right way. When you have decided that you must mark, then use the punch in a position where the component is least stressed, and where the raised metal round the punch mark will not upset the working of the part. For instance, if done too heavily, or too near the edge of a flange, it will raise the metal on the face of the flange, which will have to be removed before an oil-tight joint can be made. The worst example of the marking addict is the man who files nicks into the webs of his connecting-rods to indicate with which cylinder they correspond. The correct method in this case is a number punched on one of the big-end bolt bosses where the metal is least stressed. The question of indentations, being the possible place for future trouble to start, is a very important one. We were once in conversation with an old associate of Sir Henry Royce and asked him if the chassis serial number could be found stamped on any part of a Rolls-Royce frame. His reply was an almost indignant: "Stamped on the frame? No, sir, that would be a sure way to start a fracture." If only temporary identification is needed, then masking tape, of the type used by body painters, can be wound round the component and a number or note pencilled on to the tape.

Removing the Steering-box

Reverting to the job in hand, the next large piece to be removed is the steering-box and column, complete with wheel and any controls which may pass through the column. If the bulkhead is still on the chassis, then this can now be removed. Disconnect the controls at the bottom of the column and also free the drop-arm from the drag-link. If the ball-pin is held into the drop-arm by means of a nut and taper, do not try to remove the ball-pin at this stage. It will probably be very tightly fixed into the drop-arm and will need special attention later. Take the cap off the end of the drag-link, and remove the ball-cup, take the drag-link off the ball-pin and replace the ball-cup and cap on the drag-link. Do the same at the other end of the drag-link which will then be free of the chassis altogether. The steering-box can now be unbolted and removed as a complete assembly.

Engine and Gear-box removal

The next move is to work towards the removal of the engine from the frame. Take off all the engine accessories such as the carburettor, magneto, dynamo, starter and fan. This will lighten the engine and also save any damage to the accessories which might occur when easing the engine out. Take off the complete exhaust system from manifold to tailpipe. This will probably involve some very rusty nuts and bolts being undone, and a dousing with penetrating oil the night before on all such parts will often pay dividends. If any flange joints have to be parted, remember that a chisel edge put against the joint, and the chisel then driven between the faces, is not the best of treatment for a joint which you will want to remain oil and gas tight when it is reassembled. When all the nuts have been undone, try tapping one of the components with a wooden or rawhide mallet.

23

If this does not part the flange, it is permissible to tap the blade of a thin knife between the faces to start the joint opening. If the flanges are held together with studs threaded into one component and passing through the other with nuts on the outside, it is quite possible that the studs themselves are seized into the part which you are trying to remove, particularly if this is aluminium. Try heating this gently with a blowlamp and continuously tapping all round the part. If this fails, then try to remove the studs by locking two nuts together on the projecting screwed end. If there is not enough thread for this, split a nut on one side only, thread it on the stud, and grip it with the Mole wrench, at the same time using the wrench as a spanner. Holding a red-hot piece of metal on to the end of the stud will also

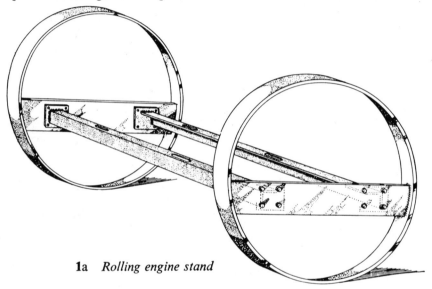

1a   *Rolling engine stand*

sometimes free it. With the studs removed it is almost certain that the face-to-face seal can be broken by judicious tapping with a mallet. A very fine design of stud extractor is made by A. P. Warren Ltd., but it is necessary to have a separate extractor for each size of stud.

Should any C-spanner nuts have to be removed, you can now buy adjustable spanners for these in a set of three at a very reasonable price. They cover all sizes of C-rings likely to be found on motor-cars. The possession of these spanners stops the use of chisels, punches or even screwdrivers on these rings which, if the wrong tool is used, will bear the marks for the rest of their lives.

If the engine is separate from the gear-box, disconnect them by uncoupling the drive-shaft. Remove the engine holding-down bolts and prepare to lift the engine from the frame. If at all possible, prepare beforehand a stand into which the engine can be placed. This need not be at all elaborate and can be built up from timber or from angle-iron. A type of stand which can be made either in the workshop or by the local blacksmith and which is of a novel design, is shown in fig. 1a. The diameter of the two end portions can be made to suit whatever engine you are dealing with, but 36 in. is a good average. The advantages of this type of stand are that it can be rolled along complete with the engine in place, and that the engine can be put at any convenient angle single-handed. If nothing but the best will do, then you can make or buy a stand as shown in fig 1b, which will fit almost any engine and which enables the engine to be turned upside down for working on the crankshaft assembly. It is preferable to keep the main

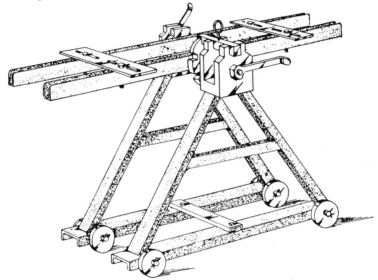

1b   *Mobile engine stand*

engine assembly in one piece at this stage and, if at all possible, try to lift it out in this state and put it on to its stand.

If you have lifting-tackle then this will be possible. If you have to rely on sheer manpower, and it is a heavy engine, then it is often possible to place a stout piece of timber or a length of steel joist across the top of the engine, and to sling the engine to this by means of a rope. Several men either side of the car can then lift the engine out or, by a series of jacking and propping movements, the engine can be lifted high enough for the chassis to be wheeled from underneath and the stand placed ready for the engine to be lowered on to it. On no account lower the engine on to the ground and drag it about on its sump. The sump is generally far too flimsy to stand this treatment, and in any case it will suffer very badly even if it does not fracture. If the engine has to be lightened before it can be lifted out of the frame, then either take off the head or the block, whichever is

25

applicable, and be careful to protect any of the machined surfaces exposed by doing this.

Next take out the gear-box, which will entail disconnecting the propeller-shaft and removing the gear-box holding-down bolts. If the design of the car incorporates a torque-tube type of final drive, it is probable that the back axle will have to be removed, or drawn backwards, before the gear-box can be removed. It is even possible that this will have to be done before the engine can be removed, but in this general description we have had to keep to the order in which the majority of cars can be taken apart.

Final Stages

The petrol tank had better be taken out next if this has not already come away with the body.

Now concentrate on removing all the brake link-work and operating mechanisms. Take care to replace all clevis-pins in their respective fork-ends and to keep as much of the assembly together as is possible. Incidentally, when removing castellated nuts which are split-pinned, do not just undo the nut and so shear off the split-pin. This ruins the last few threads of the bolt, and even if you are going to use all new nuts, the bolt may be of a special type. It is a pity to have to go to the trouble of replacing it just to save a few moments of dismantling time. Some split-pins can be very troublesome to get out, but usually the use of patience, the right size of pin punch, a pair of side-cutting pliers and a Mole wrench, will have their reward.

During the dismantling a great many nuts will have to be undone. A tool which many seem to overlook, and which greatly speeds this operation, is the nut-spinner. This goes with a set of socket wrenches

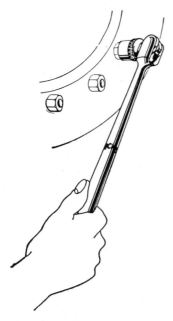

2a   *Nut spinner, position 1*

and can be used direct, as a very powerful tommy lever, and then, either still direct or through a universal joint, to spin the nut off. Both this and the adjustable C-spanners are made by Abingdon in their "King Dick" series. The use of these very useful tools is shown in figs. 2a, b and c.

We are now nearing the end of the main stripping-down. The shock-absorbers should next be taken off complete with brackets, and care taken to note any differences between front and rear. They should, in any case, be marked for the positions from whence they came. The chassis frame will now be standing on its wheels and will be otherwise bare, so that all that remains for us to do is to knock out the shackle-pins from the chassis and, lifting up the frame at each end, wheel the back axle complete with springs away to its place of storage. In the case of a front axle, it is better to remove the wheels and carry the axle beam complete with springs, as if it is wheeled along, the wheels are liable to flop over in a most disconcerting

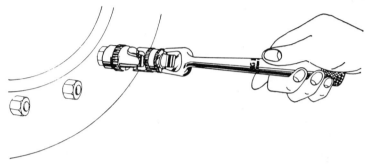

2b   *Nut spinner, position 2*

manner and you may have your fingers trapped. On cars with other than semi-elliptic springs, detach the springs, however they may be held, from the frame. If they have to be parted from their axles, then label them according to their position.

During the whole process of taking the car apart you should have made notes of anything untoward, such as cracks, fractures, peculiarities of assembly, which you might easily forget, and the position of any adjustments which you have had to disturb. Also make notes of small modifications which may make for ease of maintenance in the future.

Your car is now in a sufficient number of pieces for the work of restoration to

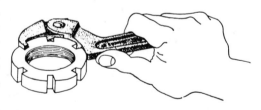

2c   *Adjustable C-spanner*

start. You will probably be in a state of mental anguish about some of the things which you have found, but this will be mixed, on reflection, with relief that at least it might have been a lot worse. As the best cure for any grief is hard work, do not ponder at this stage but press straight on to the first stages of the rebuild. The audience will now, of course, wish you the best of luck and depart, revelling in the thought that they are leaving you with a year or so of hard work on your hands. Your compensation will lie in the sight of their envy when they see the finished masterpiece.

CHAPTER III

THE FRAME

Cleaning

THE first part of the procedure is to set up the frame on four jacking stands. If you do not possess these, then four oil drums, or strong wooden boxes of equal height, will do very well. Start by removing all oil and grease, and for this use paraffin, with either a stiff brush or a compressed air paraffin spray. Whichever method you use, finish off with rag and make sure that the frame is as clean as possible.

When the car is completed, the dumb-irons and probably quite a lot more of the frame will show. Since it is impossible to get a good finish on top of old chipped paint, this will now have to be removed. This is the most dreary and monotonous part of the whole restoration work. Coming, as it does, straight on top of the excitement of buying and dismantling the car, you will feel that you will never get to the end of the scraping. The only way we have ever found of relieving the monotony is to get somebody else to do it for us. Try not to skimp this work however, as it is very important if a first-class result is to be obtained. Remember that better and more interesting things lie ahead. If you live within a convenient distance of a firm who can shot-blast articles as large as a chassis frame, it will certainly pay you to have the old paint and rust removed in this way. It will save you a great deal of time and handwork, but you must remember to protect any reamered or tapped holes and machined surfaces. Holes can be filled with corks or wooden plugs. Only those living in or near a large town are likely to be able to indulge in this luxury, and even then they will have to be lucky enough to find a firm that is equipped with a very large booth. The others will have to do the work by hand. Soften the old paint with "Nitromors" and remove with scrapers; the flat one will be used most, but the half-round will be very convenient for some of the more awkward places. Another very effective way to remove old paint is with a Calor gas blowpipe and scraper in the same way that house decorators strip woodwork.

The loose rust must be cleaned off and this is done most thoroughly with a stiff wire brush, or better still a rotary wire mop used in a flexible drive or electric drill. Rough places can be cleaned up by filing, but it is unlikely that you will be able to remove much metal in this way and, if you did, you would weaken the frame. Very deep corrosion, therefore, will have to be filled when you come to the painting. The front dumb-irons are very prominent so it will be well worthwhile to put a super finish on these. They should be polished up smooth with emery cloth.

Inspection

Now that the frame is really clean it is time to give it a thorough inspection, both for alignment and for any damage such as cracks. It is well worthwhile making a special effort of this inspection, as unless the frame is really true in every way the car will not steer in that delightfully accurate manner which gives the driver such a sense of security. Check the diagonals, corner to corner from a given datum point on each side; they must be equal. For instance, measure from the centre of the shackle-pin hole on the inside of the front dumb-iron to a similar hole on the inside of the rear dumb-iron. If the chassis is fitted with cantilever or quarter-elliptic springs, there will not be any shackle-pin holes, and in that case use some other symmetrical datum points such as the spring mountings. Even if these two measurements are equal, it is still possible for the frame to be bent in two places which cancel each other out, so that you now have to check the angles formed by the side- and cross-members. If you do not possess any instrument for measuring these angles, an easy way is to cut a piece of hardboard to the angle formed on the one side and try it for fit on the opposite side, repeating this for each cross-member. See fig. 3.

Next get two round steel rods of the same diameter as the shackle-pins, and about 18 in. longer than the width of the chassis at the point where they will be fitted. Pass these rods through the shackle-pin holes from side to side at front and rear, leaving about 9 in. projecting each side. The ends of these rods can now be rested on top of the jack stands or oil drums, and leave the frame completely free for further treatment. Also, if the rods passed through both shackle-pin holes quite freely, then you will know that the dumb-irons are straight. Incidentally, this method of supporting the frame is very convenient later on, because with one person standing at each end and by using these rods, the frame can be turned over very easily for painting the underneath. The last test is to see that the frame is not twisted. Make sure that the two stands at the front are of equal height, and likewise the two stands at the rear. The average vintage chassis frame is so flexible that, unless it is very badly twisted, it will lie quite flat on these stands. Now get a spring balance of capacity large enough to lift one corner of the frame. Lift first one and then the other rear corner with this spring balance and note the readings. Any difference in weight shown on the balance will indicate if the frame is twisted, by how much, and which way. If the difference in reading is only a few pounds and the frame is otherwise straight, this can be ignored. Large differences can only be rectified by an expert with the necessary heavy plant.

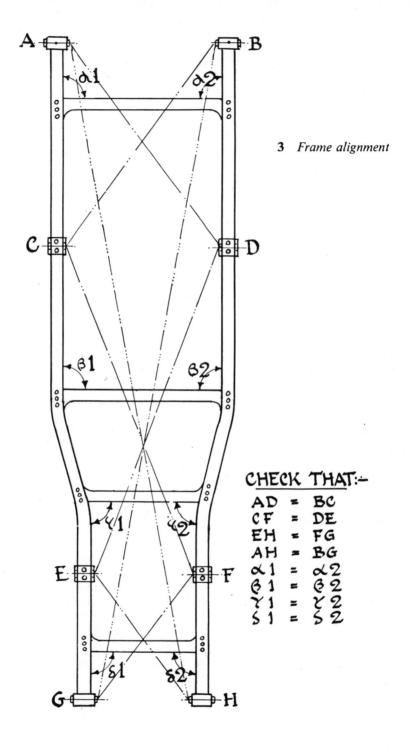

3 *Frame alignment*

CHECK THAT:-

AD = BC
CF = DE
EH = FG
AH = BG
α1 = α2
β1 = β2
γ1 = γ2
δ1 = δ2

Repairs and Modifications

If the members are undamaged but the two sides are out of alignment it is possible to pull this true with a 1-ton chain pulley block, fitted diagonally from corner to corner. Go very steadily with this and keep checking the angles between cross- and side-members. When true, check again with the pulley block slackened off, as you may have to go a little further owing to the spring in the frame.

If side- or cross-members are not badly bent, these can be straightened cold by the following method. Get a short stiff length of rolled-steel joist and attach it by chains to the frame each side of the bend to be straightened, leaving enough space for a hydraulic jack. Place the jack in the centre of the joist with its base on the centre of the bend to spread the load and then increase the pressure until the frame is straight. As with the previous diagonal trueing, check with the pressure released as you may have to go a little further to allow for the spring in the metal.

Now examine the frame very carefully for cracks. If any are found they must be welded. Never repair them with a plate, as this stiffens the frame at one point and often, in time, causes it to fracture elsewhere. When welding, the old metal each side of the crack must first be cut away and then built up again, as it will probably be crystallised. When the weld is completed it should be hammered while still red-hot to remove the stresses. This is a job for a first-class welder. Try to find the reason for the cracking. Is it due to too much cold-working done during some previous

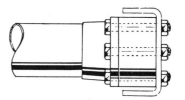

4a *Tubular cross-member with distance piece*

straightening, or has it been caused by a concentration of load due to a modification or local stiffening? If it is due to an excess of load at one point, such as badly designed shock-absorber mountings, consider the possibility of incorporating these mountings in a new cross-member which will spread the load in the correct manner without destroying the flexibility of the frame.

The correct way to make and fit a new tubular cross-member is to weld or braze flanges on to the ends of the tube and to make it a little shorter than the inside width of the chassis. This is then assembled with packing plates so that it does not have to be hammered up the frame. An even better way is to make it in three pieces, held together with flanges and a ring of small bolts. The two ends can be assembled in the frame and then the centre portion inserted afterwards with no trouble at all. These two methods are illustrated in figs. 4a and b.

The front and rear dumb-irons on Vintage cars are frequently joined at their extremities by a cross-member. This consists of one long rod, screwed at each end and forming the two shackle-pins and a tubular distance piece. This is usually dented and is often bent, and if so it will have to be replaced. These rods are frequently rusted in and, if bent as well, are very difficult to remove. In this case the easiest method is to saw a piece out of the centre and then knock out one half at a time. To remake this part get a length of bright-drawn mild steel of the correct diameter and screw-cut the two ends

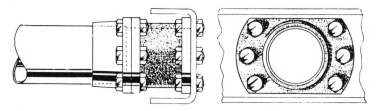

4b   *Tubular cross-member in three pieces*

in the same way as the old one. Drill the oil holes and tap with the correct thread, usually ⅛-in. B.S.P., for the nipple, then case-harden each end where the springs bear. The threads should not be hardened, and to prevent this they should be copper-plated before hardening the ends of the rod. Next you will require a length of mild-steel seamless tube of the correct outside diameter and wall thickness, and fitted with mild-steel plugs each

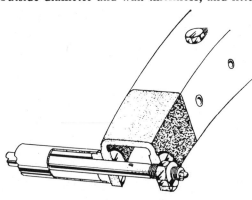

end. These plugs, about 1 inch long, should be turned out of mild-steel bar and should be a tight fit in the tube, with a small flange left at the end of the same outside diameter as the tube. They should be bored out a sliding fit on the long shackle-pin. This tube, when assembled with its end plugs, should be a perfect fit between the dumb-irons, which should not have to be strained

4c   *Tubular cross-member for dumb-iron ends*

to accommodate it. This is illustrated in fig. 4c.

Check all rivets and make sure they really are tight. If any are loose, they will usually be found on the near side of the car. Before scraping the frame it is as well to examine the paint at each end of the cross-members. If it is broken it will show that they have been moving relative to the side-members, so the rivets in them must be taken out. A faulty rivet cannot be tightened and will have to be replaced. Do not attempt to chisel off the head until it has first been prepared. You will find it very tough going and you will probably only succeed in cutting into the chassis. What is even more likely is that you will get very angry and miss the end of the chisel altogether but not your knuckle, which will be sliced off quite neatly to the accompaniment of great pain and greater temper.

The correct way to remove a rivet is to drill down through the centre of the head with a drill about the same diameter as the rivet shank. Do not attempt to drill right through the rivet as they are usually bent, so that the holes are staggered slightly, with the result that the drill will elongate the holes in the frame. If the rivet is in a position where the drill cannot be used, another way is to saw almost through the head across the centre and then again at right angles, like a hot-cross bun, after which it will respond to the attentions of the chisel a great deal more easily. The shank can now be driven out with a pin punch. If there are several rivets holding a joint and only one is apparently loose, take out all of them. The others are probably starting to become loose, although they may appear to be tight. This will also enable you to line up the holes correctly because, as mentioned previously, you will probably find they are slightly staggered. Now replace the rivets with high-tensile bolts which are a really good fit in the holes, having first reamered them to size. Use self-locking nuts. We have found either G.K.N. "Aerotight" or Simmonds "Nyloc" best for this purpose. You can use plain nuts but the bolts must be peened over, as was done for instance on Rolls-Royce chassis.

Clean all paint out of the joint before refixing. To be really sound you must have metal-to-metal contact.

If the frame was bolted together in the first place, and if it is true, do not remove the bolts, but check them all for tightness, even if they are all split-pinned.

These instructions only apply to frames which are slightly out of alignment or bent. If the frame is extensively damaged, it will no doubt also be wrinkled, which can only be got out with special equipment, and in this case it is best dealt with by an expert. If possible send it to Rubery Owen who will repair any make or type of frame. They will even make new side- or cross-members or a complete frame if necessary, but this of course would be fairly expensive. While on the subject we should mention that the authors have never found it necessary to normalise a whole frame. If the frame has had to be straightened, before passing it as correct, check that the fixing holes of major components, such as the engine and gear-box, still line up with their corresponding holes in the frame.

Any unwanted holes should be welded-up and then filed flush. If, however, welding is a problem and the hole is in an unstressed area, it can be filled up with a short bolt. If any modifications are to be made to the chassis which will require new holes, now is the time to drill them. Do not, however, drill any more than you can possibly help. Use adaptor plates wherever possible, using the old holes in the frame, the plate being drilled to take the new accessory. If it is absolutely necessary to drill a new hole, arrange for this to be in a neutral area, that is, as near as possible to the centre of either the flange or the web of the member in question. You will often find that someone has drilled holes in the top flange of the dumbirons, to fit badges or spot-lamps. This is certainly to be deprecated; they must be filled in by welding and then filed smooth. Some other mounting will have to be made up for these accessories.

It may be that you will want to shorten the chassis. This is quite permissible if two models were made. You may only have been able to buy the long one but want to rebuild your car as a short chassis. We do not agree with the shortening of chassis just for the sake of it, as this often spoils the handling of what was originally a very pleasant and comfortable motor-car. Study the frame carefully before deciding where to cut out the piece, remembering that the transmission will have to be shortened. The frame should be cut diagonally to form a scarf joint as long as possible. Make sure that everything will line up properly and have this job done by a first-class welder. Do not use plates for the reason mentioned earlier, and in any case these are not necessary as a properly cut and welded joint is as strong as the original member.

It rarely helps road holding to stiffen a Vintage frame torsionally. The suspension is usually so stiff that it is necessary for the frame to be flexible in order to keep the wheels on the ground. Certain Vintage cars have been modified successfully in this respect, chiefly in the portion between the gear-box and the rear end, by the addition of tubular cross-members, but this is a very advanced exercise. If you indulge in this type of modification you will have to be prepared to do a great deal of experimental work and go through a lot of disappointments before achieving any good results.

Instability in a Vintage car is far more likely to be due either to the car's generally bad condition or to deviation from the maker's original specification. For instance, larger-section tires can completely ruin the handling of a car expressly designed for the use of high-pressure, beaded-edge covers. One thing however will usually result in an improvement in steering, and that is the fitting of a cross-member at the extreme ends of the front dumb-irons.

A number of Vintage chassis were fitted with railway-carriage-type bracing rods. These rods do not in any way increase torsional stiffness, their sole purpose is to stop the chassis from sagging, thereby helping the bodywork and preventing the doors from flying open. After removal for cleaning and derusting they should be refitted with a small amount of pre-loading.

Now inspect the shackle-pin holes in the frame. If these are worn oval or oversize you will either have to open them out to a larger diameter and fit oversize pins, or have the holes welded up and redrill them to the original size. If you decide to open out the existing holes, make sure that an over-size pin can be accommodated in the corresponding spring eye or shackle.

Finishing

You will now be ready for the final finishing. All traces of oil should be removed by wiping down with petrol or white spirit. The metal should be treated for rustproofing with "Jenolite" R.R.N. This is applied by brush, or small components can be dipped, if a suitable tank is available, but this must not be made of iron. For dipping, the solution should be heated to about 55°C. Any loose rust should have been removed by wire brushing, since the amount of solution used depends on the amount of rust to be dissolved. The "Jenolite" should be allowed to react for a few minutes and then agitated with a wire brush. A further thin coating should then be applied, left for about 15 minutes, and then any excess wiped off with a clean dry rag. When dry, the metal surface will appear light to dark grey in colour, showing that a phosphate coating has formed, which actively inhibits future corrosion and which provides an excellent key for subsequent paint coatings.

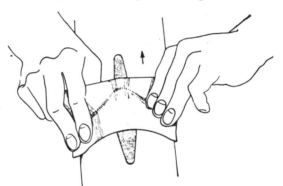

Paint should not be applied until the "Jenolited" surface is

5 *Filling a curved surface*

completely dry but, on the other hand, the surface should not be allowed to become damp as any moisture may interfere with the formation of the phosphate coating. It is therefore advisable to give the work a further coat with Jenolite Chemical Sealer. This is applied by brush while the "Jenolited" surface is still tacky. It protects the phosphate coating and neutralises any excess R.R.N. remaining in inaccessible places. The frame can now be left for 48 hours, but it should not be left longer than this before it receives the first coat of paint. Any parts not to be painted must be thoroughly greased. Cellulose paint must not be applied directly over this rustproofing. An intermediate coat must always be applied first.

The last work to be done on the frame is the painting. In the following description we have only mentioned the products of Llewelyn Ryland Ltd. There are, however, other good makes of these materials if you prefer to use them.

35

You may either brush or spray-paint the frame. If you are using an oil-bound finish, give it two coats of 303 Undercoat. If however you have any deep corrosion or dents, give one coat and then, when it is dry, fill these with Rylard Cement Filler (knifing). This is applied with a fairly flexible knife, such as is used for putty, but a strip of celluloid will be found very useful for applying it to curved surfaces. The requisite amount of filler is first put on to the celluloid which is then drawn along the curved surface, conforming to the shape and leaving the filler in any depressions, as shown in fig. 5. When the filler is hard, it must be rubbed down smooth with waterproof rubbing paper used with plenty of water. This paper is made in a number of grades, use the coarse for removing a large amount of filler and finish off with a fine grade. Repeat the filling and rubbing down until all blemishes have disappeared. Now apply the second undercoat, and if you want a very good finish, rub this down lightly with fine-grade rubbing paper and water, taking great care not to rub right through, especially on high spots such as rivet heads. This final finish will be one coat of 303 oil- and petrol-resisting enamel. This is obtainable in all colours, but the undercoat must be ordered to match.

If you are cellulose finishing the car and want the chassis to match, it is advisable to limit this to as small an area as possible. Cellulose is not really suitable for this purpose, as it is rather too brittle and likely to shell off in time. The procedure will be the same as before up to and including the last undercoat, then spray on one coat of Rylard Cellulose Sealer (Red Oxide) and then the final coat of cellulose colour.

The most uninteresting hard work is now behind you, and you have a spotless frame set up in position to receive the other components as they become finished.

36

CHAPTER IV

THE ROAD SPRINGS, FRONT AXLE AND STEERING GEAR

Springs

DURING the dismantling we left the springs, if this was possible, attached to their respective axles. They must now be detached but, before doing so, take note of any peculiarities. In particular, if the springs are semi-elliptic, notice whether the axles are bolted to the centre of the springs or whether an unequal length of spring projects on each side of the axle. It is surprising how easy it is to forget such points when everything is in pieces, only to find that you have made a mistake too late to avoid considerable dismantling.

If the springs are fitted with gaiters it is extremely unlikely that these will be any use again. It is impossible to make a good repair to the stitching if the leather is old and dirty. If this is the case, choose the gaiters, front and rear, in best condition, and remove them as carefully as possible to be used as patterns. Cut the rest off and throw them away.

Now take each spring completely to pieces by removing the clips and the clamping bolt. Be careful to grip the spring in the vice as near as possible to the centre when undoing the clamping bolt, as some springs contain a considerable amount of latent energy, even when they are off the car, and removal of this bolt without holding the leaves together in the vice can give you a good rap on the knuckles, to say the least. Keep each set of leaves and clips together so that they may be assembled back, mating leaf to leaf in their original order. Clean all the parts in paraffin and give every leaf a close inspection.

If the bottom faces of the leaves are indented, where the end of the leaf below has been rubbing, it is as well to try to remove these depressions. They can be ground out or polished out on an emery bob, or even filed if you have enough patience. These hollows are, of course, a very likely source of spring breakage, but when removing them you must spread the filing over a considerable area or you will get an abrupt change of section. If the wear is more than 0·010 in., new leaves are required to make a first-class job. We think that it is well worth polishing the working surfaces of the leaves all over but this is a matter for you to decide, depending upon the time available and also upon your patience. If you have the services of a polishing shop on tap, then definitely have them polished.

Next look at the eyes in the ends of the main leaves. If bushed, try the fit of the shackle-pins in these bushes. They should be a nice sliding fit, and if they are loose they will need renewing. Knock out the bushes which should be a tight fit in the spring eye.

Should any of the leaves be broken, or if the springs as a whole have settled, then the services of an expert will have to be called in. British Springs Ltd. will repair or replace any make of leaf spring. In the case of a spring with one or more broken leaves, send the whole spring and its companion from the other side of the car so that you will get a matching pair when they are returned. When the car was complete you should have taken note as to whether or not the springs had settled and by how much they needed setting up. Again, if only one has to be dealt with, send the pair. It is difficult to give a general guide for you to tell by how much your springs have settled. However, it will be obvious if the car is down on one side, or if the springs are over-flat when under normal load. A guide on cars fitted with Perrot shaft-operated front brakes is that these shafts should be at right-angles to the brake back plates when the car is on a level surface and under normal load. Should your conscience allow you to perform modifications on your Vintage motor-car then, as a general rule, it can be said that the nearer to flat that your springs are the more stable the car will be. We do not propose to break off into a treatise on such subjects as roll over-steer, but if your car has a tendency to wander on straight roads then check that a horizontal line drawn through the front fixing of the rear spring also passes through or under the centre of the axle. If it passes over the centre then, if possible, have the rear springs flattened until this is remedied. While considering stability, now is the time to decide whether or not to fit more clips to your springs. The lateral stiffness of the springs is considerably influenced by the fitting of these clips and, on some of the earlier cars of the period, only one clip was used front and back of the axle. At least two are necessary and on cars which are likely to be driven in a sporting manner, even more. It is possible to drill the necessary rivet or bolt hole in a leaf in the hardened condition, providing the drill is run very slowly. New clips can then be made and fitted.

Have a look at the spring clamping bolts. On semi-elliptic springs the heads are usually cheese-shaped and form the location between the spring and axle. If the head is worn, or loose in its register in the axle, make up new bolts with oversize heads and drill out the axle register to fit.

When you assemble the springs, smear the working surfaces of each leaf with a mixture of extra heavy dark gear oil and graphite. If you have difficulty in obtaining this grade of oil it is available from Rocol Ltd. called "Nimrod" E.H. Gear Oil. Having mentioned this we might as well go on to say that we wholeheartedly deprecate the use of anything but this heavy oil for lubricating any of the so-called "greasing points" on the chassis. In our experience it is a far better lubricant than any grease and has the great advantage of never clogging up the small passages communicating with the various bearings. The only place on a car to use grease is in the front hub bearings and in the water-pump bearing. In these two instances use a good-quality high-melting-point grease.

If you have decided to fit your springs with leather gaiters, and we hope that you have as they are well worth the expense both from a practical and an aesthetic point of view, they can be obtained from Wilcot (Parent) Co. Ltd., if you send particulars of the springs or an old gaiter. If you want grease-gun nipples fitted to the gaiters, which again are very well worth-while, tell them which form of nipple you are using on the rest of the chassis. Digressing again from the main theme, there are four types of grease nipple used on cars which are illustrated in fig. 6. The screw-on type

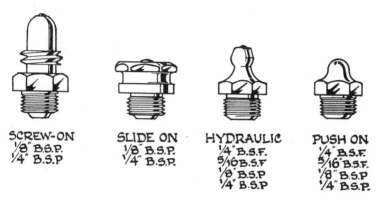

SCREW-ON
⅛" B.S.P.
¼" B.S.P

SLIDE ON
⅛" B.S.P.
¼" B.S.P.

HYDRAULIC
¼" B.S.F.
5/16 B.S.F
⅛" B.S.P
¼" B.S.P

PUSH ON
¼" B.S.F.
5/16 B.S.F.
⅛" B.S.P
¼" B.S.P.

6   *Types of grease nipples*

are no longer made but can sometimes be found at Rolls-Royce specialists. We will not advocate any particular type, but while overhauling your car it is well worth replacing all the nipples as a matter of course.

Shackles and Pins

Having completed the springs they are now ready to be put on to the frame, but we must first look at the shackles and shackle-pins. It is more than likely that new pins and bushes will have to be made. If this is so, the pins should be made from a 3% nickel case-hardening steel, such as KE169, available from Kayser Ellison and Co. Ltd., who, of course, are makers of a wide range of alloy steels covering a multitude of motor-car needs. When the pins are machined they must be case-hardened and Kayser Ellison will give, if asked, instructions as to the necessary heat treatment. If you have no local facilities for this it can be carried out by Heat Treatments Ltd. Be sure to send full particulars of the heat treatment required and the specification of the steel when sending the parts. The shackle bushes should be made of chill-cast phosphor-bronze which can be obtained at many millwrights' suppliers and metal stockholders, but if you have no such source, William Gabb Ltd. hold a large range of sizes in stock and will sell small quantities. In mentioning this firm we would also like to say that they can supply copper tube and rod, brass rounds, hexagons and sheet and also light alloy in various forms. When turning the bushes it is obvious that either an allowance must be made for the closing-in of the bush when it is pushed into the shackle or spring eye, or it will have to be reamered out after being inserted. The latter is the safest course, and if an expanding reamer of the correct size cannot be begged, borrowed or stolen from the local garage (if they have one), then the bush will have to be scraped out

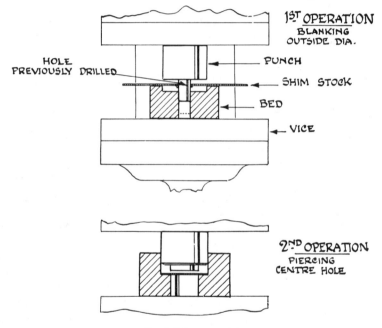

7   *Making a shim*

with a half-round scraper. The moral is, do not make the bush more than 0·001 in. interference fit on the outside and there will be very little to remove, if any, from the inside. In the case of springs with solid forged eyes, the bush can be a gentle press fit into the spring or can be left fully floating if so desired. If your car is fitted with such springs, then you are very lucky as they are a superb job. Jonas Woodhead Ltd., who have always made such springs, are willing to supply replacements or effect repairs on springs of their manufacture.

The shackles themselves should be scraped and cleaned. The faces which locate the spring sideways and the shackle in its chassis mounting should all be trued up perfectly flat. In all probability shims will have to be made to take side play out of all the spring connections. Remember that the springs are the connection between the car and the axles and that any side play will give loss of sensitivity in the handling of the finished car. Shims can be made by making a punch and bed from mild steel which will last long enough to make the small number required. Both punch and bed can be faced off in the lathe if they get too dull to cut. This job is illustrated in fig. 7. Shim steel from 0·002 in. to 0·010 in. in 0.001-in. steps is available from J. A. Hemming Ltd. in widths of 3 in. and 6 in. and in any length. Always use the thickest possible shim and not a pile of thin ones.

Should your car be fitted with "Silentbloc" bushes these should be renewed as a matter of course. They are obtainable from Silentbloc Ltd. The pin passing through the "Silentbloc" should be a nice sliding fit and the construction should be such that the centre metal portion of the bush is gripped solid when the pin is tightened, and all the movement is taken through the torsion of the rubber. If the bush complete revolves on its pin you will soon be in trouble.

Finally, prepare and paint the shackles and any portions of the springs which are not gaitered, and hang the springs on to the frame.

Dismantling of Front Axle

Now turn to the front axle. Strip this completely, keeping off- and near-side parts separate, and marking the axle beam in some way so that it is obvious which end is which. Probably the only difficulties encountered will be the removal of the hubs and the extraction of the king-pins. It is now time to make, or have made, what we shall call a universal extractor. This is illustrated in figs. 8a and b. It consists of a large flat disc of steel with a centre bolt. The steel disc is marked with a series of rings when it is being made and holes can be drilled on any pitch circle to suit the job in hand. The grooves are merely an aid to easy marking-out in the future. Such an extractor is invaluable in a number of applications on motor-car dismantling as it has great rigidity. The majority of two- or three-legged extractors have considerable spring in their legs, and if a really tight component has to be removed are fairly useless. Using the above type, holes are drilled in the disc to line up with holes already existing in the component to be removed. Bolts are then passed through both sets of holes and the disc secured. The centre bolt of the extractor is then wound in and if this alone cannot exert sufficient pull to perform the extraction, a really heavy blow on the head of the centre bolt will generally free the most obstinate part. The hubs can then be removed in this manner by bolting into either the wheel-stud holes or the brake-drum fixing holes. If the hubs are of the Rudge Whitworth variety and the correct Rudge extractor is not available, the universal extractor can be used as in fig 8b by making a collar to go behind the wheel-locking ring.

41

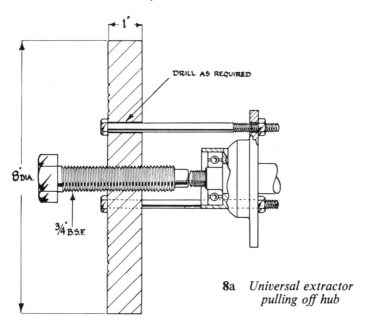

8a   *Universal extractor
pulling off hub*

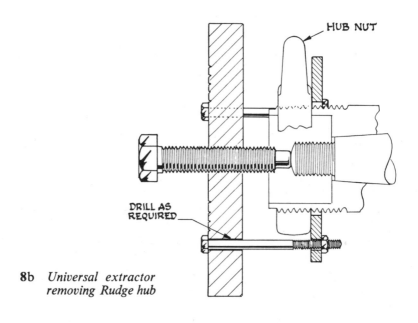

8b   *Universal extractor
removing Rudge hub*

The king-pins are usually removable downwards, in which case it is merely a matter of releasing whatever holds them in place and tapping them out of the axle. They may be rusted into the axle, when heating the axle with a blowpipe around the king-pin boss will generally help. It is very necessary to support the axle on something really solid, if force has to be used. If the king-pin has to be drawn out upwards, it will generally be tapped in the centre for an extractor. In this case make up an extractor as shown in fig 8c using a length of studding to screw into the king-pin. This studding is a very useful commodity to have in the workshop as it often saves making up long bolts. It is available in all sizes from Bridges Ltd. in lengths of 12 in. They also supply high-tensile bolts in all standard sizes, "Nyloc" and "Aerotight" self-locking nuts.

Inspection and Repair of Axle Beam

Clean and scrape the front axle beam. Then hold it in the vice for inspection. It is important that both spring pads be in the same plane and that an extended line joining their centres either passes through the centre line of both king-pin eyes or, in some cases, lies an equal distance from each king-pin eye. It is also necessary that, viewed from the front or rear of the car, the king-pins make equal angles with the vertical. Set squares placed on the spring pads and test bars about 12 in. long put in the king-pin eyes can be used to check these points as shown in fig. 9. On cars fitted with transverse springs, the shackle-pin eyes must be parallel with one another, and vertical lines taken from the front faces of the shackle eyes must be an

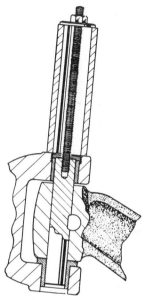

8c *King-pin extractor*

equal distance from the line joining the centres of the two king-pin eyes. If the axle is bent then, if it is of a light section, try straightening it cold in the vice. Generally a long length of tube put over the end of the axle will give sufficient leverage to do this. On heavier axles, heat will have to be used. Heat the axle to a dull red where you require it straightened and pull in the appropriate direction. On no account plunge the hot axle into water when the operation is complete, as the beam may be made of an alloy steel which will harden on quenching and become very brittle. Examine the king-pin eyes to see if they are bell-mouthed or in any way unsuitable to hold the king-pin firmly. If they are, reamer them out while realising that oversize king-pins will now have to be made.

If the connections for the shock absorbers are integral with the axle

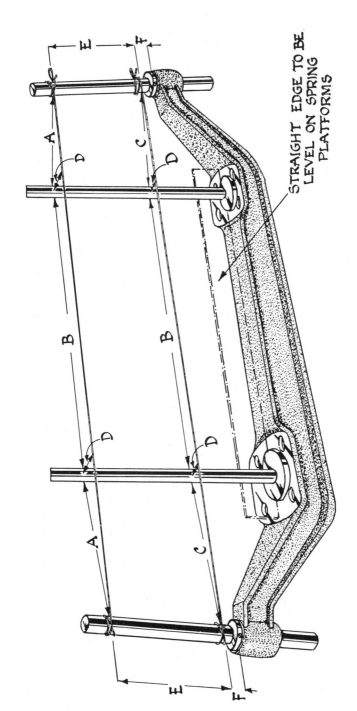

STRAIGHT EDGE TO BE
LEVEL ON SPRING
PLATFORMS

9   Front axle alignment

beam, see that they are in good order. In passing we would like to say that we think that it is permissible, even on the most thorough restoration, to fit shock absorbers of a different design to those fitted originally if these have proved useless over the years. They should, of course, be replaced by a type suitable to the age of the car and, if you have this in mind, you may have to modify the connecting points at this juncture. We deal with this subject more fully in the appropriate chapter.

If the beam is badly dented, file out these dents where possible and, if the axle shows when looking at the front of the complete motor-car, fill any damage as with the frame, and get as good a paint finish as possible.

Next examine the method of holding the axle to the springs. If this is done by U-bolts of the square type and they are not in first-class condition, we recommend that you throw them into the scrap bin. They are a very poor engineering design and can either be replaced by a plate over the spring and four high-tensile bolts or by round section U-bolts, with a semi-circular portion joining the two legs of the U. In the latter case you will have to make up a semi-circular chair for the U-bolt which will sit on top of the spring. This can be an aluminium casting or can be turned as a pair which can be cut diametrically to form two chairs.

The U-bolts themselves can be turned from KE805 in its normalised condition (50 tons per sq. in. U.T.S.) and bent cold round a suitable former after screwcutting. No heat treatment is necessary. If, during your trials of the car, you found that the castor action was not to your liking and that tilting the axle either one way or the other put the matter right, then now is the time to make a permanent job of the necessary wedges to fit between axle and springs. These can be made from any metal and the appropriate taper milled or even filed on.

Now fit the axle on to its springs using self-locking nuts which can easily be checked for tightness from time to time without having to remove split-pins.

Stub-axle Overhaul

Start now to overhaul the stub axles. If the king-pins are loose in their bushes, measure the pins for wear and examine for roughness. New pins can be made from KE169 and case-hardened according to the steel-maker's instructions. If no grinding facilities are available, turn them up with as good a finish as possible and polish them with emery cloth after heat treatment. The king-pin bushes can be made out of phosphor-bronze or mild steel which is case-hardened after machining. The latter appears to be a very good material for these bushes as, on some makes of Vintage cars which fitted them, it is practically unheard of to have to replace either the pins or bushes even after twenty-five years. Such bushes cannot, of course, be reamered after being drawn into their housings and the correct clearance must be left in the original machining. An extractor of the same type as shown in fig. 8 can be used for removing the old bushes, putting a nut and

45

washer on to the end of the stud which was previously screwed into the king-pin. The new bush should have a lead of about $\frac{1}{8}$ in. of a diameter which will slide into its housing. This will allow the bush to be started into the hole true. It should then be drawn in with a long bolt. Hammering a bush into its housing generally results in the bush tilting and thus becoming distorted. If there is a felt-washer oil seal on the king-pin this will probably have to be replaced. Cooper and Co. (B'ham) Ltd. can either supply the felt in sheet form or will cut washers to any size in their M.W. grade of felt. In the latter case, specify the diameters of the shaft and housing and the dimension of the space to be occupied by the washer and they will allow for the necessary compression of the felt when they make the seal.

Check the fit of the hub inner races on the stub axle. These should be a *light* tap fit. If, for some reason, the races have been turning on the stubs and are now loose, the stubs will have to be built up. If it is only a matter of a few thousandths, up to say 0·005 in. on the diameter, it is possible to electro-deposit hard chrome fairly accurately on to the places required. On a thin deposit it is possible to get the final accurate dimension by polishing with emery cloth. This is a slow and tedious business, but if no machining capacity is available it can be done. Deposits larger than this are always very rough, and if done with chrome, must be set up in a grinding machine and ground to size. An alternative to this is to have the shaft built up by metal spraying which can be done in almost any metal. In this case a mild-steel deposit is perfectly adequate. The deposit from metal spraying is always rough and will have to be turned down to a finished size. Brita-chrome Ltd. will deposit chrome up to any required thickness and Metal-lisation Ltd. are specialists in metal spraying.

Steering Connections

It will now be necessary to remove the steering-arms from the stub axles if this has not already been done. Before doing so, however, check if these arms are in any way bent. This is rather a difficult subject on which to generalise but it usually is possible to get leading dimensions from a given datum on each stub axle to the centre of the ball-pin, or swivel-pin hole, on the steering-arms. These must, of course, be the same in each case. An instance of how to get a measurement would be to put a straight-edge across the brake back-plate securing flange, projecting out as far as the end of the steering-arm. A measurement could then be taken from this straight-edge, and at right angles to it, to the centre of the ball-pin socket on the steering-arm. This measurement must be the same on each stub axle. Another check is a straight-edge laid across one of the inner faces of the king-pin bosses and a measurement taken down to the top of the ball-pin. If both these checks were identical on each side, then the steering-arms could be considered correct as, had they been accidentally damaged, it is hardly likely that they would have been bent by the same amount. To check the arm on to which the drag-link connects and where the drag-link is fore and aft, the ball-pin in the arm should be over the centre of the axle beam with the road wheels in the straight-ahead position. If the arms have to be straightened it is generally easier to do this while they are attached to the stub axle and small amounts can be done cold. If you have to resort to heat never quench them, let them cool slowly.

Having checked the steering-arms they can now be dismantled from the stub-axle assembly. You may have some difficulty in removing them if, as in many cases, they are drawn into tapered sockets. There is a very good way of freeing any taper like this which is well worth remembering. Lay the outside of the boss in which the taper hole is situated on an anvil or other suitably heavy block of steel. Then strike the side of the boss diametrically opposite very hard with a heavy hammer. It is best to have someone to help with this operation and then a piece of brass can be held against the boss and this struck with the hammer to avoid damage. One or two heavy blows will generally free the tightest taper, but it is essential that a really massive block be used to hold up the component. The same method can be used to release the ball-pins from the steering-arms if they are fitted by means of a tapered shank. This is illustrated in fig. 10.

We hope you will be really fussy about all the steering connections, as they are literally a matter of life and death. We recommend that all the steering-arms are filed and polished, examined and then sent for magnetic crack detecting. The ball-pins should be treated likewise, and if they are at all worn in the neck under the ball, they should be scrapped and replaced. Any small ridges on the actual ball surface can

10 *Removing a ball-pin from its taper*

be stoned off. The magnetic crack detection can be done by Commercial X-Rays Ltd. If new ball-pins have to be made, use KE169 and have them case-hardened to a depth of only 0·005 in., as this will give a maximum amount of tough core. They should be highly polished, particularly in the neck where the greatest loads occur. If you turn up these ball-pins yourself and wonder how to get a truly spherical ball portion, you will find that, having turned the ball to a semi-circular template as accurately as possible by normal methods, the ball can be finished by holding the open end of a suitable diameter tube up against it while it is still turning in the lathe. The bore of the tube does not have to be any particular size but must be smaller than the diameter of the ball, and the outside should be turned down to a feather edge like a leather punch. If this is held in both hands and forced against the ball, metal will be removed until the ball is touching all round the end of the tube and the ball will then be truly spherical. A

47

piece of silver steel, or other steel which can be suitably hardened, should be used to make the tube. This is shown in fig. 11. Assemble the steering-arms back into the stub axles and put these on to the axle beam.

Next look at the track-rod and drag-link. These are generally tubular, and if they are badly dented the tubular portion should be replaced, using the same gauge of bright-drawn, seamless, mild-steel tube as was used before. If solid ends are brazed on these can be cut off, bored out and a new piece of tube pinned and brazed in. Examine the ball-cups, they will probably have ridges in their hemispherical surfaces. These can be removed by very careful grinding with a high-speed hand grinder, or the cups can be remade using case-hardened mild steel. Prepare and paint or plate the track-rod, and fit it to the axle assembly, leaving the final adjustment of the track until a later stage. When tightening the ball-cups on to the ball-pins see that, in their final position, the balls have only a minimum of movement against the pressure springs. The movement should have a

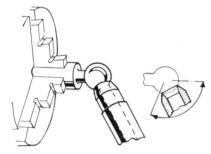

11 *Finish turning a ball*

fixed stop the length of which should be adjusted so that not more than 0·010 in. of movement against the springs is allowed. The springs have two purposes, one to take up wear and out-of-round in the ball-pins, and the other to introduce a small amount of friction into the steering system. Cars which are not fitted with spring loading in the steering connections, and occasionally those which are so fitted, are prone to low-speed front-wheel wobble, particularly if they have been fitted with larger and heavier tires and wheels than those originally supplied. The cure for this is either to increase the spring pressure in the steering connections or to introduce some small amount of friction into the system by other means. The weight of the car is sometimes carried on ball thrust races in the king-pin assemblies. If these are replaced by plain thrust washers or if a steering damper is fitted, the low-speed wobble can generally be eliminated. Reducing the castor angle will also tend to diminish the tendency to wobble. Be perfectly certain, of course, that the ball-pin is free to turn in its housing and does not jam at any point. Should you be at all doubtful of the ball-pins and not be able to remake them, then it seems reasonable in the interests of safety to replace the whole track-rod assembly by one using a modern type of swivelling connection. Finally, consider whether you would like to fit leather gaiters to the track-rod and drag-link ends. Some Vintage cars were so fitted and there is no doubt that such protection helps to keep the joints in very good condition. These gaiters can be obtained from Wilcot (Parent) Co. Ltd., providing that all dimensions of the joint are given.

Steering-box and Column

We now turn to the steering-box and column. Before dismantling, swill out the box with paraffin and check the amount of play in the box when undisguised by thick oil. With the drop-arm held solid, anything more than 1 in. at the rim of the steering-wheel is undesirable. If the box is adjustable for mesh, try, at this stage, to reduce play to a minimum compatible with having no tight spots at the full-lock positions. There are many types of steering-box and those found on Vintage cars are generally of ample proportions. Many today are still in a perfectly satisfactory state even though they are not adjustable. There is nearly always an adjustment for end-play in the column and this should be taken up first, before checking the free movement in the actual gearing. If there is excessive play and no adjustment, all may still not be lost. On worm and worm-wheel boxes, it is often possible to cut a new key-way in the worm-wheel shaft to reorientate the worm-wheel and drop-arm, and thus to use an unworn portion of the wheel. On a worm-and-nut box, the nut is sometimes white-metal lined and new metalling will put matters right. If the nut is bronze, then it can be carefully tinned internally with soft solder, screwed on to the worm, packed round with clay, warmed up to the melting point of the solder, and white metal poured in.

If new gears have to be made they are naturally expensive, and you will do well to see if you can find a replacement pair in better condition than your own. If this is impossible Schofield & Samson Ltd. or G. H. Turner & Co. Ltd. can cut gears to the old patterns.

Having made this check, now dismantle the complete box and column. Clean all parts and, if there are any ball-races, you will find the best way to clean them is wash them out under the hot-water tap after having swilled them in paraffin. This removes all grit and they will spin perfectly freely. Ball bearings cleaned in this manner must be oiled immediately after washing or else they will rust. Check all plain bearings for play and remake or replace wherever necessary. For good results it is necessary that there shall be no play nor any undue friction in any of the steering-box bearings. If your car is unfortunate enough to be fitted with one of those dreadfully ignorant felt-bearings at the top of the column, replace this with either a phosphor-bronze bush or, if possible, make up a housing and fit a ball-race. This can improve the feel of the steering immeasurably. If the drop-arm is fitted on a taper, this can be removed in the same way as we described for removing the ball-pins. Should the arm be loose on its taper, this can often be rectified by grinding it in on to its shaft with very fine grinding paste, finishing with metal polish and checking the fit with prussian blue. The key in this position must be a first-class fit in both shaft and drop-arm. If the drop-arm is fitted in taper splines, and the box has limited movement, see that it is correctly centred when replacing.

The steering-column and box is often a major component under the

49

bonnet and can be brought up to a show finish. This is dealt with in a later chapter, but bear it in mind before you start assembling. The upper reaches of the column and the wheel being inside the body will, of course, have to be brought to the same state of perfection as the inside of the car. If the column is to be plated, now is the time to make friends with the nearest plater. From now on you will be visiting him very frequently, and if you want to keep friendly with him you will take your parts in the best possible condition, leaving him a minimum amount of polishing to do before he can plate. Also remember that the more polishing that has to be done, the more shapeless the article will become. It is far better to file or machine out rust pocks or dents than to leave it to the polisher who, after all, has only a polishing mop with which to do his work and cannot hope to keep corners sharp and surfaces flat if he has to remove much metal. Insist that any steel work is copper plated before nickel or nickel and chrome are deposited. It is possible to get a beautiful-looking job with no undercoat of copper, but this will not last very long if exposed to the weather. If the column was celluloid covered and this is damaged, and you cannot get a new piece of celluloid, then it will either have to be plated or painted. Do not paint the shaft until it has been put through its bearings for the last time as this will ruin the paint and you will have to do it again.

The Steering-wheel

The steering-wheel is always something of a problem. Some of the older Vintage wheels were very clumsy to handle and it seems a pity to have to put up with this. If you are a purist you will obviously refit the original wheel. If it needs a new covering of celluloid, Exceloid Ltd. may do the work. Bluemel Bros. Ltd. can supply certain types of new wheel which are of a very Vintage character and are, in fact, identical to those fitted to some of the later Vintage motor-cars. A wooden-rimmed wheel can be repaired by letting in sections of the appropriate wood, often walnut. A very pretty, completely new, wheel can be made by cutting the rim and spokes in one piece from a sheet of $\frac{3}{16}$-in. duralumin and riveting a wood rim on to either side of this. The boss is then riveted to the centre of the spokes.

There are usually some control levers above the wheel and these must be refurbished. The teeth of a notched quadrant generally need sharpening with a small file, and the whole assembly should be brought up to a first-class condition. If the levers are fitted with knobs which are either lost or broken, or the horn button needs renewing, these can be remade in ebonite, hard wood or plated brass. You can get stick ebonite in a range of diameters from Heaven Dowsett and Co. Ltd., who can also supply the complete range of plastics, such as "Tufnol" and "Perspex", in a wide variety of sizes.

Apart from plating or painting, a finish which can be very effective for these controls is that of oxidised copper. The pieces are first copper-plated, and then dipped in a solution which oxidises the copper into a semi-matt black, and should be lacquered. This finish can be produced by most electro-plating firms.

Before putting the complete column back on to the chassis, have a look at its point of mounting. It is essential for good steering that this be as rigid as possible. If the box is bolted on to the top flange of the chassis frame only, then put tubular distance pieces between top and bottom flange and bolt the box on with long bolts passing right through the frame. The top mounting of the column can often be improved with great advantage by a steadying bracket off the bulkhead joining the column as high up as possible.

You will have noticed that nothing has been said in this chapter about cars with front-wheel drive or independent front-wheel suspension. This has been intentional, as neither of the authors has had any practical experience in the overhaul of such cars. One last point which we would like to mention before leaving the front axle: if you are going to fit front brakes to a car not previously so equipped, or if you have greatly increased the braking power of the front brakes, then you may consider fitting radius rods to the axle to prevent the castor angle becoming negative under heavy loading. You will have to design them to suit your particular car, and you will have to pick pivot points on the chassis from which arcs, inscribed through the fixing points on the axle, as nearly as possible coincide with the paths of those points during axle movement. Under no circumstance have these rods in front of the axle under compression, as this induces front-wheel tramp under heavy braking.

CHAPTER V

THE REAR AXLE AND SHOCK-ABSORBERS

Dismantling

THE axle may be a large and heavy one, in which case before stripping it down, you will find it a great help if you make two rough wooden stands to hold it, otherwise you will find that it is a most difficult piece of gear to handle.

Having fixed the axle to your liking, next drain off the oil and refill with paraffin. Now rotate the shaft to dissolve all the oil and drain again. The gears being free of oil, take hold of the propeller-shaft connection, lock the axle shafts and test for back-lash. More than 10° free movement is excessive. It should not be assumed that an axle is perfect because it is quiet and has a normal amount of back-lash. We well remember an axle which was the quietest example of one particular make that we had experienced. We made the fatal error of presuming that everything inside was beautiful, and put it away thinking that when the day came it would entail very little work. When the axle had been flushed out and gaily turned over in a most confident manner, the owner turned very white and had to be revived with the necessary stimulant, as there were loud noises of loose pieces inside. The back cover was removed in record time, only to find that three bolts were broken and the differential housing was cracked through in six places. There were no spares available so a new differential was designed and made to overcome the weakness that had caused the trouble, new planet-wheels had to be made, but the crown-wheel and pinion were in perfect condition. The whole job took about three weeks instead of a weekend.

Whatever the design, the rear hubs and companion flange on the bevel-pinion or worm-shaft can usually be removed with the universal extractor as made for the front axle. Now remove the half-shafts and then take off the nose-piece or torque-tube and back cover, if one is fitted, and strip down the differential and bevel pinion assemblies. Carefully mark any meshing adjustments. If these are screw threads, mark the nut position and make a note of the number of turns required to remove it. Note particularly if any gaskets have been used, and if so, their thickness. Any deviation from the maker's original practice may result in alignments being upset. Take note of the sequence of assembly as this may save a lot of unnecessary work later on. Now thoroughly clean all the parts, the axle casing inside and out. and remove old paint. If the transmission is by chains, make notes of the positions of the sprockets if they have to be removed either to straighten or to fit a new shaft.

52

Examination and Repairs to Casing

Make a thorough examination of the casing. This is usually steel, but it may be in part an aluminium casting. If there are any cracks they will have to be welded. Examine any brazed flange joints and rivets and replace them if they are loose. If the brake camshaft bushes are worn, extract the old ones and turn up new ones out of phosphor-bronze cored bar, and if the shafts are worn at their bearings and new ones are not available, they must be turned down, hard-chromed and then ground to size. The brake back plates are often in bad shape and are either rubbing on the brake drums or allowing the mud to get inside. If so, remove them and planish out all dents and irregularities, refitting them when the axle is back on the car.

If the axle is of the torque-tube type and the tube is clamped into the axle casing, make absolutely certain that the tube is held really firmly in the axle casing when it is clamped up. Play often develops here and, if loose, the case must be bored out and the tube built up by metal spraying and turned down to fit. The case can be lapped out with a cylinder hone.

If a torque-arm is fitted with an open shaft, and ball-type connections are used on the chassis anchorage, these must be free to move but must have no play or they will produce a lot of noise. Treat these in the same way as steering joints except that if they have to be replaced it may be better and easier if they are changed to "Silentbloc" bushes. These can be obtained from Silentbloc Ltd.

Some axles are assembled with long bolts holding both nose-piece and back cover and this type is very liable to have the flanges cracked due to slight crushing of the axle casing. Further cracking can be cured quite easily by fitting thick-walled duralumin tubes inside the casing so that the bolts pass through them. The tubes must be a good fit and tapped into place so that when the nuts are tightened on the bolts, no distortion takes place.

If the car has an open propeller-shaft, now is the time to paint the axle casing and fit it to the springs as, if it is a heavy one, the final assemblies are done much more easily in this position. The fitting to the springs may be by U-bolts or plate and bolts, and this assembly should be treated in the same way as for the front axle.

If the car is fitted with a torque tube, the painting is best left until the axle is all assembled, but if fitted with cantilever springs, the mountings should be examined at this stage and any worn rollers replaced. Examine all ball-races and make sure that none have been turning in their housings: if this has happened the housing will have to be built-up by metal spraying and then machined to size. The ball-races should be a nice press fit and not tight.

The Differential

Examine the inside of the differential; any wear on shafts or bushes is obvious and can be measured. Replace any worn bushes, making new ones from phosphor-bronze, new shafts can be made from KE169, case-hardened and ground to size. If the spider is worn and a new one is not available, it must be ground down, hard chromed and then ground to size. Wear in the gears is difficult to measure, so when the pins and bushes have been put in order assemble the differential only and put in the axle shafts. Then, holding the outer case of the differential and one axle shaft, test the free movement of the other shaft. This should be practically nil, otherwise with the magnification of this play due to the axle ratio, the play at the propeller-shaft will be excessive and the result will be a loud clonk in the transmission every time the drive reverses. If this play is due to wear in the sun-and-planet wheels, do not despair as new ones can be made by Schofield & Samson Ltd. at quite reasonable prices. If the play is due to spline wear at the axle-shaft connection, it will generally be found that the shaft has worn, as this is softer than the gear-wheel. If the shaft is otherwise good, these splines can be built up by metal spraying and then recut by milling or filing to fit.

If the axle shafts run in bearings in the differential and the shafts are worn, they can be built up with hard chrome and ground to size. Examine the shafts for twist at the end of the splines as this is the place where fracture usually takes place; if there is any sign of twisting they must be scrapped. Should you be unable to get any new or second-hand shafts, make new ones from KE805 steel. After machining they must be heat-treated to 80 tons per sq. in. U.T.S. Schofield & Samson Ltd., or any other firm with a suitable milling machine, can cut the splines.

If the axle shaft is bent, and this is quite possible if the car has a semi-floating axle and has been in a smash where the blow has been taken on one of the back road wheels, it can be straightened with a screw press (the local garage should have one) and two V-blocks. Place the shaft with the bend midway between the two V-blocks which should not be too far apart and bring the press down gradually, so that you do not overdo it, and keep testing the shaft until it runs true between the centres of a lathe.

Examine the crown-wheel and pinion or worm and wheel. If wear has taken place, it will show as ridges at the root of the teeth. A little wear will not matter, but if the wheel is case-hardened make sure, by testing with a file, that the wear has not gone right through the hardened skin. If you are unfortunate and this is the case, then the wheel is at the end of its useful life. Should the car be one that was made in large numbers, you will probably be able to get spares. It may be that only one wheel has worn, and if you cannot get a new pair it might happen that you could replace only the worn one. In this case the drive would be quite satisfactory but it would undoubtedly be very noisy. Odd wheels should be lapped-in together with flour emery, but this is a very difficult procedure unless an elaborate rig is made up. The operation must not be done in the axle casing as the emery will not only ruin the ball-races but will get into all the crevices in the casing, from which it will emerge when the car is run and play havoc with the whole mechanism. If you have a spare nose-piece, this can be used as a lapping rig. If no spares are available a new crown-wheel and pinion can be made by Schofield & Samson Ltd., but this firm cannot cut spiral bevels. However, a straight-cut pair of bevels is better than no car and, if a little more noisy than a pair of spirals, are otherwise perfectly satisfactory. Schofield & Samson Ltd. can also make worms and worm-wheels.

Check all bearings and replace any that are in bad condition, reassemble the crown-wheel and pinion into the nose-piece, putting the adjustment back into its original position. If play is still considerable, try to reduce it by adjustment. While this is the correct procedure, unfortunately when a pair of gear-wheels have been run for a considerable time in one position, they usually rather noisy when adjusted to a new position. If the adjustment position has been lost set the wheels right in mesh with the outside of the teeth in line as in fig. 12. Now manipulate the adjustments, keeping the outside of the teeth still in line but to give the small amount of play necessary, this should be just audible if the crown-wheel is rocked with the pinion held firmly. If the bevel pinion is now smeared with a thin coat of engineer's blue and the whole assembly rotated, the marking on the crown-wheel will show if the adjustment is correct as in fig. 13.

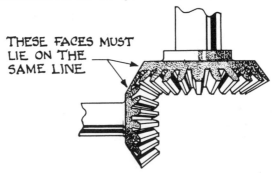

THESE FACES MUST LIE ON THE SAME LINE

12 *Setting bevel gears*

The above does not apply to hypoid axles, where there is no general rule, and with which it is even more important to note the original setting.

On worm axles there must be absolutely no side-play in the mounting of the worm-wheel and this must be dead on the centre line of the worm. Usually there is no adjustment provided here, but if any wear has taken place the bearings must be rectified to eliminate all side-play. The thrust bearing on the worm is generally adjustable, there must be no end-play here or there will be a frightful noise each time the load is reversed.

Many axles were fitted with screw-type oil seals. The clearance in these has usually enlarged with wear, so that each time the car stops a small amount of oil is lost from the nose-piece and oil also tends to creep out of the ends of the half-shafts and deposit itself all over the brakes. This fault can be cured completely by fitting synthetic-rubber oil seals made by George Angus and Co. Ltd. A housing can be turned up out of duralumin and either riveted or held by a ring of small B.A. pins on to the original casing. The method of doing this will depend on the design of the part to be modified. A typical arrangement is shown in fig. 14. Get the Angus catalogue before you start designing this modification. They have a multitude of standard sizes of oil seal but cannot make any non-standard

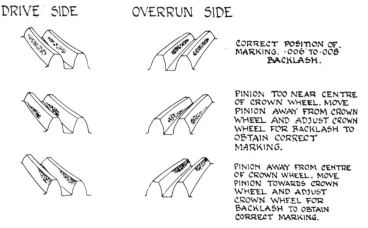

DRIVE SIDE   OVERRUN SIDE

CORRECT POSITION OF. MARKING. ·006˝ TO ·008˝ BACKLASH.

PINION TOO NEAR CENTRE OF CROWN WHEEL. MOVE PINION AWAY FROM CROWN WHEEL AND ADJUST CROWN WHEEL FOR BACKLASH TO OBTAIN CORRECT MARKING.

PINION AWAY FROM CENTRE OF CROWN WHEEL. MOVE PINION TOWARDS CROWN WHEEL AND ADJUST CROWN WHEEL FOR BACKLASH TO OBTAIN CORRECT MARKING.

13   *Correct marking for spiral bevels*

sizes. The shaft on which the seal bears must be highly polished and is even better if hard chromed. When fitting these seals to the outer ends of the

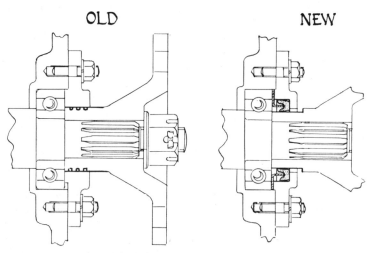

OLD   NEW

14   *Using a modern oil seal*

half-shafts, care must be taken that its position does not cause the outer bearings to run dry.

If gaskets are to be fitted a good and tough material is "Gaskoid"

Jointing made by James Walker and Co. Ltd. This material does not require any jointing compound and is made in six thicknesses, these are $\frac{1}{100}$ in., $\frac{1}{64}$ in., $\frac{1}{32}$ in., $\frac{1}{16}$ in., $\frac{3}{32}$ in. and $\frac{1}{8}$ in.

Many owners of old cars are in doubt as to what grade of oil to use in the back axle. There is no need to use the steam cylinder oil as originally recommended by the makers. Modern light oils will be found quite satisfactory, and even if this does not muffle all the noises it will result in rather more of your possibly somewhat limited horse-power arriving at the back wheels. The axle has now been assembled, painted and fitted to the springs and the next items in the rebuild are the shock absorbers.

Shock-absorbers

Over the years only one type of shock-absorber has proved to be really effective and long-wearing for Vintage-type cars with small axle movement, and that is the double-acting friction-type of which the best known is the Hartford. Most other friction types acted in one direction only and were called snubbers; these are quite useless. Designers at the time were obsessed with the idea that the damping must be on the return movement only, hence the great variety of snubbers. The only type of double-acting, double-armed friction shock-absorbers which are any good are those with universally jointed connections at chassis and axle. Originally these were double wooden-bushed bearings, and later on "Silentbloc" bushes were used. The type in which the friction discs are mounted on the chassis and connected to the axle with a rod using ball-joints or "Silentbloc" bushes at the ends, are also satisfactory. Single bearing type, whether with or without friction discs at the ends of the arms, are no good at all, as distortion renders them inoperative when cornering.

There have been quite a number of vane-type hydraulic dampers but these are no good, as the clearance between the vanes and the body has to be very close and varies with the temperature; this type also wears out very rapidly. On cars with a larger axle movement than is normally found in the Vintage era, piston-type hydraulic dampers are satisfactory. If you are fitting these to a car that has not previously had them, see that as much as possible of the available stroke is used when the axle moves over its normal travel. The shorter the movement of the plungers the more critical the setting will be, and the worse will be the effect of wear. For this reason they are not so good as the friction type on Vintage cars.

If you have the Hartford type, strip them down and take out the rivets. You can now derust and paint between the blades, replacing the rivets with bolts. Rubber bushes can only be replaced by the manufacturers as they have no outer shell, but the wood-type bushes can be turned up out of boxwood; these should have no play—just a good working fit. Spare parts, or new Hartford shock-absorbers, can be supplied by Jonas Woodhead and Son (Scotland) Ltd., and the reconditioning of old ones can be done by this firm or by Sorber Accessories Ltd.

When reassembled tighten each damper to an equal poundage with a spring balance, this will be the zero position and further adjustment should be done by an equal amount on each front and each rear damper. When fitting the "Silentbloc" bushes to their mountings, the centre must be gripped firmly so that the movement is taken through the rubber; the tightening of the mounting bolt must also be done when the arms are in the normal position and *not* with the chassis jacked-up or an extra heavy load in the car, so that the torsion in the rubber bush is equal in both up and down movement of the axle. When fitting new shock-absorbers, make sure they are large enough for the work. It is better to have them too large than too small.

If you are making new mountings they must be as rigid as possible, as they have a great deal of work to do and if they are flimsy they will soon break. They should also be mounted on the frame as near to a cross-member as possible.

Any type of shock-absorber should be made to act on the axle as near the road wheel as possible. The reason for this is that usually only one wheel is deflected by a bump, and the control that the shock-absorber concerned has over the axle movement then varies as the square of the distance that it acts from the centre of the axle beam. It is usually difficult with the double-arm-type Hartford to fit it any further out than just out-board of the springs. This position is usually good enough for most purposes. With one-arm type and piston hydraulic dampers, the connection can often be fitted much further out if a little ingenuity is used. This is non-Vintage practice but it is quite legitimate on Thoroughbreds. Piston-type hydraulic dampers should be sent to the makers for reconditioning. If they are obsolete fit new modern ones, but always consult the manufacturer who can best advise you on the type and setting required on your particular application.

CHAPTER VI

BRAKES, HUBS, WHEELS AND TIRES

THIS is probably the most important chapter in the book. If those of us who use old motor-cars want to avoid being frowned upon by the powers-that-be, then the ability to retard one's progress is a greater virtue than to accelerate it, pleasant though this may be. Hence the vital necessity of having the brakes in first-class condition, which will not only placate the police but may be the means of preventing an untimely end to some very pleasant motoring.

We cannot avoid getting a little out of order in the sequence of over-hauling the car in this chapter, as obviously the brake back plates have to be fitted before the hubs, and the shoes and drums afterwards, but for the sake of clarity we will deal with the brakes first.

Mechanical Brakes

Starting with the pedal and hand lever, see that both these have their fulcrum bearings in good order. If they are loose, either rebush them with phosphor-bronze or, if no bush was originally fitted, bore them out sufficiently to take a bush, which need not be more than $\frac{1}{16}$ in. in wall thickness.

It is worthwhile being rather fussy about the condition of the pedal pad. We dislike rubber pads as they can be very treacherous in wet or snowy weather. The best type is a metal pad with deep serrations cut in it or, as second best, a number of large-diameter holes drilled in it. The latter method also has the advantage of cutting down the vibrating mass of the pedal and increases the life of the fulcrum bearing. You can easily make the wood pattern for a cast-aluminium pad yourself and with a little in-genuity can work the initial letter of your car into the centre, which adds considerable tone to the finished article. The clutch pedal can, of course, be dealt with at the same time.

The handbrake lever generally looks well polished and plated. Before doing this, however, check the action of the ratchet mechanism, replacing any worn pins and, if necessary, sharpening up the teeth of the ratchet quadrant with a file. The pawls are generally badly worn and these can be remade in mild steel and case-hardened.

Proceed now to overhaul the brake-operating mechanism with a view to eliminating all back-lash and lost motion. There is no doubt in our minds that the best mechanical brake-operating mechanisms are those which employ rods and shafts, as these are the least subject to stretching under heavy load and can also be made to have very little frictional loss. If your car has open cable operation it might be well worth considering at this point whether at least some of the cable could be replaced by rods.

Dealing first with rod-operated systems, carefully examine all the rods, fork-ends and clevis-pins. The fork-ends and levers can be drilled out and oversize clevis-pins made from mild steel followed by case-hardening. If any of the threads on the rods are corroded, scrap the rods and remake them. Mild steel is generally perfectly adequate for these, and if of any size over $\frac{1}{4}$ in. diameter it is definitely satisfactory. If you have any doubts, make them from KE805 in the 55-ton per sq. in. U.T.S. condition. You will find it an advantage to cadmium-plate these rods which can be subsequently painted if necessary, leaving the threads unpainted for ease of future adjustment.

Any cross-shafts in the mechanism must obviously have freedom of movement without any play in their bearings. There are certain cars, which fitted cross-shafts with plain bearings at either end, which had no provision for self-alignment. This, of course, is dreadful, as any chassis whip will immediately put a tremendous amount of friction into the operating gear. If your car happens to be so afflicted, you will be well advised to make up some sort of spherical plain bearing on each end of the shaft concerned, or better still to mount it in self-aligning ball-races.

There are many types of compensator to be found on Vintage and Thoroughbred cars and it is impossible to deal with their actions individually. However, their adjustment or setting is generally dealt with in the manufacturer's instruction book, which should be carefully studied, as the good working of the brakes will depend on the compensator being correctly set up.

Some Vintage cars have a straightforward mechanically operated brake system, which has no compensation for the fact that the energy is being fed into the system from the driver's side of the car, with the result that the majority of the braking is done by the drums on that side. That is, of course, due to the twisting of the cross-shafts under load and, if your car is of this type and the cross-shafts are of a small diameter, it is perfectly permissible to increase their diameters to as large as possible, in the interests of equal braking on all wheels.

Coming now to the brake camshafts, make sure, once again, that they run nicely in their bearings with no play. Look at the fulcrum pins of the shoes on each back plate. These must be rigidly held and if there is any sign of looseness this must be rectified, or you will suffer from the brakes grabbing. If the front brakes are Perrot-shaft operated there must be no back-lash in the universal joints or play in the bearings at either end. Perrot shafts are usually one of two designs, either they have a cross-pin type of universal joint or they are of the claw-and-ball design. In the former case, if there is appreciable wear, the forks can be drilled out and oversize pins made from KE169 case-hardened, but in the latter case you have got a real job on hand. The only way of tackling it is to build up the claws by metal spraying and carefully file both working faces flat and parallel. The grooves in the ball will also have to be filed out until the claws are a good working fit in them. A very good idea, and one which was standard on some Vintage cars, is to make up leather gaiters for the Perrot shafts, seeing that they are well oiled with extra heavy gear oil before putting on the gaiters. While talking of lubrication perhaps we should mention that, as none of the fork-ends and clevis-pins on the braking system have any proper means of oiling, we find it best to assemble them with a smear of "Ragosine" anti-scuffing paste, which contains molybdenum disulphide and which will last as a lubricant for a very long time.

The same principles apply when overhauling a cable-operated braking system. Get rid of any lost motion and friction wherever possible. If you are dealing with open cables running over pulleys, it will be as well to start

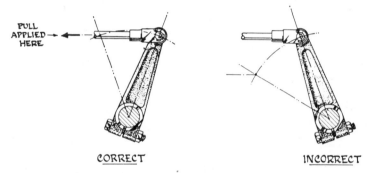

PULL
APPLIED →
HERE

CORRECT   INCORRECT

15 *Setting of brake-operating levers in " off " position*

with new cables unless the old ones are absolutely flawless. Cables of all sizes are made by Bowden (Engineers) Ltd. but they prefer that those requiring small quantities go to Thomas Richfield and Son Ltd., who also stock a considerable range of end fittings and can make up complete cables to your requirements. If the pulleys on your car are rather small in diameter, tending to kink the cable, try to redesign them bearing in mind that the larger the pulley the less will be the friction. In our opinion no cable and pulley system can ever be satisfactory, because it is absolutely necessary for frictionless operation to have pulleys between 20 and 30 times the diameter of the cable, and this is impractical on motor-cars.

On "Bowdenex" cable systems, that is, where the operating cable runs inside a flexible metallic conduit, it is essential that the cable lies along an easy running line and that all bends are of the maximum radius. In all probability, it will pay to replace all the cables and here again Thomas Richfield can oblige. If the old conduits are not fitted with lubricating points, then see that the new ones are, as regular oiling will help greatly in ease of operation and also stop the possibility of the cables rusting.

If your mechanical braking system is not of the cam-operated type but is, say, Girling, see that all the moving parts in the shoe-expanding mechanism are in as good order as possible. If your car is fitted with the system known as "Bendix" in this country, we suggest that, if at all possible, you would be wise to convert it to some other method of operation.

Finally, when setting up any mechanism see that all operating levers are set to give their maximum leverage when the brake is on, and that they are not already over the dead-centre position before any pressure is applied. Correct and incorrect settings are shown in fig. 15.

Hydraulic Systems

Apart from some very rare exceptions, all hydraulic brake-operation systems up to 1939, were manufactured by Lockheed. This firm, now Automotive Products Ltd., is very willing to help those who require replacements for existing systems in the way of cup washers, flexible pipes and other parts of their manufacture and they will also supply standard components for those who wish to modify an existing braking system. Do not, however, hope that they can undertake the conversion of an old mechanical system to hydraulic operation, as obviously each conversion of this type requires the making of special pieces, which, as makers of proprietary modern brakes, they are unable to carry out. Check all the pipe work very carefully. If there is any sign of chafing or kinking of a pipe, replace it. Bundy steel pipe (available from Benton and Stone Ltd.) should be used, and a special tool is required for flaring the ends of the pipe. It is not sufficient to knock a tapered punch down the end of the pipe as the correct flare has the pipe turned back inside itself to give a double thickness. This tool is expensive and not really worth buying for the small amount you would use it. Any large garage should be able to lend you such a tool or do the job for you. On no account use sweated-on petrol unions in a hydraulic braking system. All flexible pipes should be renewed as a matter of course, and so should the cup washers unless they are absolutely perfect. Scrupulous cleanliness is essential in the assembly of all the components.

Servo Systems

Very few cars are fitted with mechanical servo systems and the method of adjusting these can be gleaned from the instruction book. Needless to say all wear should be removed from any of the moving parts and the servo clutch relined with the appropriate lining.

Vacuum servo systems are much more common. We are only familiar with the Clayton Dewandre type and have found them to be very reliable and long wearing. The Clayton Dewandre Co. Ltd. will overhaul any of their servo motors for which they still have spares, but in all probability you will find that yours merely needs cleaning out and carefully re-assembling with a smear of oil on the moving parts. A few drops of oil should be introduced down the air intake every thousand miles to keep things in good order.

If your car has a good robust braking system which is rather heavy to operate, you might consider fitting a vacuum servo motor which can be done quite easily while the car is in pieces. Be sure to provide a very rigid mounting for the motor and connect it to the induction manifold with a pipe of at least $\frac{7}{16}$-in. bore; a smaller pipe will result in a lag in operation. It is desirable to fit a gauze breather to the air intake to stop grit entering the mechanism. We have found several of these servo motors in breakers' yards and all have been in excellent condition, having apparently far out-lasted the vehicle to which they were originally fitted.

Brake Shoes and Drums

There will probably be some wear between the cam and the shoe ends. To check the amount of this wear, strip the linings off the shoes and assemble them on to their back plates in the fully closed position. They should now form part of a perfect circle which can be checked with a large pair of calipers or even a steel rule. If they do not, then packing must be applied to the ends of the shoes to bring them truly circular again in the off position. This is shown in fig. 16. The packing can be made of mild-steel strip case-hardened, the method of fixing depending on the design of the shoe. Certain very high-class cars provide an adjustment at this point to eliminate packing.

Next turn to the pull-off springs. These should be of the same tension for either side of the car, but the fronts and rears may differ. The tension can be checked by hooking a spring balance on to each shoe when assembled and noting the reading when the shoe is pulled just clear of its expander. If the springs are obviously stretched, or are of unequal tensions, fit new ones which can be made to pattern or drawing by Quality Springs and Productions Ltd.

There are many makers of brake linings, but we have always had excellent service from British Belting and Asbestos Ltd., the makers of "Mintex". They will advise the best type of lining for your particular application; remember to tell them whether your drums are steel, cast iron, nitralloy or what have you. It is best to send the shoes for them to fit the linings; they have depots in most large towns. To determine the thickness of lining required, measure the diameter of the shoes in the off position, the internal diameter of the drum, and halve the difference. This can only be decided when the drums have been dealt with.

The condition of the brake drums is the final key to perfection in any set of brakes. The working surface must be absolutely smooth; if it is not then the drums must be skimmed out until all grooves have disappeared. There

63

are many firms who can do this job if your lathe is not large enough, but if skimming will leave the drums very thin then you will have to resort to other methods. Either the drums can be lined with nitralloy which can be done by Laystalls Ltd., or they can be built up by metal spraying and skimmed out to their original standard size. You may be able to get a set of drums cast in Mehanite or other suitable brake-drum iron. We have had this done and the resultant improvement in braking over the less-rigid steel drums is very marked. Unfortunately this was one of those jobs which was done as a very great favour and the source of supply must remain for ever locked in our bosoms.

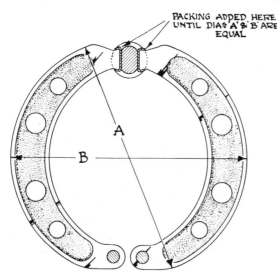

PACKING ADDED HERE UNTIL DIAS 'A' & 'B' ARE EQUAL

A

B

16 *Packing the ends of brake shoes*

Finally, chamfer down both leading and trailing edges of the brake linings and fit the drums. If you want good brakes straight away, blue the inside of each drum, rotate it with the brakes rubbing and then file off the high spots on the linings, repeating the process until a good rubbing area is obtained.

Hubs

Having cleaned out all the glutinous mess which always seems to accumulate inside hubs, remove the ball-races and note whether they are still a good tap fit into their housings. In the case of taper roller-races it is not necessary to remove the outer races unless some damage is suspected or new races are being fitted. Should the race be loose in its housing this will have to be built-up and re-machined. If the rear hubs are held on to the axle shafts by taper and key, remove the key and, bluing the bore of the hub, see that it has a 100% bearing on the shaft. If not, grind it in on its taper with a very fine grinding paste, followed by metal polish, until a perfect fit is obtained. See that the key is also a good fit in the key-way. If the drive is by splines, check these for having no back-lash. If they have, rectify it or you will soon be in trouble.

If the wheels are of the bolt-on variety, the wheel-securing nuts should be tried on the studs and if they are sloppy the nuts and studs should be replaced. Check the fixing of the studs in the hubs. Should they be loose it is probable that the tapped hole in the hub flange will be worn, and studs which are oversize on one end will have to be made. These are best made from KE805, but if they are of sufficiently robust size, mild steel will do. The nuts usually look better for being plated either in nickel or chrome, depending upon the finish of the remainder of the car.

Hubs of the Rudge-Whitworth type, if worn, can be built up and re-splined by Hofmann & Burton Ltd. This also applies to wheel centres of the same type. It is very important on a Rudge hub that the locking ring is not coming up to the end of its thread, instead of tightening on the wheel. To check this with the open-ended type of locking ring, put a wheel on to its hub and tighten the locking ring. Then measure the length of the male thread projecting through the ring on the outside. Remove the wheel and replace the locking ring until the same amount of thread is projecting and see how many more turns are necessary to take the ring to the end of its thread. If this is less than one turn it is permissible to skim up to $\frac{1}{8}$ in. off the inner face of the locking ring to rectify matters. This condition arises from wear on the wheel tapers, the locking-ring tapers, and actual stretching of the hub after many years of use.

If felt oil seals are used on the front hubs, see if it is possible to convert to a more modern type, but, if not, replace them with new felts. If the front hubs are on taper roller-races, it is necessary that these should have a slight amount of end-play when cold. Some designs are such that when the retaining nut is done up tightly there is the right amount of play, and this should be checked without grease in the bearing, when an audible clonk can be heard if the hub is pulled backwards and forwards. Other designs are such that the nut is done up until there is no play and then slackened off one flat, and the split-pin put in. This does not sound very good, but seems to work satisfactorily in practice. In this case a self-locking nut must not replace the castellated one with split-pin, and a new pin must be used every time.

The locking rings of Rudge Whitworth hubs are generally in a rather sorry state. Do not send them off to the plater in this condition but carefully file out all the blemishes and bring each ring to a state of symmetry before having them plated. This remark also applies to the dust covers often fitted in the centre of this type of hub. Should you have to make a new dust cover for any reason, Charles Eades Ltd. can engrave any lettering required if a sample or accurate drawing is sent with the job.

Finally, pack the front hubs with a good high-melting-point grease and assemble them on to the stub axles. The rear hubs are probably lubricated from the rear axle and if so will not require any grease.

Wheels and Tires

There is now only one more job to do for your chassis to become mobile once again, and that is to overhaul the wheels. Before saying anything about these, however, we propose to make a plea to you not to alter your tire size from the original. Especially with Vintage cars, we feel that many have been spoilt, and we have done this very thing ourselves, by fitting fatter tires on smaller wheels without apparently reaping any advantage other than the doubtful one of making the car look slightly more modern. Many a car has had its steering ruined by having large-section tires fitted, whereas the handling and comfort of many others on high-pressure beaded-edge tires leaves little to be desired. This does not necessarily apply if the car is to be used competitively when, of course, the question of available sizes of racing tires may come into the picture. All normal beaded-edge sizes of tires are still available from Dunlops.

If the wheels are steel artillery type or pressed steel, they may be shot-blasted and any deep pitting filed out. If the pitting is very deep the wheels are unsafe and must be scrapped and others found to replace them. This also applies if such wheels are out of truth as there is no satisfactory way of getting them to run perfectly true again. Cracks, however, can be carefully welded and filed off smooth. Wire wheels are best sent to a specialist, of which there are several depending on your locality, who can rebuild, shot-blast and prime the wheels ready for their final coat of paint. They can supply new rims for most well-base sizes. Before applying the last coat of paint see that the rims are drilled for the fitting of balance weight bolts. In our opinion if the car is capable of over 60 m.p.h. it is very well worth balancing the wheels. Four equally spaced holes should be drilled in the rim between adjacent spokes and filed out to receive the square under the head of a standard $\frac{1}{4}$ in. × 2 in. coach bolt. The bolts are held in position by the rim tape and a large quantity of lead and fibre washers of about $1\frac{1}{4}$ in. diameter should be obtained to put on these bolts with a plated cap nut and plain washer to hold them in place. The wheel is, of course, balanced after the tire is fitted, and each wheel can be put in turn on one of the front hubs and weights added to the correct bolt until the wheel ceases to stop in one particular place when rotated and allowed to come to rest unhindered. The tire should be marked with a dot of paint opposite the valve so that, should it be removed, it is always replaced in the right position. When new tires are fitted this must be repeated—obvious, you may say, but judging by the number of cars one sees with the balance weights covered in several layers of paint it seems likely that some owners do not even realise the purpose of these weights.

The only really lasting finish for wheels is stove enamel. This will stand up to the very abrasive actions of mud, snow and salt and also resists the tire lever better than anything else. There is a stove enameller in most large towns who will usually be able to match the colour scheme of your car, but for those living in the Midlands we recommend Metal Treatments Ltd.

If your car is fitted with wooden artillery wheels, they must be scraped down to the bare wood (a piece of glass is a good tool for doing this), priming and repainting each wheel after careful examination. If any of the spokes are loose or look rotten, they must be replaced, and it will be best to seek the services of a wheelwright to perform this task. Wooden wheels are remarkably free from troubles on the whole, and it will be exceptional if yours require anything but cleaning and repainting.

CHAPTER VII

THE ENGINE

O^F all the parts of a motor-car the one with which the reader will be most familiar will be the engine. We do not propose to go into every detail of a full engine overhaul as in many instances it is general engineering practice which may be learnt from books on that subject. We shall merely cover the main outline of a typical rebuild, laying stress on those details which are sometimes overlooked.

Dismantling

The engine was probably fixed on to the stand when it was removed from the chassis. If for any reason this was not done then this is the first operation to be carried out, making sure that the engine is well bolted in the stand, otherwise when it is turned over something dreadful is bound to happen. The accessories have already been removed so, before you start any of the interesting jobs, give the entire engine a thorough external cleaning. Use a stiff brush and paraffin or a "Cleanmaster" if you are fortunate enough to have one. Start at the top and work downwards.

If the cylinder-head is detachable it should be removed first. It may happen that the head is still immovable when the nuts have been removed, in which case you have two courses of action. Either you can leave the head in position until the crank, rods and pistons have been removed and then, with a stout piece of timber passed through the bore to take the blows of a hammer, you can tap off the head moving it a little at a time up each bore so that the head is lifted squarely. Alternatively, make up a hollow end mill with $\frac{1}{32}$-in. walls and a bore just to pass over the outside diameter of the studs and of a length to pass right through the head. Using this tool you can cut away the corrosion between the head and studs right down to the cylinder-block without straining anything. Remove the cylinder-head gasket carefully and keep it intact as you may need it as a pattern for future replacement. If the head is not detachable, then you must next remove the cylinder-block. Have at least one helper when you do this so that he can hold the pistons and rods when they emerge and prevent them falling over, with possible damage to the piston skirts. Be sure to lift the block squarely otherwise the rods will probably be bent.

If the engine is o.h.v. leave the rockers and valves in position for attention later, and if o.h.c. leave the camshaft in position at this stage, but in this case you should have taken notes of the timing before lifting the cylinder-block or head.

Now remove the pistons and see that they are marked, No. 1 being at the front. Make notes as to which way round they are fitted, e.g. number markings to the off-side or near-side.

Now dismantle the crankcase assembly. This part will probably be done with much greater facility if the crankcase is inverted in the stand. Before disengaging any gears make sure that they are marked for their relative timing positions. In the case of a chain-driven camshaft it may be best to rotate the engine with a protractor on the crankshaft and draw up a valve timing diagram if such data is not available. Take note of any shim packings and peculiar assemblies, and if necessary make sketches of these so that you will reassemble them in the correct way. Have a number of small boxes to take the various parts and leave them oily until the time comes for assembly.

The Crankcase

Thoroughly clean the crankcase inside and out, taking particular care of any oil ways. If the case is aluminium and you are going to polish it, now is the time to do the work so that you can get rid of all the grit and dirt before any assembly is done. If the case is iron, scrape off all the old paint and file up any very rough parts of the casting and generally prepare the outside for painting. The final coat, or better still stove enamelling, will have to be done just prior to the final assembly. We shall now talk of the crankcase as if the cylinder-block was detachable; if, however, the two are in one casting then you must read the part of this chapter dealing with the cylinder-block and do both lots of work together.

Examine the crankcase for cracks. Should there be any and you propose welding them, the work must be done by a first-class firm and afterwards checked very carefully to make sure that no distortion has taken place. It might be better to have the cracks repaired by the "Metalock" process as this will avoid the risk of distortion. If the case has been broken by a thrown rod and the hole is in an unstressed portion, you must first file out the aperture to get rid of any cracks radiating from it. Patch with $\frac{1}{16}$-in. sheet steel for cast iron and $\frac{1}{8}$-in. aluminium for a cast-aluminium case, and fit with a row of pins tapped into the casting. Use many small pins rather than a few large ones. Seal with "Hermatite" or a "Gaskoid" joint. The alternative is to have a patch welded in and to file the surface off smooth.

Clean the crankshaft with diesel oil or T.V.O. The shaft should be immersed and left for several days, as this treatment will dissolve the sludge in the oil-ways. If there are any removable plugs in the ends of the crank-pins take these out first. All oil-ways must now be blown out with compressed air, if you have none then you must take the crank to some place where there is a supply and blow out each oil way until no more sludge comes out. This part of the procedure is vital, and if you are in any doubt re-immerse in the solvent and blow out again. The hollow crankpin acts as a centrifuge and separates out sludge and carbon from the oil and it is easily possible for the oil-ways to be severely cut down, if not blanked off, after years of running. This procedure does not apply if the lubrication of the big ends is by dippers.

Measure the crankpins and main journals and also their respective bearings. The correct clearance in both cases is 0·0015 in. to 0·002 in. measured on the diameter, and if the clearance is much greater than this then new bearings are needed. If the pins and journals are absolutely round new bearings only are needed, but if they are oval the crank must be ground and the bearings remetalled. This is not work that can usually be done in the home workshop as a lot of tackle is required. There are many firms who can do this work, but we recommend C. E. Smith Ltd. and you must send the crankcase, crankshaft and rods. If the little-end bearings are worn they should be done at the same time. Some so-called bearing experts will send back the crank assembly with all the bearings tight. This is quite wrong, and if you should be so unfortunate the bearings will have to be blued and scraped until the crank will turn by hand and the rods will fall under their own weight when the bearing caps are fully tightened. Check the end-play of the shaft and the end-clearance of all bearings. As the crankcase expands in length due to heat, the crankshaft must be located by one bearing only and be free to move through all the other bearings, the effect of the expansion getting progressively larger as the bearing concerned is farther away from the crank location. Allowing 0·015 in. clearance on each side of each bearing will generally be sufficient to allow for this expansion. This point is sometimes overlooked by professional remetallers. If all seems well, just check the bearing that takes the end-thrust of the crank against the clutch withdrawal pressure and make sure that this bearing is correct. There should be no more than 0·003 in. end-float in the crankshaft. Big-end bearings should have 0·004 in. to 0·006 in. end-clearance, except in the rare cases where rod side location is effected at the little-end, in which case 0·020 in. clearance will be necessary. Wash and blow out the oil-ways in the crankshaft after it has been ground.

Do not commit the dreadful crime of filing the bearing caps to take up the bearings, it is almost certain that you will not file them flat enough to make a perfect mechanical joint, and in any case the white metal will be of uneven thickness round the bearing.

Balancing the crankshaft together with the flywheel and clutch very often improves the smoothness of the engine and is well worth doing while the engine is in pieces. For this purpose send it complete to either Dunbar and Cook Ltd., Laystall Engineering Co. Ltd. or C. E. Smith Ltd. who are all well-equipped for this work.

Examine all the other bearings in the crankcase; the camshaft bearings should again have 0·0015 in. to 0·002 in. clearance and no end-float. The camshaft, like the crankshaft, should be located by one bearing only. Any idler bearings should be repaired if necessary. If the tappets are in the crankcase, check the clearance in the guides. Should they be badly worn, the tappets can be ground down and new guides made from cast iron or phosphor-bronze following the original specification. The tops of the tappet adjusting screws must be dead flat for accurate adjustment of the clearance. If these have hollows worn in them they can be ground flat, but make sure you have not gone through the case-hardening. If you have, then they must be rehardened.

Carefully examine the joint between the sump and the crankcase. If there are any raised blemishes they must be scraped out to get a perfect, oilproof seal. Any depressions, unless they are right across the face, can be left alone; the others can be filled with "Loy" cement and scraped off flat.

The oil seal at the rear of the crankshaft is generally of the screw type with a small clearance in the crankcase. If the rear main bearing has worn the clearance will almost certainly have suffered, so that there will be a bad leak from this point. The only way to effect a repair is to build up the case and sump with welding or metal spraying, and rebore to the correct size. This must be done in the same set up as boring the main bearings.

The Oil Pump

If this is of the gear type there must be no play in the drive spindle. Should this be worn it can be ground and the body fitted with a phosphor-bronze bush and reamered to fit the spindle. The gears must have no end-play, but if there is any, it can be rectified by facing back the body of the pump at the joint. New gears, if they are necessary, can be made by Schofield & Samson Ltd. Plunger-type pumps must have the plunger a perfect fit in the bore with no side-play when dry. Look at the ball-valve seatings and balls; they must be renewed if pitted. Inspect the internal oil piping and test it with air pressure for leaks under water. If this piping is in bad shape, remake it, and be sure that it is adequately clipped or vibration will cause fractures. In any case, heat the pipe work to a dull red heat and allow it to cool in order to anneal it. The pressure relief valve should have a good seating for the ball and a new ball if it has pitted. If the spring has collapsed a new one can be made to your pattern by Quality Springs Ltd.

Timing Gear

The timing gears should have no back-lash, but if badly worn they will have to be replaced and, if no spares are available, they can be made by G. H. Turner & Co. Ltd. Bevels must be set up in exactly the same manner as described in Chapter V. If the drive is by chains and sprockets, the chains must be tested for wear by putting them out straight on the bench, fixing one end, and pulling then pushing the other end. Measure the amount of play and if there is more than $\frac{3}{16}$ in. per ft. the chain must be scrapped. New roller chains can be obtained from Renold Chains Ltd. Most sizes of silent chain are not now available and it is well worth considering modifying such a drive to roller chain. T. D. Cross Ltd. can make the necessary sprockets.

71

Check the chain tensioner; if this is of the idler-sprocket type examine the bearing and the correct working of the tensioning mechanism. When the chain is in position there should be plenty of movement left to take up the slack, which will gradually increase as time goes by. If the tensioner is of the Weller-type spring blade, and replacement is necessary, a new blade and also a new tension spring can be made by Quality Springs Ltd. Timing chains with adjustment should be adjusted until there is only ⅛ in. up-and-down movement midway between the sprockets on the slack side. When the chain is fitted and adjusted, rotate the engine slowly and if there are any dead-tight spots then the sprockets are worn and will have to be replaced. These can be obtained from T. D. Cross Ltd.

The Connecting-rods

Examine these very carefully for dents and scratches, and should there be any, polish them out. If you are in any doubt, have them crack-tested by Commercial X-Rays Ltd., and if they are made of duralumin have them X-rayed by the same firm. If they are drilled for little-end lubrication, clean out the oil-way thoroughly. Try the fit of the gudgeon-pin in the little-end. More than 0·001 in. up-and-down play is too much and new bushes will have to be made. These can be either of phosphor-bronze or duralumin. Draw out the old bush and fit the new one with a draw bolt, in the same manner as described for

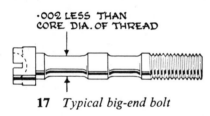

·002 LESS THAN CORE DIA. OF THREAD

17   *Typical big-end bolt*

king-pin bushes. If the rods are of the pinch-bolt type, make sure that the bolt has not stretched; and, if it has, replace it with a new high-tensile bolt.

Plenty of side clearance is needed for the little-ends to allow for the expansion of the cylinder-block and also for any possible offset of the cylinder bores relative to the centre line of the connecting-rods. The big-end bolts should be carefully examined for stretch, using a thread gauge. If you are in any doubt it is best to scrap them. New ones can be made from KE805 steel in 55–60 tons per sq. in. U.T.S. condition, but no higher. On no account replace the big-end bolts with ordinary high-tensile bolts. If you are making these bolts it may be as well to make some improvement in their design. A typical well-designed bolt is shown in fig. 17, which is waisted to give greater resistance to shock loading and a more even distribution of stress. The nuts must be in good condition and if the bolts have stretched new units will be required. If you have a torque limiting spanner available and new bolts are made, make one extra and tighten it up to higher and higher torque readings in 2-lb. ft. stages, each time loosening off and checking the length with a micrometer until a reading is reached which has permanently stretched the bolt. When tightening the bolts in assembly you then tighten to the last reading which did not stretch the bolt and all will be well. If this somewhat complicated procedure cannot be carried out, then tighten with the normal spanner for this size of bolt and not an extra long one. Do not overtighten to reach a split-pin hole. The nut must be removed and faced back in the lathe until a slot in the nut corresponds with the split-pin hole without undue tightening. For this reason self-locking nuts or tab washers are really better than split-pins.

Check the rods for straightness by fitting them on to a long piece of bar equal in diameter to the crankpin and another long bar fitting the little-end; the distance apart of the two bars must be the same at either end. If it is necessary to straighten a rod do so in the vice, with three pieces of aluminium arranged as in fig. 18. Balance the rods one against the other on some accurate scales, using the

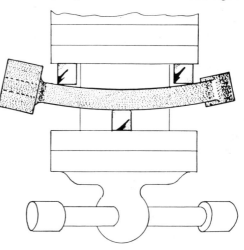

18 *Straightening a connecting-rod*

lightest one as the weight and removing metal from the heavier ones from such places as the flash lines, the centre of the web and the big-end bolt bosses until all are of equal weight. When finally fitted to the crankshaft and tightened, make sure that the rods are still free.

We have had no experience of ball-and-roller type crankshaft assemblies, but, needless to say, there must be no play whatsoever in these, and it will be as well to consult a bearing specialist if you are in any doubt.

The Flywheel

The flywheels of Vintage cars are often of enormous weight and can be reduced with advantage. We are not recommending this as a necessity, but many cars which have had their flywheels reduced seem to run just as smoothly, and tick over just as slowly, as before this modification. They have, of course, enhanced acceleration. We cannot possibly lay down any rule regarding the amount of reduction in weight, but it is being conservative to say that any flywheel and clutch assembly weighing over 120 lb., on any car with under 1½ litres capacity per cylinder, could be safely reduced by 20 lb. on the outer rim. If a great deal of tuning is proposed with the idea of getting much higher revs., it should be remembered that many early cars had cast-iron flywheels and there is a great danger of these bursting if run too fast. If this sort of tuning is proposed, a steel flywheel must be fitted.

The clutch face of the wheel must be smooth and free from ridges. If these are present either turn or grind it smooth. The teeth in the starter ring are generally badly worn, but these can be built up by welding and then filed up to a template made to an unworn portion of the ring. A new starter ring can be made by F. B. Willmott Ltd. and shrunk on after the old one has been machined off, but be careful to see that the new ring is true on the wheel.

Check the bolts holding the wheel to the crank. If they have stretched, scrap them, and make new ones in steel as for the big-end bolts. They must be a good fit in their holes. Check the mating faces of the wheel to the shaft and remove any burrs that may be found. If the wheel is on a taper, check that it is a good fit by blueing.

After you have fitted the flywheel to the shaft make sure that it will run true by rotating it and using an indicator clock or scriber point on both the face and periphery.

The Clutch

While the clutch is in a dismantled state it is as well to reline it unless the lining is in perfect condition. Relining, other than in leather or cotton, can be done by B.B.A. Group Ltd. If the clutch is of the cone type it will be as well to use the same material as the original lining. Should the lining material be cork this can be re-corked by C. Cantrill Ltd. You must send the plate for this purpose as the corks have to be ground off flat after fitting. Leather clutches can be relined by W. G. Eaton.

If the clutch is of the reverse-cone type, see that the ring into which the cone beds is in good condition, as if not it must be ground out smooth and at the correct angle. With a plate-type clutch the pressure plate must also be smooth. Check that the rivets or bolts holding the splined hub on to the clutch plate have no play. They must be a tight fit in their holes. Examine the splines; it is possible that there are ridges worn in them which will upset the operation of the clutch. If this is so and the ridges are not too deep, they can be filed out, but if they are very bad, this will cause excessive play and these parts will have to be replaced. See that the spigot and spigot bearing are in good condition. If this is a plain bearing it will probably be lubricated from the crankshaft and fitted with some type of oil-flow restrictor. Check this and also the oil seal. It is usually a great advantage to fit a modern synthetic oil seal here. There may not be enough space to fit a cup type, but, in any case, it should be possible to accommodate an O-ring and this will generally suffice.

Examine the clutch spring or springs. If during the testing of the car the clutch showed signs of slipping and no oil was found on the friction surfaces when they were dismantled, then the springs have probably become weak. Old springs can be packed up with washers, but make sure that this leaves enough movement to allow the clutch to disengage. It is far better to have new springs and these can be made by Quality Springs Ltd.; you must send a sample and state how much longer you require the new ones to be. Should the clutch be a Borg and Beck, Automotive Products Ltd. will overhaul any model of this type or they can supply any spares.

Check the withdrawal mechanism. If it has a ball thrust race this part will probably have to be replaced; they are often in poor condition due to lack of lubrication and general corrosion. Should the withdrawal fingers be worn they will have to be built up by welding and then filed to their original shape. It is essential that these fingers all bear on the withdrawal bearing equally, so that the pressure plate is true with the flywheel surface. Take up the individual finger adjustments to obtain this state.

If a clutch brake is fitted, see that it is working correctly and reline it if necessary with "Mintex". Leave this slack, as it cannot be adjusted satisfactorily until the car is on the road.

We have had no experience of fluid drives or centrifugal clutches, but the latter are generally of a straightforward and easily understood design and there is very little to go wrong with a fluid drive.

The Sump

Thoroughly clean the sump both inside and out and attend to any mating faces in the same way as you treated the crankcase. This part will probably be fitted with gauzes and if these are torn or damaged they will have to be replaced. If they are in good heart, clean them well and refit them, making sure that they cannot come adrift. New gauze can be obtained from Wm. Gabb Ltd. If the drain plug has been damaged, and they frequently seem to be in this state through the use of the wrong size spanner or a cold chisel, you will either have to make a new one from brass bar or better still stainless steel. New ones can be obtained from Enots Ltd., who can supply any size up to and including $1\frac{1}{4}$ in. in B.S.P. sizes only.

Pistons

Examine the gudgeon-pins for ovality and check their fit in the pistons. There should be no play in an aluminium piston when cold and 0·001 in. is the correct clearance with a cast-iron piston. If the car has been standing for a number of years, there may be a ring of pitting on the gudgeon-pin between the little-end and the piston. In this case scrap the pin, as it will be very liable to fracture. If the pistons are to be renewed, fit new gudgeon-pins at the same time. If the pistons are cast iron there will probably be no wear in them or the bores, but treat them very carefully as the skirts are easily broken. Replacement of worn pistons may be one of your greatest

75

difficulties if the car is obsolete. Send to one of the better-known piston stockists, for example Associated Engineering (Sales) Ltd.; it is quite possible that they may have a piston which can be adapted to your engine. For instance, it may be possible to obtain pistons for your bore diameter with the correct gudgeon-pin to crown dimension, but, with gudgeon-pin bores too large, these could be bushed down to the correct size with duralumin. Alternatively you might find pistons with all the correct dimensions except for a slightly greater compression height which would be quite satisfactory and would give an improved performance.

While not wishing to turn your car into a " dicer ", it must be remembered that modern fuels are infinitely better than those of twenty-five years ago, and a higher compression ratio, within reason of course, will not make the engine any rougher and should improve the petrol consumption. If you are carrying out this modification, make sure that the top piston ring does not come out at the top of the cylinder bore. If this happened you would be in frightful trouble as, even if there was no other damage, you would have great difficulty in removing the piston should it be in a fixed-head engine.

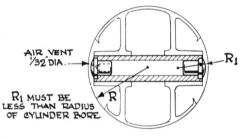

19   *Gudgeon-pin end pad*

Check the fit of your pistons in the bores. To do this borrow an internal micrometer for measuring cylinders and take readings all down the bores, noting the maximum diameter. The correct clearance for solid skirt round-turned aluminium pistons when cold is 0·0015 in. per inch of bore diameter and for cast iron 0·0005 in. per inch of bore diameter. A little wear can be tolerated, say up to 0·003 in. per inch of bore diameter. With any more wear than this, a rebore is necessary. It is possible that, if oversize pistons cannot be obtained, your old pistons could be used again if the cylinder-block was bored and sleeved. In this case the ring grooves should be turned out and new rings fitted. There should be no actual clearance that you can measure between the ring and the groove. It should be a nice sliding fit and the correct gap is 0·002 in. per inch diameter of the bore. Rings and gudgeon-pins can be obtained from Reid Watt Ltd., who have a wide range in stock. If you are still in trouble, there are firms who advertise in motoring papers who will make special pistons. Finally a wood pattern could be made for castings to be run off in a suitable piston alloy, and you could then do the necessary machining. You would, however, need very good machining facilities for this job. You can also make your own gudgeon-pins; these should be made from KE169 steel, case-hardened and tempered to Kayser Ellison's instructions and finally ground to size. If the gudgeon-pins are fully floating and you are using end pads, these should be made from duralumin. They should have a domed head with the dome of a smaller radius than the radius of the cylinder bore to give point contact, otherwise the pads will tend to be revolved in the pin and will eventually come out. The pads should have a shank about $\frac{1}{4}$ in. long, which is a 0·001 in. interference fit in the pin (see fig. 19). Drill the pad with a $\frac{1}{32}$-in. hole off-centre, this is to prevent any pressure being built up in the hollow pin. If new pistons are being fitted you may find it better to change to circlip location for the gudgeon-pin, and in this case Seager square-section circlips must be used and there must be no end-float of the pin between its circlips. Last, but not least, all piston assemblies must be balanced as was done for the connecting-rods.

The Cylinder-block

First clean this component and then remove any water plates or core plugs, if they are detachable, and clean out the water-jacket. If there are no detachable plates a satisfactory method of cleaning is to immerse the whole block in a bath of "Skalene". This preparation is obtainable in $\frac{1}{2}$-gal. or 10-gal. quantities from W. Canning and Co. Ltd., or your plater may possibly use it and will do the job for you. This cleaning fluid does not attack iron in any way but gets rid of all rust and lime deposits. Another cleaning solvent is chromic acid but this is very dangerous to the skin. Having done the cleaning, should the block be cracked externally due to having been frozen up—now is the time to effect a repair. It can be welded but this will cause some distortion and will make a rebore inevitable. It is often possible to drill small holes at each end of the crack to prevent it spreading and then to patch. An even better way would be to have the crack repaired by the "Metalock" process; this will give a very strong repair without causing any distortion. Cellulose filler or iron cement may be used to seal any leaks but, whatever process you use, when you have finished the repair, air-pressure test the block under water at 3 lb. per sq. in. maximum. If the cylinders are to be rebored or sleeved, send the block for this treatment. C. E. Smith Ltd. can do the reboring or sleeving, but of course there are many other firms who specialise in this work.

Now before any further work is done the block should receive its exterior finish. We have found that painting with Llewellyn Ryland's Cylinder Black is very satisfactory as this paint is resistant to hot oil and wears very well. An even better finish would be to have it stove enamelled and you could then choose from a range of colours.

If the head is integral with the block, or if the engine is a side valve, do all the work to the ports and valves which we shall describe later in this chapter before you send the block to be rebored and, of course, before you repaint.

Check all tapped holes in the block. If there are any stripped threads they will have to be drilled out and tapped the next size larger. An alternative to this is to use the Heli-coil stainless steel thread insert, which will provide an excellent new thread in any metal. These are obtainable from W. Bridges Ltd. Cylinder-head holding studs should all be tight in the block and any with doubtful threads must be replaced. A useful tool for removing studs is the extractor made by A. P. Warren Ltd.

Water plates, if they are in a bad condition, can be remade and are best in stainless steel, hard copper or brass. Aluminium is not a good material as it is so liable to corrode. These plates should be sealed with a paper gasket and "Hermatite" or thin synthetic rubber, and if polished and held by a row of stainless steel pins they will look very smart. Core plugs of the screwed-in type can be turned up from stainless steel or brass bar.

The Cylinder-head

Take out the valves and note their positions, unless they are all to be replaced, as you will not know if they are marked until they have been cleaned. An easy way to keep them in order is to prepare a length of wood about $\frac{1}{2}$ in. thick of sufficient length and width to take a double row of holes into which the valve stems will fit. The holes can be marked and you can place the valves in these complete with springs, washers and collets as you remove them. Next remove the rocker gear, or the camshaft if the engine is o.h.c. Take note of the position of all parts and whether they are marked. Check the valves in the guides; the correct clearance is 0·002 in. for the inlet and 0·004 in. to 0·005 in. for the exhaust. If the guides are worn they must be replaced. In this case remove them either by driving out with a punch or drawing out with a draw-bolt extractor.

Now clean and polish the ports, removing the carbon with a scraper and steel-wire brush in the flexible drive. Then remove all excrescences and roughness in the casting with a riffler and small grinding wheel in the flexible drive. A small low-voltage lamp, which will illuminate the ports, and a small mirror will be found very helpful in some cases. Be careful not to touch the valve seats or you will score them. Examine the head round the valve seats. If these seats are badly sunk due to continuous grinding-in of the valves, the excess metal must be removed down to the level of the valve seat in order to restore the proper gas flow. After removing this metal, polish up the head as smooth as possible. An excrescence will form a point for the build up of carbon which will become incandescent and cause pre-ignition. Should the valve seats be badly pitted they must be recut before grinding. You can possibly borrow the necessary cutter from your local garage, or alternatively you can buy one as it will always be useful. The new guides must be in position for the recutting as well as for the grinding. If there are no new guides available they can be made from cast-iron stick which is obtainable from British Piston Ring Co. Ltd.

Valves and Valve Gear

The valves, if they are badly pitted, can have the seats ground up true in a valve-grinding machine and any good garage can do this for you. However, if this makes them too thin on the edge they will be no use and will have to be replaced. If you have any difficulty in obtaining them, new ones can be made by W. G. James, Ltd. If the valves are not stamped on the head with their appropriate markings stamp them now, and then grind in the valves using fine carborundum paste. When this is completed remove all traces of grit and place the valves in the head. With the head inverted and the valves held on their seats by their own weight only, pour in a little paraffin, and if you have done the work properly there should be no leaks. The valve springs have an enormous amount of work to do, so it is advisable to replace them in any case. They can be obtained from Herbert Terry Ltd. and when ordering you must send a sample.

Check all the rocker gear for play in the bearings and examine the rockers for fractures. If there is any play in the bearings, either grind down the shaft and rebush the rockers or build up the shaft with hard chrome and grind and then reamer out the rockers and the shaft supports to fit. Clean out all oil-ways and check that the tappet adjusting screws are in good condition. If they are not, repair or replace them.

If the engine is o.h.c. examine the camshaft bearings; if they are worn, new bearings will have to be made from either phosphor-bronze or dur-alumin. If these are of the split type, the new ones will have to be scraped in line with the bearing scraper.

The camshaft itself rarely needs any attention but examine it carefully, and if the cams are ridged stone them down as smooth as possible. Should you be so unlucky as to have a very badly worn camshaft and the engine is obsolete, your only hope is to search for a good secondhand one as having a "one-off" camshaft made would be very expensive indeed.

If the engine is of the push-rod type examine the push rods carefully and if they are bent they must be straightened. This is best done with the rod held at its bent portion in the three-jaw lathe chuck.

Assembly

You are now ready for the main engine assembly. Place the crankshaft in the crankcase and bolt up the main bearings, remembering not to over-stretch the studs to reach a split-pin hole but to face back the nuts as for the big-end bolts. Fit any internal oil pipes and fit the connecting-rods to the crankshaft. Now bolt on the sump which may be complete with the oil pump; if not fit this afterwards. Use a "Gaskoid" jointing gasket or thin tough paper and "Hermatite" and make sure you have an oil-tight joint. Turn the crankcase the right way up for the fitting of the next components unless it is a very large engine, in which case it will be better to bolt it straight into the chassis.

Fit the rings on the pistons. To do this cut several strips of thin tinplate about ¼ in. wide and about 5 in. long, expand the ring over the piston having these strips between the ring and the piston and equally spaced but with one strip directly behind each end of the ring which will now slide along easily to its correct groove. The strips can be now withdrawn. Handle the rings with great care as they are easily broken.

Fit the pistons to the connecting-rods. The method of doing this will depend on the type of gudgeon-pin fixing you have, as in some cases it will be easier to fit the piston to the connecting-rod before this is fitted to the crank. If you have fully floating pins and circlip location, put one circlip in the piston and place this on to the rod, then insert the gudgeon-pin and fit the second circlip making sure it is right into its groove. You will need a pair of circlip pliers for this purpose.

The next part of the proceedings is to lower on the cylinder-block if it is a separate component. Prepare a paper gasket for the base and fit this on to the top of the crankcase. Now get a strip of hard-rolled metal about 0·048 in. thick sufficiently wide to cover all the piston rings, and of the right length so that when you have formed it into a tube it will fit the outside of the piston with the joint almost closed. Outside this sleeve fit a worm drive hose clip and tighten this so that the rings are contracted into their grooves but the sleeve will slide down the piston as it enters the cylinder bore. This is illustrated in fig. 20. You will require two clips for a four- or six-cylinder engine. Use plenty of engine oil on both piston and bore. With someone to hold the pistons and with two of them at t.d.c. and the crank fixed, you can now lower the cylinder-block, making sure that it goes down quite straight. As soon as the first set of rings are in the bores you can remove the sleeves and fit them on the next pistons to be inserted, and when they are all in the block can be lowered completely into place. The next operation is the fitting of the cylinder-head. If the engine is obsolete you may have some difficulty in obtaining a cylinder-head gasket. First try all the stockists, and if this does not produce any results do not despair but make a gasket from

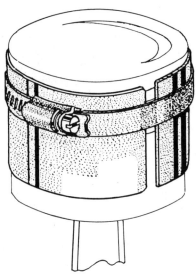

20 *Piston-ring compressor*

copper sheet. Use 0·048 in. (18 S.W.G.) copper and when finished heat it to a dull red heat and allow it to cool. In this case, unless the mating surfaces of the block and of the head are in perfect condition, they should be ground. Tighten down the nuts evenly in the correct rotation, starting in the centre and working outwards towards either end.

The Rocker or Valve Cover

This is a part which, if nicely finished, can look very handsome. Now is the time to do this work and for details of the different finishes we refer you to a later chapter. A good material for gaskets for these parts is "Nebar" sheet cork jointing, which is much tougher than ordinary sheet cork. This material can be obtained from James Walker and Co. Ltd. Cap nuts should be used here, as they not only look better but also form a complete oil seal which an open-ended nut does not. Normally cap nuts are best used on all external engine applications as they look well and do not catch in the cleaning rag when the engine is being wiped down. If a nut which was previously split-pinned is being replaced by a cap nut, a "Nyloc"

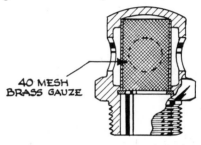

40 MESH BRASS GAUZE

21 *Typical rocker-cover breather*

cap nut, which is self-locking, should be used.

It will often be found that the engine is not sufficiently ventilated and the fitting of a gauze-protected breather in the rocker cover, or valve side cover on s.v. engines, will be found a great advantage in keeping the inside of the engine free from sludge and corrosion. Fig. 21 shows a typical design.

Induction and Exhaust Manifolds

If the inlet manifold is exhaust- or water-heated, the jacket must first be cleaned out. Then thoroughly clean the induction tract itself. Whatever finish you are using for the exterior must be done next. Before fitting, make sure that the ports line up with the engine ports. Having cleaned the the mating surfaces, check the alignment by blueing the face round the engine ports and the face of the induction pipe and then put the two together with soft white paper between and bolt up. Remove the manifold and cut out the marking on one side of the paper. If this cut-out does not correspond on the other side of the paper you must rectify one or other of the ports until it does. Repeat the process with each port. Now fit the manifold using a gasket of "Gaskoid", "Nebar" or "Hallite".

The exhaust manifold should next be cleaned out and the ports checked in the same manner as just described. The next job is to choose the finish you are using and to have this done. Really the only ones which will stand up to the heat are metal spraying or vitreous enamelling. In the case of sheet metal or tubular fabricated manifolds, chromium plating will last fairly well. Use copper and asbestos washers on flanged joints, and if the connections are screwed smear well with graphite for future ease of dismantling. Always use brass nuts to hold exhaust manifolds.

The Carburetter

Strip the instrument and clean it thoroughly. Check the float chamber mechanism and repair it if necessary; the conical part of the needle should have no ring worn in it and if it has then it must be re-machined true. The seating should be as narrow as possible; if it is too wide face it back with a suitable cutter. Test the float by immersing it in hot water, any leak will be shown by bubbles of air expanding out of the puncture. Should there be a leak, drill a small hole to drain out any petrol and repair by soldering, but be careful to use as little solder as possible as the weight should not be increased. To recondition a cork float it should be warmed to expel all petrol and then given a thin coat of shellac. The outside of the body of the carburetter can be polished or plated.

If the carburetter has had much use and if the jets are original, they are sure to be worn, due to the passage of countless gallons of fuel, and they must be replaced with the correct sizes. The S.U. Carburetter Co. Ltd. and the Zenith Carburetter Co. Ltd. are still in existence and can supply the following spares:

S.U.

Complete carburetters, new, back to 1930.
1919–1930 some parts only.
No spares for slopers or bellows type.
Post-1930 inquiries to W. H. M. Burgess Ltd.
Pre-1930 inquiries to S.U. Carburetter Co. Ltd.

Zenith

Parts back to 1930 only.
Reconditioning of Solex carburetters of certain types.

Parts now obsolete will have to be made. The correct internal diameter of jets can be ascertained by asking the makers, if they are still in existence, quoting the number stamped on the jet. If the makers no longer exist the size will have to be found out by trial and error of the carburation, probably more error than anything else unless you are very "genned" up on this subject, so unless your car is a very rare collector's piece it will be better to fit a modern instrument.

The butterfly valve spindle must be a good fit in its bearings. If it is worn the body can be reamered out and bushed, or an oversize spindle fitted, but this is a very difficult operation as the disc must fit the bore properly or you will have most erratic throttle control.

If you propose to fit a new carburetter we recommend that you use an S.U. as this is the most easily adjustable and satisfactory carburetter we know.

The Ignition System

If this is by magneto, clean the instrument externally and then strip it down. Do this very carefully and remember to remove the H.T. pick-up brush-holder before taking off the drive end-plate, or you will break the slip-ring. Take careful note of the internal timing of the distributor, carefully clean all the internal parts and keep well away from all iron filings while dismantling, as once these get in they are impossible to remove without de-magnetising. If the magneto is original and old it will probably pay to have the armature rewound as corrosion often starts in the centre of the winding, which is very hard to see. Rewinding will also get over any possible shellac troubles later on. There are many electrical equipment experts who can arrange for your armature to be rewound, such as Electric Service (B'ham) Ltd. who can in fact overhaul the complete magneto and supply spares such as bearings and contact-breaker points.

The bearings are seldom worn but these will have to be checked for play. Should they be worn, new ones will have to be fitted. The contacts should be cleaned with a stone and the contact breaker arm bush replaced if it is loose. This bush and a new cam follower, if it also is worn, can be made from "Tufnol". Contact-breaker points for magnetos are made from platinum and those for coil ignition are from tungsten.

Clean up the slip-ring with metal polish and check the distributor spindle for play, if it is worn you should rebush its bearing. Examine the distributor carbon brush, if any; this will probably be worn but, if so, a new one can be filed up from a dynamo brush.

Make sure that the taper on the end of the armature shaft is in good condition and examine the distributor cover for cracks. If you find any your only hope is a new or good secondhand replacement. It is important that there be no looseness in the cam-ring; if this should be in bad condition it is sometimes possible to build up the spigot on which it runs with white metal and a soldering iron, carefully easing down with a file until the cam-ring runs freely but has no play. Now reassemble, packing the ball bearings with a meagre amount of H.M.P. grease, and finally have the magnet re-magnetised.

In the case of a distributor for coil ignition, check the centre bearing; if this is worn replace the bush or even running will be impossible to obtain. Check the rocker bush, points, follower and distributor cap in the same way as for the magneto.

If the rotor end is badly burnt it must be replaced; it is also a good idea to replace the condenser in any case. These are easily obtainable and any modern condenser will do from an electrical point of view, but a little ingenuity may be required to fit it nicely as it will possibly be a different shape and size to the original. See that the auto-advance, if fitted, is working freely and that the springs are in good condition, and finally put a smear of oil on the cam.

Robert Bosch can do a certain amount of repair work on old equipment of their manufacture.

If you are at all doubtful of the coil, discard it and fit a modern one. Also, if your magneto is in a very bad condition, you might consider fitting a coil and distributor. Delco, Remy and Hyatt make a conversion for tractors which can be obtained from Electric Service (B'ham) Ltd. and this can be very easily adapted. If your engine is a slow-running one, this modification should result in a better performance and starting.

Fit all new H.T. leads in any case and use the plastic-covered type of wire as it is oil resisting. If these leads are not fitted as standard in a conduit, see if this can be done as it is a great improvement to the tidiness of the engine. The conduit can be made from metal or "Tufnol" tubing.

Consult the plug manufacturer's chart for the correct sparking plugs and fit a new set regardless, setting the gaps to 0·019 in. for magneto or 0·025 in. for coil ignition.

The Water Pump

Strip the water pump and thoroughly clean and inspect all parts. If the body is an aluminium casting you will probably collapse at the sight of it as it is usually very corroded. It is sometimes possible to give it, and your own enthusiasm, a new lease of life by skimming the corrosion out of the inside and making up a new rotor to fit the enlarged dimensions. It may be possible to build up the case by welding. The new rotor should be made from gunmetal or brass. If the body is cast iron or gunmetal it will probably be in a good condition, or only require rebushing and a new rotor spindle. Make the spindle from stainless steel and the bush from phosphor-bronze.

The string-packing type of gland, universal on Vintage cars, can often be replaced with advantage by a synthetic rubber U-washer which requires no attention. No type of gland will hold water if the spindle has worn in its bearing. If the graphite impregnated string packing is to be retained it can possibly be obtained from the local garage and, if not, from James Walker and Co. Ltd.

Do not overtighten the gland as it can absorb considerable power and when lubricating the spindle use H.M.P. grease and never overdo it, or the excess grease will clog the radiator.

The Fan

This component will probably only need cleaning and attention to the bearings. If it is made of aluminium, it looks well polished; and if of steel, paint it a distinctive colour or have it stove enamelled. If the pulley is worn it may be possible to turn it off and shrink a new one in place.

Check the V-groove by laying a belt in it, the belt should not touch the bottom of the groove when pressed in. New rubber belts can be obtained from most good garages and link belts from T. Whittle and Sons Ltd.

The Air Pump

This part rarely gives any trouble. Check the valves, springs and seatings and rectify if necessary. If the piston is loose in the cylinder, hone or bore out and make an oversize piston. There should be a filter gauze on the air intake and some means of occasional oiling.

Installation

The engine can now be removed from its stand and lowered into the frame. Make sure that the engine bears equally on all its frame mountings and, if it does not, pack accordingly. Its alignment with the gear-box, if this is separate, can only be checked finally when the latter is in position. If rubber mountings have been used these will almost certainly need replacing and are best made from synthetic rubber which is oil resisting.

Any fibre or leather washers needed during the overhaul can be made by R. H. Nuttall Ltd.

Exhaust Pipe and Silencer

With the engine now in place we will finish off this lengthy chapter by discussing the exhaust system. It will usually be in a parlous condition if it is original, and will probably be well worth entirely remaking. There are many firms who can bend large-diameter tubing and it is a very difficult job to tackle in a home workshop if a presentable article is to result. If you feel that your exhaust system could do with redesigning, remember that there are only two practical types of joint to use for connecting the various sections together: one is by welding or brazing which is permanent and the other is the flange joint which is held together by a ring of nuts and bolts. Any type of sleeve or clipped connection is useless and will always give trouble. We feel that the correct design for an exhaust system is one in which the silencer is securely mounted on the chassis and the pipes at either end are flexibly connected to it with flanged joints. This arrangement allows a certain latitude in the dimensions of the pipe work and also relieves the engine manifold of any undue stress due to chassis flexing and expansion of the pipe under heat. Twelve inches of flexible metallic tube either end of the silencer is quite adequate and this should be brazed on to the rigid piping with a 1-in. length of engagement. There are various grades of flexible metallic tubing, only one of which is suitable for exhaust piping. As they all have very much the same outward appearance make certain that you are supplied with the correct grade. Number 2 quality flexible-steel tubing, made by the United Flexible Metallic Tubing Company Ltd., which is available through most motor factors, is the only type which we have found really suitable and long-wearing. On no account saw two slits in the flexible pipe and try to hold it in position with hose clips, as this joint will inevitably leak.

There are several good proprietary silencer-makers who advertise regularly and who can make a silencer to your dimensions. You can make your own, preferably as a replica of the original, if you have welding facilities.

A really satisfactory finish for an exhaust system, unless it is made of stainless steel, is aluminium spraying. An alternative is Hot Paint supplied by Ram Research Ltd. in a variety of colours, but we hope that you will choose black. The flexible portion of the system must not be metallic sprayed or it will lose its flexibility and Hot Paint is ideal in this case.

If your car was unbearably hot for the front passenger due to the exhaust pipe warming the floor-boards, it will pay you to lag this portion of the pipe with asbestos tape. An even better cure is to fit an asbestos-lined metal shield between the pipe and the floor-boards, with an air gap of about 1 in. between the pipe and the shield, and a further gap between the shield and the floor-boards. This was standard practice on certain high-quality cars and is very effective.

You will now be ready to start the engine—you hope—but if it needs running-in due to a rebore and new bearings, and you are strong-minded enough, it is better to leave this until the car is ready for the road. Much time is wasted rigging up a petrol and coolant supply and it is bad to run a reconditioned engine for a short time and then to leave it for months. Put some oil in the sump and the bores and turn it over occasionally, making sure that it has plenty of oil when you do start it.

CHAPTER VIII

THE GEAR-BOX AND PROPELLER-SHAFT

IF you were able to road test your car before dismantling you will have a fairly good idea of the condition of the propeller-shaft and gear-box. Ailments in either of these two mechanisms are usually very apparent when the car is driven, either by excessive noise, jumping out of gear or complete absence of one of the speeds in the case of the gear-box, or by vibration at speed and clonking when the drive is reversed if the propeller-shaft is at fault.

Inspection of the Gear-box

If the gear-box is working well and is not excessively noisy we do not recommend that you dismantle it. You must, however, have a good look inside and confirm that everything is as good as it sounds. First clean the box externally and drain out the oil. Fill up with paraffin or petrol and either shake the gear-box thoroughly or rotate the shafts for a few minutes and drain again. Examine both drainings and the inside of the drain plug for any pieces of metal and try to identify anything which you find. In a sliding-gear type of gear-box it is quite usual to find minute particles of gear teeth which have rubbed off the ends of the gear-wheels. This need not be cause for alarm unless there is a considerable quantity or the fragments are large. Next remove the top cover. In the rare cases of a gear-box with no removable top or side cover large enough to reveal the whole inside, we feel it desirable to dismantle at least enough of the box to satisfy yourself that you have looked at each working part. While we realise that some gear-boxes live in the back axle and that they will be overhauled with this component, we crave the indulgence of owners of these cars and hope that they will have read this chapter before starting on the back-axle rebuild.

Considering first the case of the more normal sliding-gear type of box, look at all the gear-wheels and dog-clutches, turning the various wheels so that each tooth can be seen in turn. It is quite probable that the edges of the teeth which engage when changing gear will be burred or worn back, so reducing the overall width of the teeth. A small amount of this is permissible and providing 75% of the width of the original tooth remains it can be left. It is desirable, however, to stone off any sharp or burred edges, and to do this the gear-wheel must be removed from the box. If the wear exceeds this amount, then either a new wheel must be made or possibly a second-hand replacement found. The same remarks apply to dog-clutches in the case of gear trains with constant-mesh wheels.

Next test the gears for correct engagement. This is particularly easy to do where the box has a right-hand gate change when the gear-lever can be left in place with the gear-box lid removed and the whole sequence of gear changing performed. Each pair of gears should be fully in mesh when the respective selector plunger locates in its indent on the selector rod, and at the same time the gear-lever should be just clear of the end of the particular quadrant in the gate. In the neutral position all moving gears must be well clear of engagement, as if this is not so it is possible to touch other than the one to be selected when passing through the gate. Some gear-boxes have their gears located in mesh by means of notches in the gate itself and not with spring plungers. On this type look for wear in the gate locks, rounding off of the edges of these locks and lack of spring loading on the gear-lever to make it enter the locks, all of which can cause jumping out of gear.

Returning to the actual driving mechanism, next look at the selector forks which embrace the sliding gears or dog clutches. These must be a nice running fit on the gear-wheel collar, and excessive side play of more than 0·016 in. will spoil the feel of the gear change. Now lock the output shaft and, exerting a good torque on the input shaft, check each gear in turn for back-lash. Any free movement can be due to either play between the gear teeth, looseness of the gear wheels on their splines or keys, or up-and-down play in the gear-box bearings. A very small amount of play will naturally exist between the teeth and this is quite permissible, but any excessive amount must be traced to its actual source and steps taken to rectify the trouble. Should the gear-box have synchromesh on any of its speeds then the only practical way to know whether this is in good order is to test it on the road. If it is possible to override the synchronising action when changing gear at normal speeds for the car concerned, the box will have to be stripped. We cannot deal with epicyclic gear-boxes in this book, as each type has its own peculiarities which require considerable explanation and specialised description, but if your car is fitted with such a box and it requires overhaul we would recommend that you read Chapter XXI in *The Motor Vehicle* by K. Newton and W. Steeds (Iliffe, 1950). Do not be alarmed at the thought of dismantling such a gear-box, but do keep a very careful check on the order in which the parts are assembled.

Should your gear-box have any of the faults outlined above then it will have to be dismantled. If it passes your inspection then replace the lid, using either a "Gaskoid" or "Nebar" washer.

Repairs to the Gear-box

Take care on dismantling the box that the usual notes are made concerning any peculiarities of assembly. If the layshaft is adjustable for mesh, i.e. if its centre line can be moved relative to the centre line of the mainshaft, take particular note of the position of this adjustment which is provided only as an aid to manufacture. No advantage will be gained by attempting to experiment with this setting unless there are signs that it has been the subject of previous experiments by other owners. Use the universal extractor for removing the drive coupling from either one or both ends of the box, depending upon whether it is in unit with the engine or separate. In the case of a somewhat flimsy coupling be careful to drill the extractor bolt holes as near to the boss as possible to prevent buckling the coupling.

Dealing first with possible gear-wheel repairs and replacements, let us say immediately that if there is any chance of finding either separate gears or a complete box in better condition than your own, then in all probability it will be cheaper to buy this than to get new gears cut. If your gears have badly worn teeth or are loose on their splines it is virtually impossible to repair them, and new or replacement gears are the only solution. If you decide that new gears have to be made use KE805 heat-treated to 85–90 tons per sq. in. U.T.S. after machining. There will be very little distortion if any and they should not have to be finish ground after heat treatment.

In the case of sliding gears fitted to their shafts with detachable keys instead of splines, it is often possible to effect an improvement by renewing these keys. Normally the gear is unworn and only the keys have suffered. In this case make new keys from either Key Steel or KE805 in the 70-80 tons per sq. in. U.T.S. state. The keys must be a very good fit in their keyways and a sliding fit in the gear-wheel. Should the old key be loose in the shaft then fitting a new key alone will be no good. The key-way is bound to be bell-mouthed and must be trued-up in a vertical miller or key-seating machine. The new key will then have to be stepped in order to obtain the right fits in both shaft and gear-wheel. A new shaft can also be made from KE805, heat-treated after machining to 80 tons per sq. in. U.T.S., which may have to be straightened after heat treatment. This can be done by first checking the shaft between centres on the lathe, then laying it on V-blocks under a fly or mandrel press and straightening it a little at a time, checking each time in the lathe.

If play has developed in the spigot bearing between the input and output shaft and this a plain bearing, the spigot on the output shaft will probably have to be turned or ground round and parallel before making a new bush for the input shaft. If this is a roller or ball bearing a new bearing will probably rectify matters, but the spigot may have to be built up with hard chrome and ground back to its standard size if it is worn.

The ball- or roller-races on which all gear-box shafts revolve are practically all standard sizes and can be obtained from any of the well-known ball- and roller-race manufacturers in both inch and metric sizes. Coiled spring rollers or Hyatt-type bearings are obtainable from Salters Ltd., who are manufacturers of this type of bearing. If there is any up-and-down play in a ball-race it must be removed. The bearings must, of course, be the correct fit in their housings and on their shafts and if not, the necessary building up with hard chrome or metal spraying followed by machining to the correct size must ensue. Ball-races should be a light press fit into their housings and a light tap fit on the shaft. If they are any tighter than this then ease down the appropriate part. Never use a heavy hammer on a ball-race to put it back on a shaft even if you had to use one to get it off.

If the gears are not selecting properly, that is if they are not fully engaged when the selector mechanism enters its lock, then either the selector forks are worn or bent, or the gear-lever is wrongly assembled so that its gate is restricting the movement of the selectors. The selector forks are invariably made from aluminium-bronze which is exceedingly tough and wear resistant. The most likely cause of trouble is that the forks are bent due to ham-fisted gear changing. They can be straightened cold, a little at a time, with constant checking until the gear engagement is restored. Be very careful when doing this that the prongs of the fork which embrace the gear-wheel do not become distorted, and check that the gear-wheel revolves perfectly freely in the fork when the assembly is complete.

If the gears tend to jump out of engagement and this is found not to be due to either bent selector forks or worn teeth of either the gear-wheels or dog-clutches, it can be possibly traced to wear in the spring-loaded plungers or in the indents in the selector rods into which they engage. Both these items should be sharpened up if necessary and the springs which operate the plungers replaced if they have become weak. Each plunger should snap into its indent when the gears are fully engaged. In the case of a gear-box where the locks are on the gate, these again must snap into place.

Any play in the gear-lever mechanism should be eliminated if a nice feel is to be attained, and this can generally be done by building up the worn parts concerned and rebushing worn bearings. A poorly working reverse catch can be a constant source of petty annoyance and its easy movement and positive locking should be realised before passing the gear-change mechanism as perfect. The gear-lever will, of course, be visible and has to be brought up to a high degree of finish. Fettle it up, and either paint or, better still, plate it to match the rest of the car. If the knob is battered a new one can be turned up from ebonite, ebony or other hard wood or, as an alternative, there is a very good range of plastic knobs used on modern machine tools, one of which can often be adapted. E. Perkins and Co. Ltd. can supply these knobs. Ball change levers often rattle when old. This is generally due to their spring loading becoming weak—an easy matter to rectify.

Any oil seals which have shown signs of leaking must be replaced. As in the case of the back axle we definitely recommend the substitution of modern oil seals, but if you find this impossible, replace any doubtful old type seals with new material.

If your gear-box is separately mounted from the engine it will quite possibly have a Hardy disc-type shaft coupling on the input end. See that the spider that carries this disc runs true. If the disc is old or worn replace it with a new one which can be obtained in any size from Hardy Spicer Ltd.

Should the case of the gear-box be cracked, this can be repaired by the same process as described in the previous chapter for cylinder-blocks, i.e. welding, plating or "Metalock". As the box will not be seen on the finished car, painting with two coats of oil-resisting paint when the box is assembled will be perfectly satisfactory.

Finally see that the drain plug resembles something better than a shapeless piece of brass. Either carefully file up the hexagon to the next smaller size or better still, mill it down if you have the equipment. Failing this, buy a new one as we hope you did for the engine sump.

Fitting Gear-box to Chassis

If your gear-box is of the unit-construction type you have merely to bolt it on to the back of the engine, making sure that the two mating faces are clean and free from bruises. With the separate type of box a little more care must be taken. Put the box in place and make up a pointer which can be attached to the input shaft coupling and will run round the back face of the flywheel. Rotate the gear-box shaft with its pointer and pack the gear-box until the pointer moves round the flywheel at exactly the same distance from it for the whole 360°. The position of the pointer must be checked in two planes, both for running axially true with the flywheel and in a fore-and-aft direction. A considerable amount of patience is often needed to get this setting right, but patience will be rewarded in a smoother-running engine and longer life of the universal couplings. If the couplings are Hardy discs see that they are neither in tension nor compression when bolted up. If they are, then the fitting of spacing washers or the shortening of the coupling shaft will be necessary.

Multi-speed Chain Drives

The same remarks apply to these as to gear-boxes with regard to the necessity of lack of play in the selection mechanism and full engagement of the dog-clutches. The sprockets should be checked for wear, sharp-pointed or hooked teeth denote wear and the necessity for replacement. T. D. Cross Ltd. can make new sprockets but these, being "one-off" jobs, are naturally fairly expensive. On the larger type of sprocket they can often turn off the old teeth, weld on a ring and recut new teeth which is more economical than making an entirely new wheel. The lay-shaft sprockets must run freely but with very little side-rock on the shaft, and all keys and key-ways must be a good fit with each other. Both lay-shaft and back-axle shaft should be tested for running true and, if bent, they can often be straightened. A new lay-shaft or back axle can be made from KE805, heat-treated after machining to 80 tons per sq. in. U.T.S. and straightened after heat treatment. Test the chains for wear as described in Chapter VII, but in the case of these rather heavier chains, up to $\frac{1}{4}$ in. per foot play is allowable. When the chains are in place adjust the tightest to have $\frac{1}{2}$ in. up-and-down movement at its slackest point. The others will have to be to the nearest half link, as in no case must the back axle be put out of line to obtain better overall chain adjustment.

General Remarks on Gear-boxes

When the box is finally installed fill it with oil to the correct level and rotate it to distribute the oil into the bearings and round the wheels. We do not recommend the use of the old heavy-grade gear oils in Vintage gear-boxes, as modern light oils are perfectly satisfactory and absorb very much less power.

Quite apart from the overhaul, the owner may often wonder why it is easy to change gear on some types of box and practically impossible to make a quiet change on others. It seems to us that this can only be due to two factors—the size of the gear-wheels and the number of teeth in their peripheries. Thus the greater number of teeth that are passing a given point per second, the harder it will be to gauge exactly the speed at which both sets of teeth are passing that point at exactly the same speed, and the more accurate will have to be that gauging to get a silent change. This seems to be borne out in practice in that boxes with small wheels and coarse teeth are very much easier to change gear upon than those with large-diameter wheels and fine teeth.

The adjustment of the clutch brake will have to wait until the car is on the road, but this is a crude device at the best of times, particularly on large heavy cars with high inertia in the rotating parts. Unless the car is to be used competitively, it is kinder to the gear-box to leave the clutch brake fairly slack and to take a little longer over the upward changes.

A modification which is well worth adding to the gear-box, and quite in keeping, is to put a breather in the lid. Choose a place not directly opposite a pair of gear-wheels, drill and tap a hole and fit a gauze-protected breather much in the same way as we recommended for the rocker cover of the engine.

The Propeller-shaft

The propeller-shaft is a vital link in the transmission line which is generally neglected and often in poor condition on an old car. In Vintage days there were a multitude of varying types and designs which, of recent years, have gradually died out, until only one type remains and this is fitted to practically every car made today. This type is made by Hardy Spicer Ltd. in this country, and if your shaft is beyond economical repair you will be best advised to seek their help. Hardy Spicer Ltd. will make up a complete shaft to suit any car but, if this is beyond your pocket, they will advise you how best to adapt a standard shaft to your existing coupling flanges. On some Vintage cars the earliest examples of the Spicer joint, made by Hardy Spicer Ltd., can be found. These are a plain-bearing, oil-bath type which, if they have been properly lubricated with steam cylinder oil, seem to last in perfect condition for ever. The roller-bearing type of universal joint was introduced in 1934 and all shafts made subsequent to this can be serviced. Unfortunately the earlier plain-bearing type, should it have been neglected, cannot be overhauled by the makers. If your shaft is of some other type and you want to retain it—and if you are a purist you will—then you will have to undertake the work yourself. The pot type, with sliding blocks working in channels cut in a circular body, or the ring type consisting of two rings bolted together and clamping four bushes in which the cross-pegs of the shaft and coupling work, can both be over-hauled, but considerable patience, careful lathe work and fitting, is needed to make a good job. Use phosphor-bronze for any bushes and KE169 case-hardened for cross-pins and try to arrive at a condition where there is neither torsional nor up-and-down play when the shaft is mounted.

If your shaft has Hardy discs these are, of course, obtainable, but this type of universal joint is really very undesirable with the considerable angularity obtaining in a propeller-shaft, and if you can bring yourself to use a modern type shaft we recommend that you do so.

When you have fitted the shaft, jack-up the back wheels and turn the shaft to check that it runs perfectly true. If it does not the resultant vibration can ruin an otherwise perfect car.

It is essential that the universal joints are kept well lubricated and clean if they are to last in good condition. While extra heavy gear oil is by far the best lubricant for these joints we do realise that on some of the cruder types it is very difficult to stop the oil slinging out under centrifugal loading. In these cases you will have to use grease, and an added refinement would be to have made up two leather gaiters for the joints which will at least keep the dirt out of the possibly under-lubricated bearings.

CHAPTER IX

THE RADIATOR AND BULKHEAD

WE propose to deal, in this chapter, with the two units which form either end of the engine compartment on all normal cars. We have had no experience of underfloor or rear-engined motor-cars and, in any case, these are greatly in the minority for the era with which we are dealing. Should you be sufficient of an individualist to have the urge to rebuild one of this type with air cooling, then there will be no need for you to read this chapter.

The Radiator

The radiator has perhaps more bearing on the presence of the car than any other single component. Many Vintage radiators were exceedingly handsome, and it will be well worthwhile putting yours into first-class condition for the sake of appearance, quite apart from the fact that it is a vital part which will have a large influence on the running of the car. It is also saddled with two responsibilities, firstly to maintain an equable temperature in the engine, and secondly to support the front end of the bonnet.

In the Vintage period radiators were made with the outer case in one piece with the core and are therefore much more difficult to repair or re-plate than those of a later period. If the radiator is very badly damaged but belongs to a car which was made in large quantities, then it will probably pay you to look for another in better condition. It is possible for an old radiator to be suffering from multiple cracking due to age hardening and if this is extensive it is beyond repair. There are many firms specialising in radiator repair, but we have found that Serck Ltd. give excellent service. This firm can undertake complete reconditioning and replating of all types of radiators and have a number of depots covering the country. They can supply new blocks for the film or gilled tube types, but cannot supply the honeycomb type as this is no longer made.

Vintage radiators were usually made from German or nickel silver and polished. We quite realise that to chromium plate an early type is not correct, but we have every sympathy with the owner who wishes to use his car every day carrying out this somewhat naughty modification. It will look much better than a dirty and tarnished radiator but is rather expensive. Maintaining a nickel-silver radiator in impeccable condition in this country with three months of rain and nine months of bad weather, not to speak of smog, entails a great deal of hard work, unless you have the perfect motor-house equipped with a man to do the cleaning.

To chromium plate it is necessary to remove the block, and since this is old it will probably resent being disturbed and it is likely that a new block will then be required. A 4½-litre Bentley radiator which is of the film type is probably the most expensive to repair. A new block would cost about £30 and plating, if done at the same time, an additional £5. Other radiators are proportionately cheaper. The post-Vintage model in which the shell and the block are separate are quite inexpensive both to repair and to replate. The one radiator which should never be plated is the Rolls-Royce, as these never seem to look right finished in chrome. The early ones were made from nickel-silver and the later ones from stainless steel.

If the radiator is undamaged then give it a thorough clean, clear out the air holes in the block with compressed air and a test-tube brush dipped in paraffin, as this part is generally very dirty. Take great care not to damage the block. Next flush out the interior with a water hose. If you have road-tested the car you will know the state of efficiency of the radiator, if not this will have to be checked. A rough test can be made by running the engine until the radiator is warm then spraying the block with water; do this before painting as it shows up better on a dirty block. The water should dry off rapidly and evenly and if the drying is uneven then the part which remains wet indicates the area where the water passages are blocked. This test is not infallible and a more certain way is to send the radiator to Serck Ltd., who will carry out a flow test at quite a moderate charge.

There are several causes of blocked water passages, hard water probably being the most prevalent. If you live in an area where you have this unpleasant commodity always fill up with rain water. Other causes are rust from the cylinder-block and corrosion from any aluminium castings in the water system and, last but not least, over-enthusiastic greasing of the water pump.

If you have some small leaks and wish to do the repairs yourself, blank off all the outlets leaving a connection for air pressure. Then immerse the whole radiator in water and blow up to 5 lb. per sq. in. and no more, with a tire pump. On no account connect the radiator to an air compressor in case you get a sudden rise in pressure beyond the safe figure. At the least, if there are some very weak places they will blow out and damage the block beyond repair, but you are more likely to meet an untimely end in a quite impressive explosion. Having located the leaks by noting the stream of air bubbles, mark the positions and remove the radiator from the water. Thoroughly clean the damaged area with a scraper and emery cloth before soldering. A large iron is required for this work as a small one will cool off too quickly.

If the leak is half-way along one of the tubes in a radiator of the honeycomb type it is possible to cure the trouble by blocking up each end of the offending tube. This is not a type of repair to be encouraged as too much of it will impair the efficiency, but it might get you out of trouble for a time.

Should your radiator have any dents they will have to be removed or the whole appearance of the car will be ruined. Small dents can sometimes be rectified, provided the surface is not chromium plated, by soldering a brass rod in the centre of the depression and using this to pull out the dent, the rod can then be removed and the surface polished off flat. A better way is to cut a hole in the back of the tank and through this to tap out the dent; the hole can be closed by soldering on a plate of brass or copper. This is tricky work and unless you are very skilled it is difficult to get a good finish. You may therefore find it better to send the job to a specialist.

If you have a honeycomb block and it is beyond repair, it can be re-placed with a new film block which will look quite good—in fact, it will probably never be noticed by anyone. If, however, you fit a modern gilled-tube type, you will have to disguise it with a dummy honeycomb front which can be supplied by Serck Ltd., or fit a stone guard which will go a long way towards hiding the change. Although neither of these methods is in keeping with the age of the motor-car, they are much better than being off the road altogether. Stone guards can be made by Joseph Nichols and Sons Ltd. to drawing or to pattern.

Make sure that the overflow pipe is clear and that the outlet is well below the engine, otherwise the engine will soon be covered with rusty streaks. Examine the pressure relief valve if one is fitted, the blow-off pressure of this part can be checked when the radiator is being pressure tested. Inspect the draining arrangements and if these are plugs you will find it much more convenient to change them to taps. If taps are fitted, make sure that they are in good condition.

The Cap

The cap is often rather battered, but it is possible that this may be skimmed and filed or reknurled and made to look like new. If it is the type made from ebonite with a metal insert it is rather difficult to repair, and you will probably find it much easier to turn up a new all-metal one. An even more difficult type to replace is one with a rolled thread, and several early Vintage cars used these. If you are not too rabid a purist you can turn up a cap from brass bar or a casting, and screw cut it with a thread form to fit the neck on the radiator, leaving the outside parallel. Although this will not be a true replica of the original cap it will certainly be more handsome. You may have one of the lever-type quick-action caps and if so it is sure to be in a bad state. They depend on all the parts being a good fit and as soon as a little wear takes place they no longer seal properly. It is possible to renovate them if you have sufficient patience but probably a better way is to fit a "Monza" quick-action cap made by Enots Ltd. You will have to make an adaptor screwed inside to fit the radiator neck and outside to fit the new cap. These are made in three sizes: 2 in. × 18 t.p.i., $2\frac{1}{2}$ in. × 16 t.p.i. and $2\frac{3}{4}$ in. × 16 t.p.i. If you wish to make a screwed cap

I RIPE FOR RESTORATION: *decrepit though this early 30/98 Vauxhall may have been, it was quite possible for an amateur to restore it to concours condition*

II, III   THE MORNING AFTER: *a 1929 4½-litre Bentley after dismantling. The success of its restoration can be judged by comparison with Plates VI and IX*

IV   *Dashboard mounting brackets attaching the instrument panel to the chassis, so that the car may be run without a body. Note also the cross-bracing (see page 98)*

V   *The instrument panel made for a rebuilt car, showing the "reproduction" instruments and lamps, and the mottled finish (see pages 109, 110 and 162)*

VI *A 1929 4½-litre Bentley engine, after restoration, on its stand awaiting installation in the chassis*

VII   *A 1932 J Type Duesenberg engine installed in front of a reproduction "period" bulkhead*

VIII   THE AUTHORS' ROLLS-ROYCE: *a 1930 Phantom II with coachwork by Barker*

IX *The Authors enjoying the fruits of their labours at Goodwood in their 4½-litre Bentley*

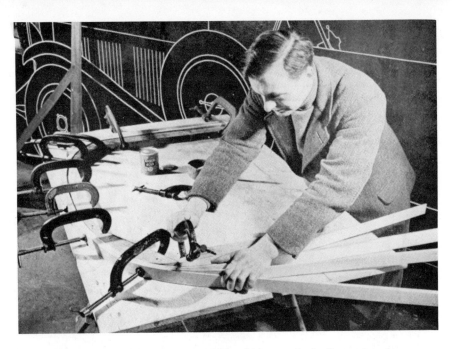

X   *The Lamination Process for making new body-frame members*
(see page 132)

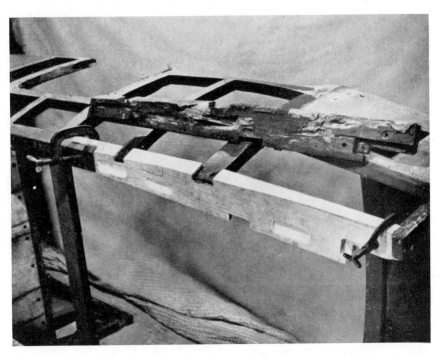

XI   *Replacing a rotten section of a main body member, showing the decayed
timber which has been removed (see page 132)*

with a cross-bar you will have to provide an adjustment to set the cross-bar in its correct position when the cap is tight.

Whatever type of cap you have can be finished in polished brass, nickel or chromium plate depending on the finish of the radiator.

Stays and Mountings

The radiator stay may be in bad condition and the bonnet hinge mountings almost certainly will be worn as they are constantly moving due to the flexing of the chassis. If these parts are beyond repair or rebushing, brass castings can be made and these are not at all expensive if you make the pattern. Build this pattern up from well-seasoned and close-grained wood and remember to allow for shrinkage and machining. Finish the wood as smooth as possible and taper the sections in the appropriate places so that it will not stick in the mould and finally paint with cellulose. If you are not fond of woodwork you could machine these parts from the solid brass.

Whatever way you approach this work it is worthwhile doing it well as it will have to take a fair amount of stress, and the good fitting of the bonnet will depend on it. The mountings should be both riveted and soldered to the radiator and should be done with a blowpipe. If this frightens you, take it to a radiator specialist who will do the job for you. The same procedure applies to the radiator mounting brackets.

The Badge

The badge may be worn through years of polishing and if it is enamelled this may be chipped, if so do not despair as it can be repaired. If this work has to be done the badge must first be removed from the shell. Should the shell and block be in one piece the badge will be soldered in position, but if it is a later radiator with a loose shell it will probably be fixed with studs and nuts.

The badge can be re-enamelled at quite a reasonable price by Marples and Beasley Ltd., who can also re-cut it if it is badly worn, but this work is rather more expensive. Remember that enamel is glass and will not stand bending, so make sure that the badge is a perfect fit before sending it to the enameller. The re-soldering of the badge on to the radiator is definitely a job for the expert. If the radiator is to be plated and the badge is soldered in position it must be fitted first.

When the radiator is complete, clean the block with cellulose thinners, mask-off the plated part and spray with Llewellyn Ryland's cylinder black. Always fit new bonnet tape; this material is available from any coach-builders' suppliers but if there are none in your vicinity it can be obtained from Albert Jagger Ltd. Fit new radiator hoses of good quality and wet the inside of the hose and the outside of the pipe for ease of assembly. Always use worm-drive hose clips as these are by far the best type.

If you require a bent hose and this cannot be obtained, a way out of the difficulty is to wind a spring in brass wire 16 S.W.G. the full length and a good fit inside the hose. It will then be found that the hose can be bent to shape in position, with the spring inside, without kinking.

The radiator should always be insulated from the chassis with at least thin synthetic-rubber packing, and when fitting make sure that tightening the fixing bolts does not put any strain on the radiator. Use "Aerotight" or "Nyloc" nuts.

The Bulkhead

As, once again, it is impossible to deal with all the various designs likely to be met with by our readers, we shall have to generalise.

If the bulkhead is part of the front of the body it will probably be made from thick plywood. This type is difficult to keep clean. It can be painted, but a far better way is to cover it with thin hard aluminium sheet cemented in place with "Evostik" and it can be finished in a variety of ways; it is then easy to keep clean.

If the car is one of the more expensive Vintage models, the bulkhead will probably be a separate component mounted on the chassis to which the body will later be joined. This part may either be an aluminium casting or a sheet of aluminium with brackets bolted to it. This type of bulkhead is by far the most satisfying to work on as they can be made to look very impressive.

First strip every detachable piece from the bulkhead and then clean it thoroughly. If there is any sign of cracks they must now be welded, and in this case make sure that no distortion has taken place and that it will still fit the chassis. Decide on the finish you require and then, if it is a casting, scrape and fettle until it is really smooth. There will probably be a few spare holes due to alterations by previous owners and if so fill these with short lengths of aluminium rod riveted over and scraped flat. If you require any new holes now is the time to decide on their position and to drill them. Some cars had their underbonnet wiring carried in aluminium conduits. If yours does not have this feature it is worth considering at this stage, as it looks very tidy and is so easy to keep clean.

If you are proposing to mount the dashboard off the bulkhead you should have made a mock-up with wood and hardboard before the body was removed so that you are sure of the shape and position of the dashboard. Should this be the case, now is the time to make the brackets from either castings or sheet aluminium; a typical example is shown in Plate IV.

Check the radiator stay and bonnet-hinge mounting and treat these in a similar way to the ones on the radiator. Also examine the bonnet tape strip and repair if necessary. Fit a new bonnet tape.

Examine the steering column attachment; in some cases this was not strong enough and if you find that your car suffers from this fault redesign the mounting to give greater rigidity, as this treatment will all help to improve the steering. Inspect the floor-board attachments and if any of the threads tapped into the bulkhead are stripped, drill them out and fit G.K.N. anchor nuts.

Should the car be fitted with a dashboard-mounted water thermometer, the pipe will have to pass through the bulkhead and will require a large hole to allow the passage of the union nut and bulb. This should have a blanking-off plate with a rubber grommet which acts as a steady for the

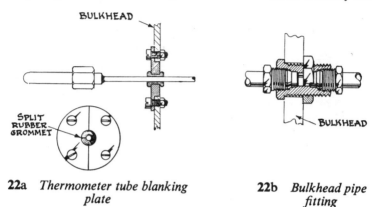

| 22a | Thermometer tube blanking plate | 22b | Bulkhead pipe fitting |

pipe (see fig. 22a). Any other pipes which have to pass through the bulkhead should be split at this point and joined with bulkhead connectors which can be obtained from Enots Ltd. (fig. 22b).

Try to blank off as many holes as possible between the engine and the cockpit as this will keep the car cooler in summer and also it will help to reduce mechanical noise.

If your bulkhead is too far gone to be repaired, it is quite possible to make one from ¼-in. duralumin plate and angle duralumin, using a riveted construction, and in this case you could anodise the parts before assembly.

CHAPTER X

THE FUEL SYSTEM

The Petrol Tank

THE position of the petrol filler is worth some consideration before starting work on the tank, for the sake of greater convenience when refuelling. For instance, if a luggage carrier is fitted, can the tank be filled with a trunk in position? If the tank has no gauge, can you check the level with a dipstick? Is the venting arrangement satisfactory? We well remember one car on which the misguided designer had so placed the air vent that, in heavy rain, the tank was filled with water. Even more remarkable was the fact that he must have known of this delightful habit in his masterpiece, as there was a warning in the instruction book always to cover up the filler cap when washing the car. A slight modification cured this trouble.

Having decided if any alterations are necessary set to work to clean the tank both inside and out. Tanks are generally made of tinned steel and, if old, often have a considerable amount of loose rust inside. Having emptied out all the petrol the rust can be easily washed out with water by repeatedly filling and emptying the tank. Care must be taken to dry out the tank immediately afterwards. The old paint should be removed with Nitromors and not scraped off dry, as this will also remove a great deal of the tin from the outside of the tank as well as the paint. If there are any dents which have to be removed, often the only way possible is to take out one end of the tank in order to support the inside surface of the metal while it is being hammered. An end will also have to be removed if any of the baffles are loose, for the purpose of securing them. This will entail unsoldering a joint and on no account use a blowpipe for this job. Such a warning seems unnecessary but people keep on blowing themselves up with old petrol tanks, and the only safe rule is to use nothing but a soldering iron near any tank, no matter for how long it has been empty. Tank repair firms take very elaborate precautions to ensure that the tank is free from petrol before using a blowpipe, and these require facilities far outside the scope of an amateur.

Next carefully examine the tank for cracks or pinholes. The bottom of a tank is often rusted through from the inside, due to having had water lying on it. The tank may be tested with air under water in the same way as was the radiator, and any small leaks not at a joint usually denote that the metal is getting very thin. It will be as well either to solder a patch on the affected area or to make a complete new portion. If you feel unable to do this yourself, Serck Radiators Ltd., or any good tinsmith, can take on

100

the repair or even make a complete new tank to the old design using the existing filler neck and other fittings. Any leaks round joints can be easily soldered up with an iron, and if the tank then passes a pressure test of 5 lb. per sq. in. it can be counted serviceable.

The filler cap should be treated in the same way as we described for the radiator cap. It should have a cork or synthetic rubber washer in good condition and, unless the fuel system depends upon a pressurised tank, an adequate vent hole suitably baffled to stop water getting in or petrol splashing out.

The mounting brackets of the tank should be strong enough to support the tank when full which is often a very considerable weight, and in the case of a rear-mounted tank, should not subject the tank to any stress when the chassis distorts. If there is any sign of the mountings pulling off the tank, an alteration to the design of the brackets may cure the trouble. Rear tanks on the better cars were generally three-point-mounted to obviate distortion troubles.

The tank is sometimes fitted with a filter. This should be thoroughly cleaned and, if damaged, new gauze fitted. If no filter is fitted in a rear-mounted tank a very suitable design of combined drain plug and filter is shown in fig. 23, where the filter can be cleaned by removing the drain plug.

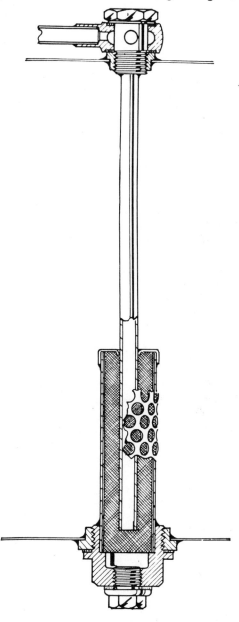

23 *Tank filter and drain plug*

101

The correct gauze for all petrol filters is 80 mesh brass or monel metal.

See that the drain plug is in good fettle and that is has a sound washer. Either thin fibre or copper and asbestos are suitable. Replace the drain plug if necessary.

Next look at the petrol outlet connection. On a gravity tank this will in all probability be a female-threaded boss into which the petrol tap is screwed. In this case have the tap in position when testing the tank and observe any leaks at this point. A new fibre washer may cure the leak, but if the face of the boss is damaged it may be possible to rectify it in position by very careful filing, or it can be unsoldered and a new boss fitted. On rear-mounted tanks the outlet is generally a male-threaded cone union connection, which can be blanked off for testing with a nut and nipple soldered on a short piece of rod or nipped-up tube. Any damage to this will require a new union which can be made either outright, or from a drain-plug collar and double-ended union of the appropriate size screwed in and then soldered.

Lastly in connection with the tank, there is the question of the petrol gauge. There are so many and divers forms of gauge that it is impossible to go into any detail on this subject.

It is an easy matter to test the gauge by filling the tank a gallon at a time and noting the reading. The mechanically operated type mounted direct on the tank are usually very reliable and any fault is easily detectable. Dash-board-mounted gauges are sometimes troublesome and seldom accurate, with the possible exception of the "Nivex" which, if in good order and the connections to the tank sound, is very dependable. The Hobson "Tele-gauge" can be serviced by H. M. Hobson Ltd., who are the original manufacturers. Most electrical gauges were made by Smiths Motor Accessories Ltd., who can still repair them.

If the tank is at all rusty on the outside, "Jenolite" it before painting. A rear-mounted tank that shows on the finished car must be brought up to coachwork standards of finish before it is remounted in the chassis.

Petrol Taps

There is only one really satisfactory type of petrol tap and that is one in which cork is used as a seating. If you wish to fit a tap, or replace a faulty or inferior pattern with a cork-seated type, these can still be obtained. A gravity system must have a tap and this is usually fitted direct into the tank. It can either be a simple on/off type or a main and reserve two-level variety. With a rear-mounted tank a tap is not a necessity unless the feed is by "Autovac" where, once again it will be screwed direct into the gravity tank. If your car has no reserve it is well worth considering the fitting of a two-way tap under the bonnet with two delivery pipes from the tank, one reaching not quite to the bottom, to stop that sinking feeling when the car comes to rest miles from home at 3 o'clock in the morning.

Petrol Filters

Many cars were fitted with filters remote from the tank. If yours is so fitted dismantle the filter and clean it out thoroughly. If necessary make a new gauze or, if it is an edge-type filter, clean each disc and reassemble with new cork or fibre washers wherever necessary. A modern pipe-line filter is quite permissible on an old motor-car and is best mounted on the bulkhead where it is easily visible. When ordering state the diameter of pipe which you are using.

Method of Supply

If your car has a gravity petrol system then you have no worries under this heading. Probably the next most commonly used system on Vintage cars was the "Autovac". This is phenomenally reliable and rarely gives trouble of any sort. It will be as well to dismantle the "Autovac", which is very simple to understand, and to clean all parts thoroughly. Make sure that all the valves are working freely, that the cone filter fitted to the inlet elbow is clean and that the inlet and suction elbows are a good fit in their tapers. These can be ground in with fine grinding paste if necessary. Vintage Racing Cars Ltd. can overhaul any model and can also supply an instruction leaflet on the care and maintenance of their product.

The S.U. electric pump may be tested by connecting it to a battery and fitting it with a short length of pipe on the suction side which can be dipped into a container of petrol. A good flow of petrol should issue from the outlet and if you put your finger over this the pump should stop working until the pressure is released. S.U. Ltd. can overhaul these pumps and supply spare parts. They cannot however supply parts for or service their older product, the "Petrolift" pump. This is very easy to overhaul at home—the only likely source of trouble being the cork float and the electrical contacts. A new float can be made by C. Cantrill, Ltd. and should be shellac coated and the contacts will usually only need stoning. Again the filter in the pump should be in good condition. A very good main and reserve system can be made using two S.U. pumps drawing from two levels in the tank, the change over being effected by a switch on the dashboard.

The same procedure can be adopted to test an A.C. mechanical pump, working the cam lever by hand, which should stop in the depressed position when the outlet of the pump is closed off. A.C. agents throughout the country can overhaul or supply replacements for these pumps.

Should your car be fitted with a pressure system, then probably the hand-operated air pump will be in a poor state. Usually a new leather is needed on the plunger (obtainable from R. H. Nuttall Ltd.), and the spindle support will need bushing. The non-return valve should also be tested and reseated if necessary. The air pressure gauge can, if necessary, be overhauled by Bailey and Mackey Ltd., who can overhaul pressure gauges of any make and also supply new gauges of various sizes and pressures. This firm also sells a very accurate tyre-pressure gauge of the Bourdon-tube type which is an asset to any motor house.

Piping

We now come to a subject on which we cannot lay too much stress if your car is to look a first-class engineering job. So often one's first impression, on looking under the bonnet of a car, is that everything has been carefully put together and then, as a complete afterthought, some old battered copper piping has been hastily dug up from the scrap box, bent back and forth until it is flattened and kinked, and then literally sprung into position between the various unions with no thought of supporting its vibrating length anywhere. The original pipework on Vintage cars was generally very neatly laid out, but when it has

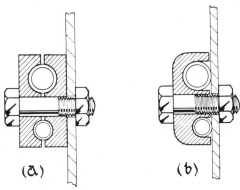

(a)   (b)

24   *Pipe supports*

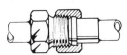

SINGLE ENDED UNION
THREADS 1/8" B.S.P TO 3/4" B.S.P
PIPE 1/8" °/DIA. TO 3/4" °/DIA.

DOUBLE ENDED UNION
THREADS 1/8" B.S.P TO 3/4" B.S.P
PIPE 1/8" °/DIA. TO 3/4" °/DIA

TEE UNION
THREADS 1/8" B.S.P. TO 3/4" B.S.P.
PIPE 1/8" °/DIA. TO 3/4" °/DIA

SOLDER TEE UNION
3/16, 1/4, 5/16, 3/8, 1/2, 5/8 & 3/4 °/DIA. PIPE

BANJO FITTING

1/8" B.S.P.	°/DIA. PIPE 3/16",	1/4" OR 5/16"
1/4" B.S.P	"	1/4" OR 5/16"
3/8" B.S.P	"	5/16" " 3/8"

25   *Types of unions*

been removed and replaced a few times it tends to get hard and misshapen. The best advice is to throw away all the old piping and to start with new. This can be of either copper or Bundy, and some thought must be given to taking each pipe in as neat and well-supported a line as possible. A very good plan on rear-tank cars is to break the petrol line along the chassis into several short lengths, each joined by a union so that the piping is easily assembled and removed. Make all bends of as large a radius as possible and bend the pipe round a suitable wood or metal former to keep the radius constant. Buy copper pipe in the half-hard condition, which allows it to be bent more easily without flattening, and anneal each piece after it is formed to shape. This is done by heating it to a red heat and allowing it to cool. Bundy tube needs no annealing as it is made from mild steel, but it must not be bent backwards and forwards too many times. It is always a good idea to put a short length of flexible pipe between a chassis-mounted pipe and the engine. Clips for supporting the pipe can be made by drilling a small block of metal and then splitting it as shown in fig. 24.

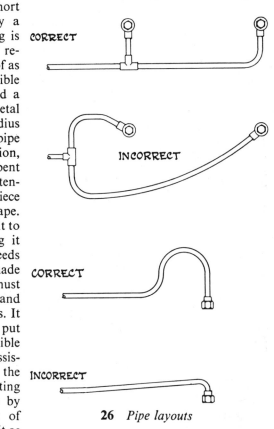

CORRECT

INCORRECT

CORRECT

INCORRECT

26　*Pipe layouts*

Under the bonnet, always try to keep the piping either horizontal or vertical to follow the lines of the engine and bulkhead. In fig. 25 we show various types of union which are made today. Two of the more common faults in pipe layouts, and their corrections, are shown in fig. 26.

Hard and Soft Soldering

In this chapter and elsewhere we have referred to soldering and perhaps a few words of advice to the uninitiated may be of help. In dealing with soft soldering, the first and most important rule is cleanliness. It is quite impossible to solder together any two pieces of metal unless they are absolutely clean and free from grease and oxide. Having got your parts to this state the next move is thoroughly to tin each piece. This can be done by heating the part with a blowpipe, and when the required temperature is reached, applying flux with a brush and then touching the end of the stick of solder to the metal. If the temperature is right and the fluxing adequate the tin should run on the surface, and further fluxing should spread it out. Where this procedure is difficult or dangerous, the same can be done by first tinning a soldering iron in the above manner and then applying the solder to the surface to be tinned with the iron, using plenty of flux and constantly reheating the iron. In our opinion the only flux any good for soft soldering is killed spirits of salts, which can either be freshly made by dissolving zinc in hydrochloric acid or bought as a proprietary flux such as Baker's Soldering Fluid. The two mating surfaces having been tinned they can now be reheated, refluxed and put together with the addition of a little more solder. Parts should always be thoroughly washed after soldering to remove the flux which is very corrosive.

For hard soldering we recommend that you use a silver-based alloy such as "Easiflow" which is made by Johnson Matthey and Co. Ltd. They can also supply the correct flux in powder form. Again cleanliness is very important and a much higher temperature than for soft soldering is necessary. Unlike soft soldering, the two parts must first be put together with a little flux, which is mixed with water into a paste. They must then be brought up to a bright red heat, more flux applied and the solder touched against the edge of the joint with the flame still playing on it. The solder should immediately melt and be drawn into the joint by capillary attraction. If it does not run immediately the temperature is not high enough. It is very important in the case of circular fitting parts, such as a pipe nipple, that a very small clearance only is allowed, the smaller the better, a good push-on fit being the best for perfect hard soldering. In the amateur workshop, probably the best blowpipe for hard soldering is the "Bullfinch" which will cope with normal-sized work providing the work-piece is standing on, and backed up by, some fire-bricks which concentrate the heat.

In our view soft soldering is quite good enough for normal pipe work, but if the nipples are hard-soldered on to the pipe it can be annealed with all its fittings in position.

Drain plugs, collars, pipe unions, copper and Bundy pipe are all available from Enots Ltd.

CHAPTER XI

CONTROLS, INSTRUMENTS AND INSTRUMENT PANEL

WHEN your car once again takes the road with you at the wheel, nothing will give you greater pleasure than to have a well-laid-out and nicely finished instrument panel before you, fitted with instruments that not only work but also tell the truth. No less important for real pleasure in driving will be well-positioned controls working with smoothness and accuracy.

Controls

Under this heading we shall deal with the minor controls such as the mixture, ignition, hand throttle and radiator-shutter controls, also the foot accelerator.

First examine the levers themselves and make sure they are a good fit in their bearings; these may possibly have to be bushed or reamered out and new fulcrum pins made. If your car is fitted with controls in the centre of the steering wheel, these will be fitted with a means of holding them in any desired position, either teeth in a quadrant or some type of friction device. Should you have the type with teeth, re-cut them and make a new hardened pawl if necessary. If they are the friction variety, make sure that they are working smoothly but will, in fact, hold the levers in position. Rectify any play in the bearings of the long tubular shafts at both the top and the bottom of the steering column. If there is any marking on the quadrants and this is in a bad state have it re-engraved before you give the parts their final finish. Charles Eades Ltd. can do any engraving for you, and this may be filled in with paint.

Your controls may be on the instrument board, and in this case their working will be greatly improved if they are fitted adjacent to one of the mounting brackets. The horn button is possibly mounted in the column and may be the type in which the wire is wound and then unwound each time the wheel is turned, finally breaking the wire and causing an electrical short circuit. If so, get rid of this system and fit the button in some other convenient position. Should the levers be fitted with detachable knobs and these are either in a bad state or missing altogether, new ones can be turned up from hardwood, ebonite or metal or they can be bought from Perkins Ltd. who have a large range of sizes and colours.

Make a careful study of the control-rod linkwork; it may pay you to scrap it and make a new layout as there were very bad examples on some of the early cars. The secret of the beautiful feel in the controls of quality motor-cars is mainly due to correct layout. There should be no lost motion caused through back-lash or lack of torsional rigidity in long shafts, and for this reason push-and-pull rods are much better than torsion shafts unless these are short and of ample diameter. All the levers must work equally on each side of their dead centres and many layouts could be improved by the use of bell-crank levers, but it must be remembered to keep the number of joints down to a minimum consistent with good geometry. Always use ball joints in preference to fork ends and

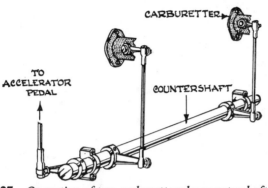

27 *Operation of two carburetters by countershaft*

clevis-pins; keep all the rods as light as possible and if any of these are in compression, a larger diameter light alloy tube is preferable. Never use spring-loaded ball joints as these introduce friction into the system; choose the adjustable type which can be obtained from Amal Ltd. For

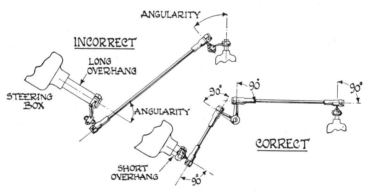

28a *Control layouts*

most of the controls under the bonnet, 2 BA size ball joints have ample strength.

There should always be a spring fitted to the throttle control close to the butterfly valve, in addition to the one on the pedal, so that should the linkage break or come adrift the throttle will be automatically closed.

If more than one carburetter is fitted, a layout which works very well is one in which each carburetter is linked up to a countershaft running in needle roller bearings, the countershaft then being linked up to the pedal.

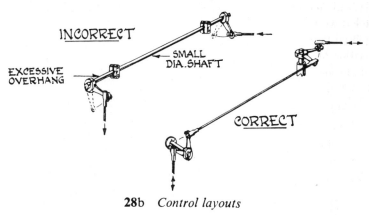

28b *Control layouts*

This is shown in fig. 27. In figs. 28a and b are some examples of correct and incorrect control layouts.

The Instruments

Unless you are lucky enough to have a car with all its original instruments, try to collect a matched set. If you are unable to find all the correct ones then a certain amount of rebuilding and alteration will have to be done to them. All the instruments must at least have dials of the same colour; these can have the glass removed and the dial and fingers can then be repainted. It is possible to have old instrument dials repainted professionally and, although this can be expensive in the case of an elaborately marked dial where the maker's trade mark and other printing has to be reproduced by hand, A. H. Bedford and Son can undertake to repaint most types of dial and can give an estimate of what the cost will be beforehand. Even aircraft instruments of the back-mounting type can be made to look quite "vintage" if mounted in such a way that only a small portion of the body projects in front of the board, and they are then fitted with a false bezel to match the other instruments.

The fronts of lighting and other switchboards can be made up from duralumin or brass, engraved in the correct manner and then black anodised, polished or plated, and the lettering filled in with paint if necessary. In fact there is great scope for ingenuity here and the gentle art of faking is most entertaining. In Plate V we show a completely new board which has been made up and on which a considerable amount of faking has been done with very pleasing results. Resist the temptation of fitting rows of switches, as this generally looks very untidy. A radiator thermometer is worth considering if one was not originally fitted—providing you are not too intolerant a purist. They are made by Smiths Motor Accessories Ltd., with different types of mounting so that you ought to be able to match it with the remainder of the set of instruments. The bezels should all be plated or painted to match; black looks best on an aluminium board and either black or plated on wood. Clocks can usually be repaired by your local clocksmith, and pressure gauges of all types by Bailey and Mackay Ltd., speedometers and revolution counters by Speedometer Supplies Ltd.

Instrument fixing is generally one of two types. Either the instrument has a small flange behind the bezel which is pulled down on to the board by means of a stirrup fitted over a stud in the back of the case, or it is held in place by several small screws in a wider bezel flange. In the latter case use countersunk raised-head screws, which should also be used wherever

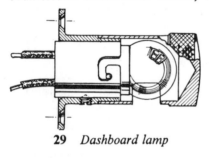

29 Dashboard lamp

possible in preference to flat countersunk screws for the sake of appearance. Since the instruments on modern cars are all illuminated from the back of the board, it is now very difficult to get well-made dashlamps. We are therefore showing in fig. 29 a design for one which will give good lighting and will look imposing if you have the necessary lathe to make it (see Plate V). The bulb-holder portion of this lamp is from a Butler "Atlantic" Spot Lamp and is available as a spare part. Last of all, do not forget to include a socket for an inspection-lamp plug.

The Instrument Board

If you are making a completely new board, make up a wooden pattern and fix this in the correct position. Arrange the instruments in a nicely balanced pattern using cards to represent them, cut out to the proper sizes and shapes and fixed with drawing-pins. Now sit behind the wheel and make sure that all the instruments are visible; if they are not, they can easily be rearranged at this stage, but be certain that you have the full set, as anything added afterwards will spoil the appearance. You can now mark out and saw all the necessary holes, being careful not to damage the surface of the board as this will only mean extra work later on when you come to the finishing, with which we shall be dealing in a later chapter.

Should the original board be in wood and in reasonable condition, remove all the fittings and repolish it. Any small unwanted holes can be plugged by glueing in small pieces of wood to match Not only use the same type of wood and as near the same colour as possible, but make sure that the grain runs in the same direction, it will then be almost invisible when polished. If the board is in a very bad state it is better to scrap it and make a new one; walnut is the best wood for this purpose. It could also be made quite nicely from plywood with a hardwood surface, or covered with leather or "Lionide" to match the upholstery. If you are going to cover it, and this certainly looks very good if well done, the material should be cemented in position with "Bostik", and the edge finished off with a rim made from 22 S.W.G. brass as shown in fig. 30, and finished to match the instruments.

If the board is aluminium, strip off all the fittings and refinish it. Any small unwanted holes can be plugged with aluminium rod riveted in and filed off flat. Should the board be too far gone and a new one is required, make this from $\frac{1}{8}$-in. duralumin or thin dura-lumin of about 0·048 in. cemented on to plywood. To do this, roughen the back of the metal with coarse emery cloth and cement it in position with "Evo-stik". The metal can be finished in a variety of ways as mentioned in a later chapter but, if an anodised finish is required, this will have to be done before the cementing.

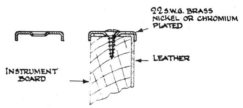

30 *Metal edging for instrument board*

CHAPTER XII

THE ELECTRICAL EQUIPMENT AND WIRING

IT is unlikely that every part of the electrical equipment will be tackled at one stage in the overhaul, but for the sake of easy reference we will deal with it all in this chapter, with the exception of that already dealt with under the heading of the engine. The thorough reconditioning of everything electrical will undoubtedly pay dividends, as the system is under its heaviest load at night and consequently this is the time when it usually chooses to break down if it is in bad condition. It is invariably also a cold and wet night, but this is from sheer cussedness and not for any technical reason!

The Battery and its Mounting

The heart of the electrical system on any car is the battery. There is very little advice that we can give on this subject that is not general knowledge, except that a bad, or undersized, battery can make an otherwise good car a perfect nuisance. If you are at all doubtful about the state of your battery have it tested, and if it is faulty discard it and fit a new one. There are many excellent makes on the market but we always use "Exide", who have a range of shapes and sizes to suit every type of car. A modern battery of a good make will stand up to any normal load, but in the case of Vintage cars where the dynamo output is often limited, it is a good idea to have as large a capacity battery as you can conveniently accommodate, in order to cope with possible long night use where the dynamo is not balancing the lighting load. If your car is to have only very occasional use, it might be well worth considering fitting an alkaline battery which, although heavier and much more expensive for a given capacity, will stand unlimited neglect and standing with no use, which a lead-acid battery certainly will not. Wood-cased lead-acid batteries are still available in all sizes from Brylite Batteries Ltd.

Having decided on the size of battery, turn now to its accommodation on the car. Some Vintage cars have a box for this purpose on the running board, and if you are not completely "purist" we would advise you to move this to another position. Not only does a battery so mounted put a very great overhung load on the often flimsy chassis side-members, but it is very tempting to small boys to play with when the car is left in the street. Small boys are very electrically minded these days, and as we all know the short-circuiting of a large battery can produce a very interesting pyrotechnic display. Probably the best place for the battery is underneath the rear floor of the car on the side remote from the exhaust pipe, as it is cool and out of the way. Be sure, if you have to reposition your battery, that you are going to be able to get at it easily, otherwise it will be neglected.

The battery box is often in a foul state, having suffered with years of acid attack and general neglect. If yours is like this, it is well worth making a new one from acid-resisting materials. We show a typical construction in fig. 31 which is made from duralumin angle and "Tufnol" sheet. A sheet of rubber is put on the floor of the box, which somewhat insulates the battery from excessive vibration. The battery box is best supported between two chassis cross-members, but if none are conveniently placed, two tubes can be arranged across the frame and flange connected into the two side-members. If you decide that your existing box can be restored, and it is made of steel, paint it well with anti-sulphuric acid paint which is available from W. Canning and Co. Ltd.

The Starter Motor and Dynamo

Although an easy way out with these two instruments is to pack them up and send them to an expert for overhaul, it is often quite easy to do all that is necessary yourself. Your road test will have shown whether or not they are working satisfactorily, but even if they appear sound they must be stripped down for examination and cleaning.

Troubles in starters are usually due to worn brush gear or a bad commutator. When the motor is stripped and cleaned, examine these components carefully. It will always pay to fit new brushes if the old ones are worn, and as there is a multitude of sizes, many of which are no longer obtainable, you will possibly have to buy the nearest size, and either carefully file or machine them to fit your brush holders. The commutator will probably need skimming. This must be done in a lathe and with a nicely ground tool get as smooth a finish as possible, turning out all the burnt surface. Finish off with metal polish and never use emery cloth, as the emery will embed itself into the copper. The mica separators must now be undercut below the level of the commutator segments, and the best tool for this is a broken hack-saw blade with the set ground off the side of the teeth. This can then be used as a scraper, the mica cut back, and all burrs removed from the sides of the segments. While the armature is in the lathe, see that it runs true and that the spindle is not bent. If the spindle is bent and is beyond straightening, the armature will have to be sent to an expert who can make a new spindle and rewind the armature on to it. Electric Service Co. (B'ham) Ltd. can arrange for this to be done. See that the armature is not touching the pole pieces and tape-up any bare internal wiring. Check the bearings for wear and if necessary replace them. Plain bearings should be made from phosphor-bronze, and ball-races for obsolete starters are nearly always available from one of the ball-race manufacturers.

By far the most common type of starter drive is the "Bendix". A brutal mechanism, it nevertheless serves millions daily with fair reliability. It is

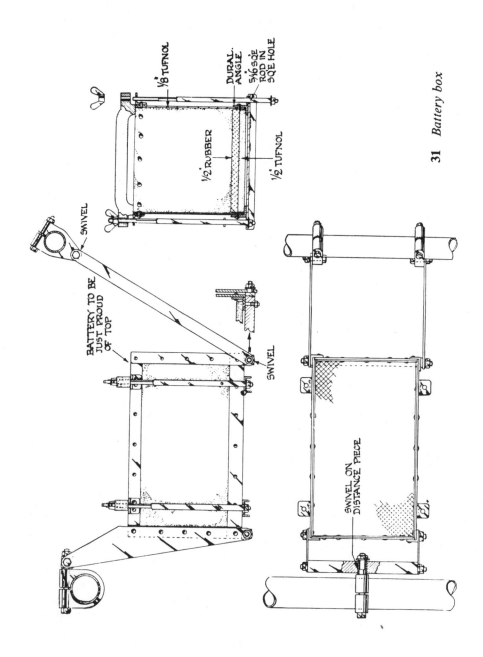

1/8 TUFNOL

DURAL. ANGLE

5/16 s.QE. ROD IN SQE HOLE

1/2 RUBBER

1/2 TUFNOL

SWIVEL

BATTERY TO BE JUST PROUD OF TOP

SWIVEL

SWIVEL ON DISTANCE PIECE

31 *Battery box*

important that the pinion and buffer spring are in good order, and most of these are still currently in stock or a very similar pattern can be used or adapted. Never oil a Bendix drive or it will eventually stick. There is usually sufficient oil vapour under the bonnet to keep it from rusting. A very much kinder type of starter drive is the axial, where the whole armature slides, carrying the pinion into mesh before the full starting current is applied to the motor. This is particularly beneficial on a large engine and is currently used on the heavier commercial vehicles. Bosch, Simms and C.A.V. make such starters and, although very expensive to buy new, can often be found in breakers' yards in good condition. If your car has a large engine and you are in "Bendix trouble", it might be worth considering the fitting of an axial starter. A small range of varying size pinions is available from the manufacturers should a change be necessary. A point to watch is that the pinion is fully engaged with the flywheel ring when the armature is in its extended position.

When the starter is reassembled, the brushes can be bedded-in by wrapping a piece of fine emery cloth round the commutator with the emery side outwards, and rotating the armature backwards and forwards with the brushes in position. Get rid of all dust after this operation.

The starter can finally be tested by mounting it in the vice and clamping on to the pinion a steel bar 12 in. long. A spring balance hooked on to the end of this bar and suitably anchored to the bench, will now read directly in pound-feet the torque of the motor. Couple the starter to a battery for as short a time as possible; the reading should be somewhere between 15 and 24 lb.-ft., depending on the size of the engine for which it is designed.

Some Vintage cars were fitted with dynamotors: that is, one machine permanently connected to the engine which served both as a starter and as a dynamo. Although very silent in operation these were really a failure, as their weight is usually at least as great as that of a separate starter and dynamo combined, and secondly either the instrument is geared correctly from the generating angle, and therefore lacks the torque to turn over the engine when really cold, or it is too highly geared as a dynamo and absorbs a great deal of power from the engine. If you are making a perfect restoration, keep your dynamotor, but otherwise think carefully about the possibility of replacing it with separate instruments. The perfect starting arrangement is to be found only on the Rolls-Royce of pre-war days, where a chain-drive starter with solenoid-operated clutch ensures complete silence and mechanical perfection.

The starter switch should be cleaned and its contacts brought up to a polished state. It is often a good plan to replace manually operated switches on the instrument board with solenoid operation, as this cuts down the length of heavy cable required and also the voltage drop between battery and starter. A suitably "period" instrument board switch can usually be found to operate the solenoid circuit.

If your car is fitted with the strange system known as "Startix", we think that you would be better off with a straightforward system of push-button control, unless you are a collector of electrical phenomena.

Much the same remarks apply to the overhaul of the dynamo as to the starter, so that we shall not repeat them. In the case of the dynamo, however, care will have to be taken that the various field connections are rejoined to the right brushes. Most Vintage cars are fitted with three-brush dynamos of the constant-current output type. The current output can be varied by adjusting the position of the third brush; moving it in the direction of rotation increases the current. Poor output may be due to a dirty or scored commutator, bad brushes, poor connections or weak brush springs, and all these points should be checked before adjusting the third brush, as this is an adjustment and not a cure for other ills. Later cars fitted with voltage control have two-brush dynamos, as do certain Vintage cars fitted with continental electrical equipment.

When the dynamo has been overhauled it can be put in the lathe and connected through its cut-out, ammeter and battery, and tested. It should cut-in at a speed equivalent to less than 25 m.p.h. in top gear, and the third brush can be adjusted to give the output which you desire.

Cars using constant-current dynamos were normally fitted with a "half-and-full" charge switch. As it is very difficult to know when to use the various charging rates, we feel that it is not departing too far from the original design of the car to consider fitting a constant-voltage generating system. If you can find a Bosch dynamo of Vintage days it will have a built-in voltage control unit, and you will be still using a period instrument. On post-Vintage cars we have no hesitation in recommending the fitting of a modern dynamo and voltage control unit.

Never run a constant-current dynamo unless it is connected to a battery, or unless you have disconnected the field winding. With no battery connected, the voltage can rise alarmingly and do considerable damage to the rest of the electrical gear on the car.

Both starter and dynamo can be finished to match the engine.

The Cut-out or Voltage Contro

Both these items are normally very reliable and apart from cleaning the contacts carefully and seeing that there are no potential short-circuits, there seems little one needs do to either of them. If your cut-out is dog-eared Delco Remy Ltd. still manufacture them, and replacement is probably easier than repair. Most voltage control units are replaceable by modern types.

Lamps

The condition of the lamps on your car is important from an appearance as well as from a functional point of view. Examine the shells for dents. These can often be tapped out on a wood block, but damaged rims are generally very difficult to repair at home. Here a professional metal worker can quickly restore the original shape, and Serck Ltd. specialise in lamp repairs. Examine the mountings on head-lamps, as these are sometimes loose and need re-riveting. If you decide to plate your lamps, perfection of the shells is even more important as the very smallest dent will show up when they are polished. Replate the reflectors if they are discoloured. Several firms advertise in the motoring journals who can do this silver plating quite cheaply. In the case of glass reflectors, these should be cleaned with cotton-wool soaked in methylated spirits and, if the silvering has deteriorated, they can be resilvered by any firm which specialises in doing this work on household mirrors. Make sure that the bulbholders are in good order and that the cork seals between rim and reflector are unbroken. In the case of lamps with frosted glasses, if one of these is broken, it is no use replacing it with household frosted glass as the optical properties are wrong. Most of these special glasses are now unobtainable and we feel that possibly the only solution is to fit both lamps with plain glass. The older pattern plate-glass fronts with bevelled edges can be made by any good glass dealer who has facilities for cutting and bevelling plate glass. Should your car be blessed with indifferent lamps, and especially if you are likely to be travelling fast at night, we have found that the Marchal 1767–300, which is still a current model, is exceedingly good, has a Vintage character and will not spoil the appearance of any pre-war car. Like all modern lamps these have aluminium vacuum-plated reflectors which give a superior light and do not deteriorate like those which are silver plated.

If your car has non-dipping lamps, then we think that the best arrangement is to choose and fit a suitable driving lamp and to arrange for the dip-switch when operated to turn off the head-lamps and turn on the driving lamp. Here again Marchal make a range of driving lamps, the smallest of which is quite powerful and has a flat-topped beam which will not annoy other drivers, but which enables you to press on fairly quickly.

The side-lamps will have to be dealt with in a similar manner to the head-lamps. If they are damaged beyond repair, the Lucas VS45-6 commercial-vehicle side-lamp is quite a good substitute with a Vintage appearance. More modern cars can be fitted with current side-lamps providing care is taken in the choice of a subdued design which it is not obvious to everyone has come off a Problematic Pilchard 105P! The law now requires us to fit two rear-lamps and reflectors. Either try to find a matching lamp to that already fitted to your car or, failing this, fit a pair of modern lamps. Be particularly careful in your choice, as with the side-lamps, that you do not fit a bulbous, vulgar pair of lamps that will ruin the back view of the car. A fairly undateable type is the Lucas ST38 or alternatively you may care to fit a pair of Model 8 Rubbolite rubber-cased lamps which have a very Vintage appearance. You will have to make your reflector mountings to blend into your own particular scheme.

Very good replicas of certain Vintage side and rear lamps are now available from Complete Automobilist Ltd. It is possible to replace the red glass of any rear lamp with a piece of plastic reflector material cut from a modern commercial vehicle reflector and so keep the appearance of your car unchanged.

Horns

The electric horn is usually a very reliable piece of equipment. As it can contribute to the general character of your car, do not be content with any old buzzer that will get past the law. We favour the Klaxon or Bosch horns and if you can find either of these by all means fit them. The overhaul of the Klaxon is very straightforward and they are generally in a reasonable condition internally. The adjustment of the vertical type, which is by revolving the eccentrically mounted motor housing is a little tricky, but once set will not need touching for a long time. The adjustment of the horizontal type is clearly marked. The diaphragm may be cracked, in which case the makers can supply a replacement. Grease the striker before assembly and see that the brushes and commutator are in good order.

Vintage Bosch horns should be used in pairs and tuned separately, one with a low and one with a high note. All horns depending on a vibrating diaphragm energised by a solenoid have contacts which should be cleaned and adjusted when the instrument is overhauled.

On more modern cars, a pair of wind tone horns can give a pleasant sound, and these should always be wired through a relay as the current consumption is too high for the horn button switch to handle.

The Fuse-box

The fuse-box is an essential piece of equipment which is sadly lacking on most modern cars. In our opinion the type of fuse which uses ordinary fuse wire is by far the most practical. Should your car lack a suitable fuse-box, one of the good old-fashioned type which is still in production is the C.A.V. type 5ML. This is robust and quite in place under the bonnet of a Vintage or modern car. Another solution is to use an ex-R.A.F.-type fuse-board which can be obtained from certain ex-government stores. These use cartridge-type fuses, however, and have to be hidden out of sight. The cartridge fuse can be repaired by unsoldering the old wire and soldering in a new piece of the required gauge.

The Wiring

If you have completely overhauled your car, we hope that you will throw away that rotting and diseased old wiring which you took off at the beginning of the job, and start again from scratch. Draw up a wiring diagram and run all the wires in plastic sheathing which renders it oil resisting. The standard size of wire to use is 28/0·012 single cable and the P.V.C. sheathing is available in 5-, 8-, 12-, 15- and 20-mm. sizes, depending on how many single cables you wish to run down each sheath. Solder tags on to the ends of each cable where a cheesehead screw is used as the terminal. Where a grub-screw terminal is used, solder the end of the wire up into a solid piece to stop it fraying. The wiring must be clipped up at regular intervals, and it is often possible to incorporate the wiring clips with the piping supports when running down the chassis side frame. If metal clips are used, wrap a piece of sheet rubber round the sheathing under the clip as an extra safeguard against chafing. Some difficulty will be experienced in threading the cable down the sheathing, and this can be overcome by using talcum powder, as for babies, on the cable and then pulling it through with a 16-S.W.G. wire which has been put through the sheathing first; one end is attached to the cable or cables to be pulled through, and the other end is held in the vice. The sheathing can then be pulled over the cables quite readily.

Always use rubber grommets when passing cables through holes in metal. These are available from electrical stockists specialising in motor-car work. Several sizes of junction-box are available and these are a benefit where wires have to be split up, such as in the side- and tail-lamp circuits. The heavy starter cable must have its lugs very well soldered on and should also be put into a P.V.C. sheath. Make sure that the battery earth connection is really clean at the chassis end and, if the engine is rubber mounted, make a starter-cable earth connection between it and the chassis.

All the necessary equipment for rewiring, together with electrical spares, can be obtained from Electric Service Co. (B'ham) Ltd. Armoured cable of the Vintage type can still be supplied by Ripaults Ltd.

Finally, consider the fitting of a battery master switch. If hidden, it is the best anti-thief protection which you can give your car, as well as being very convenient when working on any of the electrical equipment.

CHAPTER XIII

CLIPS, BRACKETS AND LEVERS

W^E have found by experience that, in no matter what condition a car may be, during the rebuild there will always be small modifications which one wants to carry out, and these will generally entail the fastening

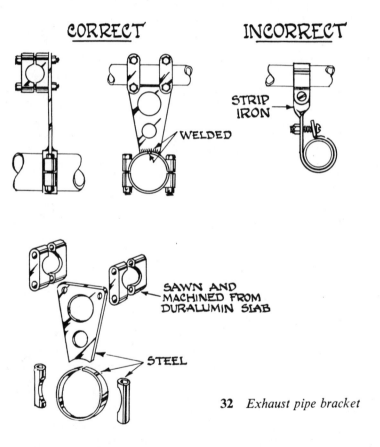

CORRECT

INCORRECT

STRIP IRON

WELDED

SAWN AND MACHINED FROM DURALUMIN SLAB

STEEL

32 *Exhaust pipe bracket*

together of two or more parts or the fixing of an additional component to some existing part of the car. This can either be done in a way which makes the modification look like part of the original design, which is the correct way, or it can very easily be made to stick out like a sore thumb. Many excellent rebuilds are spoilt by the use of poor brackets, and these may be original; even the best cars sometimes have accessories mounted in a way which looks as though a maker of iron palings had a hand in the design.

No bracket should be any heavier than is necessary, as is shown on the Rolls-Royce "Silver Ghost" chassis, an examination of which is also an education in bolt sizes.

A well-designed bracket is not only strong and light, but is also a pleasure to behold, and although fabricated from several pieces it can be made to look like a one-piece drop forging.

We are illustrating in this chapter the right and wrong way of making a few typical designs which have many variations to suit individual applications.

Always make a drawing of the part you propose to fabricate or machine; this will definitely save time in the end. It is also useful to make up a rough

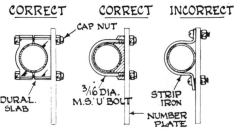

33 *Number-plate bracket for clamping on to cross-tube*

wood or cardboard model. This procedure will show you if the new part is going to look right and will also bring to light any snags.

These parts can be made from steel or hard brass, either welded or brazed together. They can also be made quite inexpensively as castings in light alloy or in gunmetal, which metal is as strong as mild steel and much easier to machine. If the casting is to be in light alloy, use L33 for low stress, or D.T.D. 304A heat-treated for more highly stressed parts. Another method to make really beautiful brackets is to saw them out of duralumin slab and then finish them by machining and filing. They can then be polished up to a high finish and if you wish they can be anodised, which will make them corrosion proof.

When fitting such brackets to the car always try to use any existing holes, and to pick these up make a paper rubbing of the holes and mark off the part from the rubbing. If there are no existing holes available do not immediately drill some, but consider if you can do without them; e.g. never drill tubes, always clamp round them. It may be possible to remake an existing piece, already bolted to the chassis, so that it will incorporate

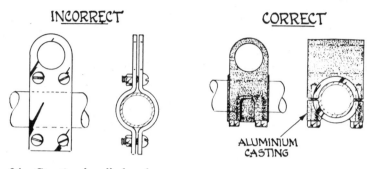

INCORRECT   CORRECT

ALUMINIUM
CASTING

34   *Starting-handle bracket*

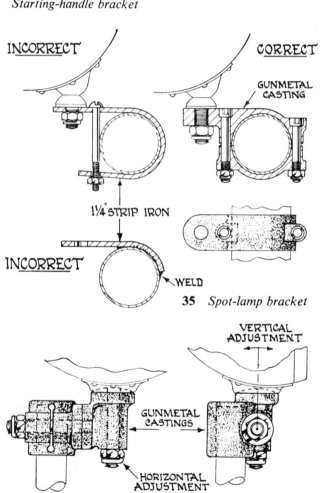

INCORRECT   CORRECT

GUNMETAL
CASTING

1¼" STRIP IRON

INCORRECT

WELD

35   *Spot-lamp bracket*

VERTICAL
ADJUSTMENT

GUNMETAL
CASTINGS

HORIZONTAL
ADJUSTMENT

36   *Universal bracket for head-lamp*

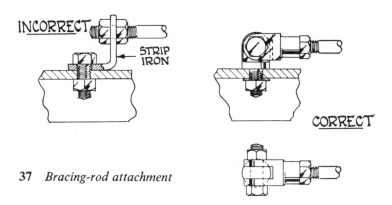

37 *Bracing-rod attachment*

the new part. Do not use pins screwed into light alloy; if possible use nuts and bolts and if this is impossible then screw in a stud so that a nut can be used. The use of many small bolts is greatly to be preferred to a few large ones. Be careful if you are using angle or T-section; if this is chopped off with square ends it will look very crude, so taper off the ends to disguise it as much as possible.

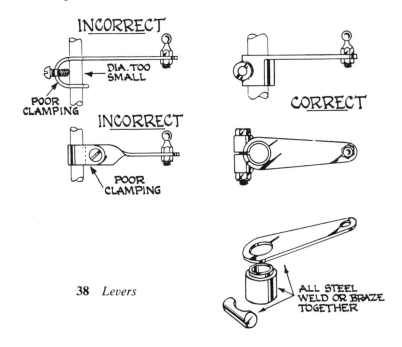

38 *Levers*

123

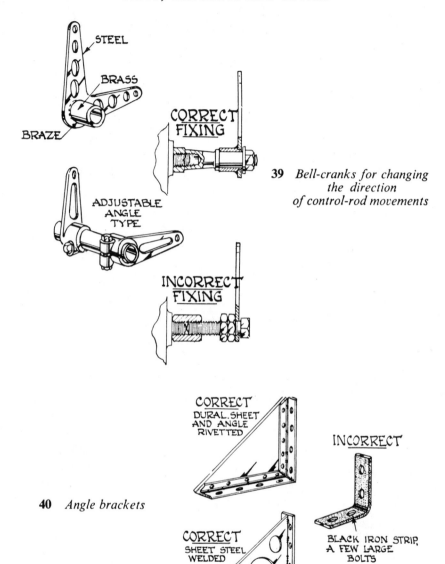

STEEL

BRASS

BRAZE

CORRECT
FIXING

ADJUSTABLE
ANGLE
TYPE

INCORRECT
FIXING

39 *Bell-cranks for changing the direction of control-rod movements*

CORRECT
DURAL. SHEET
AND ANGLE
RIVETTED

INCORRECT

40 *Angle brackets*

CORRECT
SHEET STEEL
WELDED

BLACK IRON STRIP.
A FEW LARGE
BOLTS

WELD

When designing your brackets remember the use of triangulation, as this method will give you great strength with very little weight. Never make brackets or clips by bending up strip iron, as not only do these look unsightly but they do not clamp properly and are very liable to fracture.

A word of warning to the designer of such parts—bear in mind the type

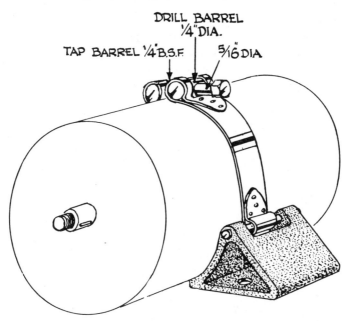

41 *Dynamo-mounting strap*

of car on to which they are to be mounted. Obviously what looks completely in keeping on a Grand Prix racing car will appear absurd on a Doctor's Coupé. We have shown a few typical clips, brackets and levers in figs. 32–41, which we have made for various cars, in the hope that they may give you a lead to the solution of one or more of your design problems.

CHAPTER XIV

MUDGUARDS, RUNNING-BOARDS AND SPARE-WHEEL MOUNTINGS

WE have now reached a stage where work on the chassis is complete with the exception of any final adjustments which may prove necessary after the test run. We are advocates of taking the chassis on the road before fitting the body, as it is very much easier to make adjustments and minor alterations with the body out of the way. If you can rig some temporary mudguards, a driving mirror and a horn, and also see that the seat is securely attached to the chassis, you can drive on the road quite legally in the daytime providing you have a Road Fund Licence and are insured. Aside from any practical advantage, driving a chassis is good fun and also provides a break in your labours before setting about the coachwork.

Mudguards

Many Vintage and Thoroughbred cars are spoilt by being fitted with mudguards which are a different shape to those used originally. Before you do anything to your mudguards be sure that they suit the car. One sees many cars, particularly sports models, which have been fitted late in life with cycle-type wings and these, in our opinion, are not an advantage. The wing line contributes greatly to the general appearance of the car and it can easily be completely ruined by casting away the running-boards and fitting four practically similar mudguards. The reduction in weight can be an advantage to those of us who race, but from the point of view of mud protection and appearance the cycle-type wing is usually very inferior. The type of front mudguard which turns with the wheel is, of course, a mechanical monstrosity, adding greatly to the unsprung weight, and the only excuse which can be made for using such wings on your car is that they were fitted by the manufacturer.

Unless the mudguards are obviously beyond repair, the first task is *thoroughly* to clean them both inside and out and then to assess the work necessary to restore them to their original condition. Remove all the stays as it is nearly impossible to clean properly with them in place. Strip off the paint with "Nitromors"; this is absolutely essential if the mudguards are aluminium, as the metal is so soft that, unless great care is taken, you will leave scores and ridges which are hard to cover later.

Examine the stays and straighten or repair them where necessary. They are probably very rusty and will need shotblasting before painting. Check

126

that the chassis-securing bolt holes are not elongated or oversize, as you will never stop the mudguards from coming loose if they are. If necessary weld up and redrill the holes to cure this fault. Where the stay has a tapered end fitting into a socket, make sure that the taper really fits well and that the nut is not coming to the end of its thread before the taper is drawn home. Many mudguard stays are very crude and heavy, but if you feel moved to remake them be careful to see that they are sufficiently rigid, as nothing is more annoying than to find that your finished car suffers from flapping wings. While dealing with the front stays see if any provision is made for running the side-lamp wires up them. If they are tubular the wires can often be passed up through them, otherwise a $\frac{5}{16}$-in. diameter copper tube can be brazed to the side of the stay to form a conduit for the wire which, if unprotected, will eventually give trouble.

Turning now to the actual mudguards, their valances and the running-board valances if fitted, obviously all dents and blemishes must be removed prior to painting. Small dents can be hammered out with a rounded hard-wood mallet, resting the wing on a suitably shaped piece of wood held in the vice. If your mudguards are badly damaged we can only advise you to take them to a good-class sheet-metal worker as this is what we should do ourselves. Panel-beating is an art which takes a long time and expert tuition to master and cannot be learnt from a book. Any cracks must be welded-up and filed smooth. Get the mudguards into the very best condition you can before starting on the painting, because the hiding of blemishes by means of filler is often a very much more difficult and lengthy process than getting rid of the imperfections in the first place. If you have to have new mudguards made it will be practically imperative to take the chassis to the sheet-metal worker with the stays in position so that he can work to these. The alternative is to make detailed drawings from which he can work, but with the more elaborate forms of wing this is extremely difficult.

We shall deal with the painting in a later chapter but before doing this it will pay you to fit the stays to the chassis and offer the mudguards up to them. Then check that all the fixing holes are in alignment, and that when attached the mudguards are symmetrical and in their correct positions relative to the wheels and the chassis frame. You must allow for the extra weight of the body yet to be put on when considering the rear mudguards. Any adjustments can now be made without having to worry about scratching the paint. While the usual method of fixing mudguards to their stays is to use coach bolts, we feel it is permissible on the more sporting type of car to use polished hexagon-headed stainless bolts with a stainless washer below the head. These remain unpainted and the mudguard can be removed without damage to the paintwork round the head of the bolt.

We have so far only spoken of separate mudguards but if your car has wheel arches at the rear, with the wings screwed up into these arches, then remove the mudguards from the body and put them in good order, but do not replace them until the body is finally on the chassis.

When you are satisfied that all the necessary repairs have been carried out and any new holes drilled, the stays and mudguards should be separately rust-proofed, either by "Jenoliting" or "Bonderising", and then painted. Do not use cellulose under the wings as it will chip off very readily. A good tough brushing paint should be used, or one of the sound-deadening or sealing compounds of which there are many on the market.

Running-Boards

On Vintage cars the running-boards are often made of wood, covered with metal or rubber. If they are broken it is an easy matter to make new ones from seasoned ash. The metal or rubber covering and the necessary metal beading round the edge are still available from coachbuilders' suppliers such as Albert Jagger Ltd. Ribbed rubber covering can be cemented on with "Bostik C", coating both rubber and wood and allowing the cement to dry before pressing the two surfaces together. Aluminium covering should be held on with small countersunk woodscrews round the edge which will ultimately be hidden by the beading, which in turn should be secured with plated-brass, countersunk, raised-head screws. Often the existing metal covering can be brought up to a good state with steel wool or a wire brush, and the rubber covering with boot blacking. Cars of more recent manufacture often have metal running-boards with section metal strips fitted to them to form a tread. All these strips must be removed in order to repair and repaint the running board and replacements where necessary are still available from coachbuilders' suppliers together with the strip rubber filling.

The running-board mountings and the brackets attaching the mudguards to the running-boards should be treated in the same way as the mudguard stays and replaced if they are too badly rusted.

Spare-wheel Mounting

While it is obvious that, from engineering considerations only, the correct place to mount the spare wheel is at the rear of the car, where a properly supported mounting can be made; there are often aesthetic reasons for not doing this and a further outrigged load has to be imposed on the already overloaded frame in order to mount the wheel at the side. On some cars the bracket was well designed and rigid, possibly as an aluminium casting, in which case you will have no trouble; if not study the mounting and see if it can be improved. For instance, is it possible to take the majority of the weight on a new member passing right under the chassis from side to side? Any outrigged mounting should certainly be attached to the frame close to a cross-member and, if yours is not, then see if you can possibly move it until it is in a better position or whether you can add a light cross-member at this point. This is particularly important on cars with heavy wheels. The spare wheel is often mounted in a recess in the front wing. If the mudguard is of a reasonably heavy gauge and well

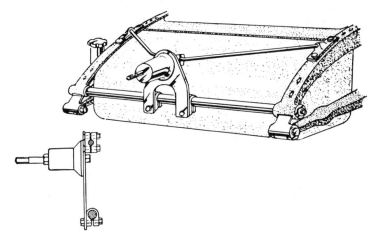

42   *Spare-wheel mounting taking the weight of the wheel*

stayed at several points, this is probably the best type of side mounting as the load is spread.

With centre-lock wheels you can often improve the look of the spare by using a centre-bolt support, with cap and wing nut, which merely stops the

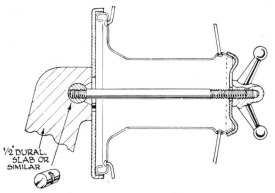

42a   *Spare-wheel mounting not taking the weight of the wheel*

wheel departing from the car, while the weight is taken on a bracket or in the mudguard well. Such a cap and wing nut can also be used on a rear mounting, which can take the whole weight of the wheel on its centre; the mounting being placed directly above the rear cross-member and suitably braced to avoid side movements. Both these arrangements are shown in figs. 42 and 42a.

On sports cars, the wheel can be carried in a cradle and fixed with three leather straps united on a centre ring. This looks well, and the straps can be made by the local saddler. Old straps, provided they are not cracked, can be cleaned with saddle soap and dressed with boot polish.

There are many and varied spare-wheel mountings, but if yours does not please you, perhaps the suggestions above may give you something to start on. Remember never to use angle iron or tubes with flattened ends if you make a new mounting, as either of these methods will mark you down as being beyond the pale with the *cognoscenti*.

Registration Plates

The size of the lettering required on registration plates has recently been reduced. If you wish to reproduce a plate identical to that originally fitted to your car the numbers and letters should be made to the dimensions shown in fig. 42b.

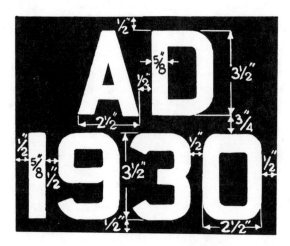

42b *Dimensions of registration numbers and plate*

CHAPTER XV

THE BODY-FRAME AND COVERING

W E now enter a completely different branch of the restoration work which is neither engineering in the normal sense of the word, nor is it any single trade, but a combination of carpentry, sheet metalwork, black-smithing, glazing and working in fabric, all gathered under the general heading of coachbuilding.

The great majority of the cars which are entitled to be called Vintage or Thoroughbred have bodywork consisting of a wooden frame covered with either sheet metal or fabric, and it is to this type of construction that we shall be referring in this chapter.

Inspection and Dismantling

If possible arrange the body on boxes or trestles at a suitable height for working, with enough room to walk all round. Now make a thorough inspection of the whole body, checking the doors, locks and hinges for fit. If you have a sports or touring car, is the windscreen rigid and in good condition? Will the hood framework clamp properly to the windscreen? Is it rigid and free from rattles when erected and will it fold down tidily? If it is a closed type of body, do the window winders work smoothly and is the glass a good fit in its channels? Should the body be in a bad state and you suspect rotten or broken framework you will have to remove all the upholstery and linings in order to carry out a thorough examination.

In the case of a fabric body, the framework is often rotten in places due to cracks in the fabric allowing the wet to get in but not to dry out. Check the wood for rot by prodding with a knife and examine all joints for loose-ness. Inspect any metal brackets; are the screws broken, rusted away or loose? On metal-covered bodies take careful note of any dents, rusting or metal broken away from the wooden frame, and rotting of the metal in the case of aluminium panelling.

If your car has a fabric body, and this also applies to the fabric roof of a closed car, it is quite likely to be in a bad state and no longer waterproof, as the cloth becomes hard and cracks, especially if it has been painted several times. It is most unsatisfactory to try patching this type of body; the covering must be stripped off and, to make a sound job, it will be better also to remove the coating of wadding and canvas as this is probably mouldy and rotten. This may seem to you to be an impossible undertaking, but it has the one great advantage that any work to be done on the body

131

framework will be much easier when the frame is nude. All the old tacks must be removed and a vast quantity will probably be found. The covering of a fabric body, unlike metal panelling, is by no means a mystic art, anyone with the ability to do good handwork can produce a very satisfactory finish provided they have the enthusiasm and patience and are prepared to do some quite hard work. When removing the old fabric take it off carefully, noting what materials have been used and how they have been applied; e.g. note where the joins have been placed and how the fabric has been taken under body fittings.

Repairs to the Body-frame and Fittings

Wherever there is any sign of rotting, the section must be cut out. If the trouble is in one of the small members then it is better to remove it and to make a new one, but if it is only a small portion of a long main member it will be quite satisfactory to cut out the rotten wood, making sure that you do in fact cut *all* the bad part away. This operation is illustrated in Plate XI. A new section can now be cut and shaped and joined on to what is left of the original member, using a scarf or halved joint. Always use well-seasoned ash for the framework, and in addition to screwing the joint, cement it with "Cascamite" glue following the instructions on the tin. All joints must be a perfect face-to-face fit before being glued together. In the case of joints and brackets which are screwed only and not cemented, put a piece of leather cloth between the faces before finally tightening the screws, as this will prevent those irritating creaks which emanate from a coachbuilt body on a flexible chassis.

If you need to replace any very curved section, you will notice that it has probably been cut from a wide plank of wood; this method is not only very laborious, unless you are fortunate in having a band-saw, but it is very wasteful of wood and very weak, as you cut across the grain. You can, of course, cut a straight member and steam it to shape, but this method is very difficult unless you have the necessary equipment. A much easier and stronger method of making these curved pieces is by the lamination process, as shown in Plate X. A number of strips of ash are obtained which should be a little wider than the finished member to allow for planing, and the thickness should be $\frac{1}{8}$ in. for a very small radius curve and up to $\frac{1}{4}$ in. for a large radius; a sufficient number of strips are used to build up the necessary total thickness. A former is now made up on a large board and the strips, which have been coated with "Cascamite" glue, are put together, pulled round the former and well clamped in position until dry, when it will be found that you have a very strong and accurate member. Where brackets are used to strengthen a joint or to attach some other part, instead of using wood screws a much more durable job can be made of it by fitting a plate on the back of the wood and using metal screws tapped into this plate. This method is a very good one for fixing the door hinges, and another very useful method for avoiding the use of wood-screws is the bolt and pommel as shown in fig. 43. The pommel should be a good fit in its hole otherwise, if the bolt is withdrawn, the pommel may rotate, making it impossible to replace the bolt. If the hinge screws are loose in the wood, never plug the holes, as this will only result in the screws coming loose again, but resort to the above method. Should the body have very wide

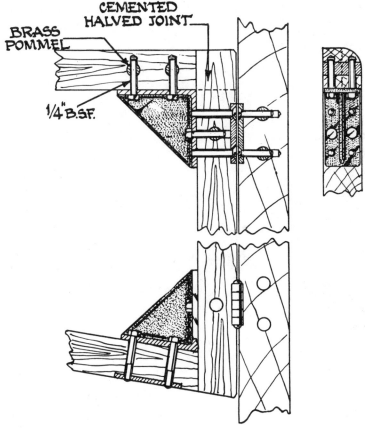

43   *Details of hinge attachment and door construction, showing the use of bolts instead of woodscrews*

doors, make a careful check of the corner joints and, if these are loose, dismantle the door and rebuild it again using strong corner brackets into which the hinges are bolted as shown in fig. 43.

The hinges are generally worn and so they will have to be repaired or replaced, otherwise the whole rebuild will be spoilt. Worn hinges can be reconditioned by reamering out the holes and fitting oversize pins, and if you are going to this trouble use stainless steel for the pins. If the knuckles are worn they can be filed flat then built up with pieces of sheet brass, brazed in position, and then all the knuckles filed to a perfect fit. If you have not the time or the inclination to repair the hinges and other body fittings, fit new ones. Most body fittings are still available from coach-builders' suppliers such as Albert Jagger Ltd. or Complete Automobilist Ltd., or from the manufacturers Hallam, Sleigh & Cheston Ltd. The same remarks also apply to the bolt and striker plate of the lock, the door handles and the rubber buffers for the doors.

If you are re-covering a fabric body, you may have noticed that in some parts the fabric had sunk in, causing the shape of the wooden members to show. If this is the case you will find it a great advantage to fill in the troublesome area with a plywood or metal panel before re-covering. The ribs will have to be rebated to take the thickness of the panel, and the metal or plywood will be held with a multitude of $\frac{1}{2}$-in. No. 4 countersunk screws. In the case of plywood, glue must also be used.

Having now finished all the repairs to the body frame, and before passing on to the covering, it is better to carry out any repairs to the floor-boards, the seat mountings if they are movable, the body-to-chassis attachments and possibly the tool-boxes.

If the floor-boards need renewing they are better made from plywood of the correct thickness to fit the rebate which accommodates them in the body. Make them a good fit to exclude draughts and engine fumes. Consider means of fixing them, as loose boards are liable to rattle and to be forced up by wind pressure; holding them in position with wood-screws is both poor and a nuisance when oiling or adjustments have to be carried out. A better idea is to fix them with sunk, wing-headed pins tapped into a suitable bracket underneath. Give the boards a good coat of flat lead paint, as if wet gets in it will split the plies. A good finish for the top of the boards is to cover them with plain brown linoleum, which can be cemented in place with "Bostik C".

If the seats are movable, make sure that the fittings are in good condition and well fixed. Not only must the seats slide smoothly but, when in the locked position, they must be quite rigid. Should the driver's seat come adrift it might be the cause of a serious accident, particularly when braking.

Bodies are usually bolted to the chassis with coach bolts—a method which we do not like. The nut, a square one with a Whitworth thread, is often rusted to the bolt, which is also rusted and which is no longer a tight fit in the wood. If the bolt has no head to take a spanner, the removal or tightening of the nut becomes a major problem. A much better mounting is to let a steel plate about $\frac{1}{4}$ in. thick into the wood frame at each fixing point, and to use cadmium-plated, hexagon steel bolts with self-locking nuts.

If the tool-box is in the body, now is the time to repair it if necessary, or possibly change its position if it is inconvenient. You should be able to get at any tools needed on a dark night without too much trouble, and the box should be watertight. Some cars were fitted with tool-boxes in, or on, the running-boards. If you have this arrangement and you are a stickler for originality you will leave it there, but it is a bad position as it usually fills with water. A much better position is inside the body, but this depends on the design of the body and the amount of space you have available.

Any steel panels should now be given a rust-proof finish with "Jenolite" and the whole body framework given a good coat of flat lead paint, both sides of any panels in the case of fabric bodies but, if the body is to have a painted finish, the outside should be given a coat of metal primer.

The Windscreen

On the majority of motor-cars which are dealt with in this book, the windscreens of both open and closed bodies were made from some type of metal channelling.

Examine the screen thoroughly and make sure that it is fitted with safety glass; if it is not the glass will have to be changed. If the frame needs plating the glass will have to be removed. First remove all the screws and then pull the glass from the channelling. The glass is fitted in the metal channel with a rubber strip and this becomes hard with age and firmly attached to both the glass and the metal. If you are in difficulties it is best to take it to one of the firms who specialise in this type of work. When the glass has been removed from the frame and before plating, fill up any unwanted holes and also drill any new ones you may require for the fitting of screenwipers or a driving mirror. Do not forget to drill and tap some holes for small B.A. screws for the screen-wiper wiring clips, and when tightening these screws after the glass has been fitted make sure that they are not too long, as if they touch the glass it will be split. Even if the screen is fitted with safety glass it will pay you to replace it should it have become badly scratched, as you will find that this impairs the clarity when driving at night.

Fold-flat screens are liable to be worn at their fulcrum points, these should be rebushed if necessary and the locking arrangement put into good condition. Some windscreen mountings on the body were very poor so that the screen was liable to flap about. If yours suffers from this trouble it will pay you to carry out some modification, as the screen must be absolutely rigid. Check the hood connections to the top of the screen and make sure that these two components do clamp firmly together, otherwise some day you may find the hood leaves you rather abruptly when doing the "ton".

All types of Vintage windscreens can be repaired, and new ones of the correct Vintage type can be supplied, by A. Price Ltd. This firm can also supply a large range of Vintage bits and pieces for the bodywork and many of the moulded-rubber sealing strips used on the windscreen.

You might also consider modifying your screen to a one-piece type if the existing one is a multipiece, as this kind is very prone to leak in wet weather, can usually accommodate only small wiper blades and is conducive to blind spots.

The Hood Frame

If the hood frame is in good condition, remove any old tacks and give it a good coat of paint, or you can sandpaper the wood sticks and coat them with yacht varnish and then paint the metal parts. Should the frame be in a bad state with loose rivets, they can be replaced, and members which should be straight but which have become bent so that the mechanism does not work properly, can be straightened. The mechanism of a hood frame is such a complicated piece of work that we do not advise you to attempt to make a new one. New frames can be supplied to fit your motor-car by Auster Ltd., and this firm can also carry out the covering.

Fabric Covering

There are coachbuilders who can do this work for you but, as mentioned before, it is work that is possible for the amateur to do himself. If you decide to do this job, make sure that the outside of the body frame is really smooth as any small projections will show through the final covering. The materials you will require are light-weight sail cloth, sheet wadding and the leathercloth for the final coating. The leather cloth should be the correct type of material for the purpose with plenty of stretch; any type of leather cloth will not do. The grain should be non-directional and fairly shallow, otherwise it will hold mud. We recommend a cloth with a nitrocellulose coating such as "Rexine"; this material has the great advantage that it can be reconditioned by painting when it becomes shabby. The type of cloth with a P.V.C. coating, although possibly easier to work, will definitely *not* take any form of paint. You will also require japanned gimp pins and "Bostik C" for tacking the material in place. All these materials can be obtained from coachbuilders' suppliers such as A. Jagger and Co. Ltd.

You have first to give the entire body a covering of the sail cloth, which must be stretched on really tightly and then tacked on the inside and along the bottom of the body. All the wrinkles must be pulled out and boned down flat. Use "Bostik C", in addition to the gimp pins, as it will be found a great help in holding the fabric when pulling out the folds on small-radius curves. For smoothing out the wrinkles a bone folder is very useful; this is a tool which is used in the leather goods trade and can be obtained from the Joseph Dixon Tool Co.

Having now achieved a coating of cloth which is both smooth and taut, the next part of the procedure is to put on a thin and even coat of wadding.

We have used the cellulose variety as it is rather easier to apply, but you may have difficulty in obtaining it. The wadding should be tacked in place with "Bostik" along the edges with a few dabs in between to hold it in place. The excess can be trimmed off along the inside and the bottom of the body frame with a pair of scissors, but for any joins which are on the surface of the body, the edges must be torn, not cut with the scissors, or you will have a hard line which may show through the top fabric.

Now you can proceed to apply the final coat of leather cloth, but great care must be taken with the finish of this operation as any blemishes or faulty workmanship will mar the appearance of the completed motor-car. First decide where the joins are to be; it is inevitable that there will have to be some joins as you cannot cover a car with one large piece of cloth. These joins must be on one of the wooden members so that they can be tacked down, and a place should be chosen which is not too obvious or they will look very ugly. Now cut your cloth one piece at a time, pull it over the edges and tack it roughly in position. It must now be stretched tight all over so that it is quite flat, cemented with "Bostik", and tacked down along the inside of the edges of the frame and under the bottom member. Use a few gimp pins, at first widely spaced and not knocked right home, so that any wrinkles can be pulled out in between the pins. Then finish off with pins about $\frac{3}{8}$ in. apart. Concave curves and corners will have to be nicked to pull them over smoothly but be sure that the nicks are not too long or they will show on the finished body. Convex curves will have an excess of material, and great patience is required and a certain amount of strength to pull these out and bone them down to a smooth finish. It will be found that the cloth works much more readily in hot weather, and it is a great advantage to have your wife—if she can stand the language—or a friend, to apply hot water with a sponge while you pull the fabric over the more difficult places. The joins should be overlapped in such a way that they will be covered by the beading, and here the "Bostik" is very important as it waterproofs the joint. The beading to use is the lead-filled spiked variety which is made in a number of sizes from $\frac{1}{8}$ in. to $\frac{3}{4}$ in. wide. This is cut to the correct length and then covered with the leather cloth cemented in place with "Bostik". The cloth must be taken round the beading and butted on the underside. Excess "Bostik" can be removed with petrol, but be careful not to use too much and wipe it off immediately the cloth is clean, as petrol tends to attack the fabric. The beading is then hammered into place with the pins that are fitted by using a piece of thick cardboard between the hammer and the beading to prevent damage to the fabric. Any spaces between the frame members that are not panelled will now have to be packed with hair and fibre mixture to hold the outer fabric. This packing is held in place by tacking cloth across the members on the inside of the body. Be very careful how you do this, as a paucity of packing here will cause a hollow in the covering to form in time and any excess will produce a bulge.

Clean up and refit the aluminium beading round the doors. If the beadings are in bad shape make new ones; the material is known as door lapping and the wooden frame of the door is rebated to take its web. It is held in place with countersunk brass screws. The beading will now have to be painted; mask off the fabric with masking tape, making sure that the tape is wide enough if you are spraying, and paint the beading to match the fabric.

It must be admitted that this part of the rebuilding is very thirsty work, but too much stimulant will tend to impair the finish and the results may be very disappointing when viewed the next morning. The fabric body has one very great advantage, and that is silence. It is not so prone to rattle as a metal-panelled body and it also helps to deaden chassis noises.

The body can now be bolted on to the chassis and the doors and windscreen fitted and, in the case of closed bodies, the movable windows will be fitted in their channels and coupled up to their winding gear. Fixed windows can be fitted with "Bostik" putty.

Metal Covering

If the panelling is badly rusted and either very thin or actually has holes in it, then it is better for you to have the repairs done by a coachbuilder. Should you take it on, you are unlikely to have much success unless you have experience of sheet-metalwork and welding. Small dents, however, can be quite easily repaired without removing the panel. If a dent is inwards, and this is the usual type of damage, the procedure is to hold a sandbag on the outside and knock out the worst of the dent with a mallet, taking great care not to go too far. Having restored the panel as near as possible to its original shape from the inside, finish off with a hammer on the outside and a steel block on the inside. The block should be as near as possible to the shape of the inside of the panel. Owing to the stretching of the metal you may not be able to remove all the dent but at least you will reduce it to a size that can be hidden by filling when you do the painting. Alternatively, and better, these small irregularities can be tinned if the panel is steel and filled in with plumber's solder, which can be filed off flush. It is possible for the amateur to make new panels and produce a good finish provided these are flat and of a simple shape or large radius curve, so that only bending is required and not actual forming. If you decide to do this work it will be far easier in aluminium. Use half-hard aluminium, as in the soft state this metal is quite useless for the purpose as it dents too easily. There will probably be some edges to be turned over, and if so the aluminium in this area must be annealed. A very simple and reliable method of doing this is first to mark out with a soft pencil the part to be annealed—the reason for using a pencil is to avoid scratching the metal. Now coat the part to be bent by rubbing the area with a tablet of soap. The metal can be annealed with the blowpipe and, as the correct temperature is reached, the soap will turn black. When this occurs move the flame at once, as if the metal is heated too much it will eventually melt.

When the panel has been prepared, tack in position with gimp pins the edges which do not have to be bent, and clamp the other edges using strips of wood and C-clamps. Only the part which has to be tapped over should be left projecting and this can be tapped over absolutely smoothly, taking it a bit at a time all along the edge using a strip of wood and a hammer. This last edge can now be secured in position with gimp pins. If you require any new aluminium beading this is easily obtained and is available in various sections and sizes.

Professional Coachwork Restoration

If you feel that your skills are limited to the mechanical side of the restoration only and that you would prefer to leave the coachwork to a professional then we can recommend I. Wilkinson and Son Ltd. The company is run by an enthusiastic owner of Vintage cars and does a first-class job.

CHAPTER XVI

BODY PAINTING

BEFORE entering into a detailed description of how to set about the painting of your motor-car we would first ask you to consider which of the two main types of finish you will use—cellulose or coach paint? While it is impractical to apply cellulose without spraying equipment, there is no denying that its use is less laborious than coach painting. Cellulose also has the advantage of not requiring very elaborate precautions to be taken against dust, owing to its quick drying properties, and the finish obtainable is very hard and abrasive resistant in comparison with coach paint. The arguments against the use of cellulose are that, in our opinion, the technique of using a spray-gun is probably harder to acquire than the correct use of a brush; the necessary spray equipment must either be borrowed or bought, and the latter is expensive; and lastly the coach-painted finish, although softer, is very tough and less likely to chip than cellulose. Finally there is the question of historical accuracy, and while it is impossible to lay down a definite line of demarkation when coach painting gave way to cellulose, it would be reasonable to say that the transition started about mid-way through the Vintage period.

Preparation

Whichever method of painting you choose, the preparation of the body-work will be the same. We presume that the body is still off the chassis and all the detachable parts are separate. It is essential for good work that the painter should be able to walk easily all round the body and that the lighting be really good. It is practically impossible to make a first-class job by artificial light unless it is of the type found in body-painting shops, where every precaution is taken to get an absolutely even intensity with no shadows. For cellulose work nothing can beat working in the open during the summer, providing there are no wind and no flies. It is impossible to coach paint outside due to dust settling, and if you have decided on coach painting move the body to the best-lighted part of the garage before starting. The correct temperature for all types of painting is 60°–70°F., so in winter you will have to heat the workshop, but beware of fire if you are using cellulose.

Having set the body in the best position, consider the supporting of such parts as the mudguards and doors for painting and rig up either boxes or trestles for this purpose. It often saves time to do each operation on every part at one time rather than to finish one piece completely and then to start on the next. In any case, you cannot rub down one part while coach paint is drying on another in the same room, because of the dust problem. Unless you are certain that your bonnet will fit when the body is replaced, its painting will have to be left until later, as usually there will be some repair or alteration needed to make it fit perfectly.

If the old paint is in good condition and merely shabby, it is not necessary to remove it down to the bare metal. Very carefully examine the whole surface and, if there are any patches where rust has started, scrape these down to the metal and remove the paint all round back to where it is really well adhered and the metal is clean and bright. Apply a coat of "Jenolite", if the metal is steel, followed by a coat of "Jenolite Chemical Sealer". If the paintwork is in poor condition on a metal body, then remove it all with "Nitromors", being careful to get rid of every trace of paint remover before starting on the next stage. In the case of a steel body give it a coat of "Jenolite" all over, followed by a coat of sealer.

Coach Painting

When we described the painting of the chassis parts we referred to the products of Llewellyn Ryland Ltd., and once again we shall do the same. The terms used for the various paints and fillers are fairly general throughout the paint trade, however, and will be understood by other manufacturers. It is essential that all paints be thoroughly mixed before use, as failure to do so will only result in a poor finish.

Starting with bare metal in the case of aluminium, or the "Jenolite" sealer on steel, first apply one coat of metal primer. No particular precautions against dust need be taken in these preliminary stages and the metal primer should be brushed on in an even coat, taking particular care that all parts are well covered.

It is next necessary to fill in all unwanted dents, crevices and blemishes and for this purpose you use "Rylard" knifing filler. Never attempt to fill a deep dent with one application, as the filler will not dry properly if you do. Use several thin coats, where necessary building up the filler until it is level with the surrounding paint. In the case of a body on which the old paint is being left on, give this treatment to the places where you have had to remove doubtful paint and follow on with the various processes which we are about to describe. Having got the blemishes filled as well as you can using the knife, rub down the filled surface with 260-grade wet-and-dry paper. It is essential to keep the paper thoroughly wet to preserve its cutting power, so have a bucket of water always at your side and constantly wash the paper in this as you proceed. Also have an old sponge to sluice the work with water and to remove the particles of material which you have rubbed off. Failure to do this will result in the paper clogging and becoming quite ineffective.

141

Having obtained a smooth surface on the filler and the surrounding area, damp the surface with water to give it a shiny appearance and examine it in a good light from all angles. It must appear to be a perfectly continuous surface with no hollows or hummocks, and if it does not appear so, further filling or rubbing must proceed until this result is obtained. On no account kid yourself that you will cover blemishes with further coats of paint, because you will not. Great patience at this stage will be well repaid later on.

When you are quite certain that all is as smooth and shapely as it should be, apply one coat of Llewellyn Ryland Brushing Filler all over the body and allow it 24 hours to dry. If you are starting with new brushes, use them now, as it is better that they drop any loose hairs in the filling stages than later on, when such a thing becomes rather a calamity. Only use the very best-quality brush, and wash it out thoroughly in the correct thinners each time you have finished using it.

Breaking away for a moment from the main theme, the best way of storing a brush for any length of time is to wash it out thoroughly and then suspend it in a jar of raw linseed oil with the bristles clear of the bottom. When it is wanted again it will wash out in thinners and be as good as new. A well-kept used brush always paints better than a new one.

When the first coat of filler is dry, rub it down with 260-grade wet-and-dry paper using copious amounts of water, as you did with the knifing filler. You should remove all the brush marks and get a dead flat surface. This done, apply another coat of brushing filler and rub down again, and then repeat once more—giving three coats of filler in all. When you are working on the top of old paint you can probably get away with one coat only of brushing filler, but you must be absolutely certain that you have a perfectly smooth surface before going on the the colour application.

You are now ready to apply the colour, and from this time on the very greatest precautions must be taken against dust settling on the work. If there is any possibility of dust dropping from the ceiling, hang a dust sheet horizontally between the body and the ceiling. All doors and windows must be kept shut while the painting proceeds and the floor should be kept constantly wet with a watering can. We will not presume to advise you on the colour to choose for your car, but if you are having more than one and are in any doubt as to the matching properties, a chat with your paint supplier may prevent a catastrophe. The quality of paint we advise is Llewellyn Ryland's Coach Painting Ground Colour which is a flat paint available in a large range of shades.

If you have had little experience of brushing paint, it is as well to practise on a vertical panel of metal held in the vice before starting on the car itself. Cover the whole surface with horizontal strokes of the brush, working from top to bottom of the panel, and lay-off with vertical strokes. On no account use diagonal or rotary strokes, as somehow these always show on the finished job despite rubbing down. The same rule applies to rubbing down and final polishing. Never use a rotary motion. Use the minimum of paint on each coat and aim to get as even a covering as possible, free from runs. As we have said before, it is impossible to fill blemishes with paint, and any attempt to do so by putting on a thick coat will assuredly result in a run.

Allow the first coat to dry for at least 24 hours and then rub it down lightly with 260-grade wet-and-dry paper. The whole operation must be repeated three times, but the last coat should consist of 75% Ground Colour and 25% Rylard Flatting Varnish which you will mix yourself. This coat is not rubbed down and will dry rather more matt than the previous coats. It gives a better surface for the final varnish than pure Ground Colour.

Lastly you will come to the varnishing. For this you will need Rylard Flatting Varnish and a very soft brush. Put on one coat of varnish and allow 48 hours for it to dry, then rub it down very lightly with 400-grade wet-and-dry paper again using plenty of water and repeatedly washing the paper. Another coat of Flatting Varnish, another rub down, and finally you will put on the last coat which is Rylard Finishing Body Varnish which you do not rub down.

Now leave the body for seven days without handling of any sort and try to resist the temptation of testing the varnish with your finger to see how it is getting on. After seven days give the whole surface a good wash down with clean cold water, which will harden off the varnish, and repeat this from time to time until the car is ready for use.

Cellulose Enamelling

Before starting on the actual enamelling a certain amount of equipment must be got together. First you will require a spray-gun and if you decide to buy one remember that, like all equipment, the best is generally the most expensive but will also give the finest results. Spraying equipment is not cheap, and unless you are thinking of doing a considerable amount of cellulosing it will probably be better to try to borrow a gun. Secondly you will require a source of compressed air, and if your workshop has no compressor and you are borrowing one, see that it is fitted with a reducing valve and pressure gauge and also some sort of water and oil trap in the air line. Wet or oily air is fatal to good spraying. Next connect your gun to the compressor, and with the valve open and the reducing valve set at 60 lb. per sq. in., see that the compressor is capable of maintaining the pressure, otherwise you will be continually waiting for it to build up, which again is liable to spoil the job. Make sure that you have an adequate length of air hose to reach right round the body without having to move the compressor.

It will be as well to practise on some spare sheets of metal before attempting work on the body then, with everything ready, start by using

Cellulose Base Metal Primer. The air pressure should be set at between 40 and 60 lb. per sq. in. and you can try out the results obtained using various pressures in this range during your practice period. You will have to thin the paint as supplied, and start by mixing equal parts of paint and cellulose thinners, which is generally about the right proportion. Practise on vertical surfaces, as these are the most difficult, the aim being to get an even coat with no runs. If the paint is too thick it will go on very rough, and if too thin, it will very quickly go into runs. With practice you will soon find out which way to set the nozzle, either a vertical fan, a horizontal fan or a circular spray, to get the best results on any given surface. Do not hold the gun too close to the work, 8 in. to 10 in. is generally suitable and, like painting with a brush, move horizontally or vertically, and not in any other direction. The gun must be kept moving the whole time and always get the spray going before bringing the gun on to the work, as it always starts by shooting out an unatomised blob of paint when the trigger is pressed.

If for any reason you are held up in your work, stir the paint in the container before starting again, and when recharging the gun always give the paint tin a very good stir as cellulose enamel is very prone to separate out into its separate constitutents. This is particularly important when using polychromatic enamels which contain heavy metal particles, as these rapidly fall out of suspension.

Reverting now to the bodywork, spray on one coat of cellulose Base Metal Primer. If you have used the "Jenolite" process, you must first spray on one coat of Rylard Cellulose Sealer (red oxide). Follow on with cellulose knifing filler in the same way as we have described under coach painting. Rub this down and get the best results you possibly can. The rubbing down is, if possible, even more important when using cellulose than coach paint, as cellulose has very little body and no filling power at all, so that the finish is entirely dependent on what lies underneath.

The next operation is to spray on three coats of Cellulose Spraying Filler. Only the last of these needs to be rubbed down, as it goes on very much flatter than brushing filler. If however you get a run or blemish on any of the intermediate coats, rub this down flat before proceeding further. Using 260-grade wet-and-dry paper and plenty of water, you must now obtain a perfectly smooth surface, as the following coats will be exceedingly thin with no filling power at all. A drop of detergent in the water will act as a wetting agent and will help to keep the surface thoroughly moist.

Any portions of the bodywork such as plating, glass, fabric or a two-colour scheme which you want to protect from the spray will have to be covered with masking tape, which is sold in various widths. On large areas newspaper is the best mask and it can be held at the edges with masking tape. If you are sticking masking tape to a painted surface, remember to see that the paint is properly hardened-off or you will remove the paint with the tape at a later stage.

You now set about the last stages of the enamelling, and if you are in any doubt, do plenty of practising before you start on the bodywork itself, as enamel runs even more easily than the undercoats. Using Cellulose Body Enamel Colour spray on three coats, allowing a few hours between each for drying. Small and intricate parts will require the paint valve to be cut down and the air pressure to be reduced. Should a whitish bloom occur on the painted surface while drying this is caused by humidity in the atmosphere and can be removed by spraying afterwards with a fine coat of thinners only. The latter requires considerable skill as runs occur very easily, so keep the gun moving quickly and only put on the thinnest coat possible.

You will next have to rub down the whole body very lightly with 400-grade wet-and-dry paper and then spray on the final coat of colour. To get a high gloss without too much polishing, a mist coat of thinners only can be applied at this stage.

The surface is now finally brought up to a very high gloss by polishing with medium-grade Cutting Paste, again taking care not to use a rotary motion. Allow 24 hours for the last coat to harden before using the cutting paste, which is applied on a soft damp cloth. When using the cutting paste on raised surfaces such as rivet heads and sharp edges, only bear on very lightly or you will cut right through to the filler. When you are satisfied that you have completely finished polishing, give the body a coating of wax polish, such as "Simonize", as a protection.

If the body of your car is fabric covered, and this also applies to the fabric top of a metal saloon, it can be painted provided the material has a nitro-cellulose coating, that the fabric is not showing signs of rotting and the coating has not peeled off nor has any areas of poor anchorage; this can be tried by scraping with the thumb nail. Should the fabric be one of those with a P.V.C. coating, renovation is out of the question as this finish will not take any type of paint. This material can only be cleaned with soap and water to which a little detergent has been added; if the appearance is still unsatisfactory your only hope is to re-cover the body or top.

A simple test to determine the type of cloth is to remove a small cutting from some suitable place and apply a lighted match to it. If it is nitro-cellulose it will burn very readily and give off a smell of burning castor oil. P.V.C., on the other hand, will either be completely fire-proof or will burn very slowly.

Having decided that you have the type of material that can be painted and that it is in good condition, the fabric will first have to be thoroughly cleaned. Wash down using soap and water and a soft scrubbing brush. Should any obstinate areas of soiling be encountered, then the addition of 20% methylated spirits to the washing water is permissible. Now dry off the body or top with a clean cloth. You now have a choice of two types of paint, either spraying with cellulose, and we have had very good results with this, using one coat of body enamel colour only and no filler or primer. Brush painting with I.C.I. Dulux 98 line Coach Finish or any good synthetic paint with its appropriate undercoat and primer is an alternative. On no account must oil-bound coach paint be used for this purpose, as one of the chemical constituents in the nitrocellulose finish of the fabric will prevent the paint from drying.

With both types of painting on fabric, you must aim at getting the maximum cover with the minimum thickness of paint.

Do not use cutting paste but polish with "Karpol" or "Simonize" Cleaner, both of which are milder in their cutting action than normal cutting paste.

Always keep your gun scrupulously clean and swill it out well with thinners after each time it is used. Do not attempt to use cellulose enamel on P.V.C. material such as cable sheathing, as the result will be a sticky mess which will never dry.

We have already advocated the use of stove enamelling for the wheels of your car and you may feel that there are other small parts such as brackets, hood irons and even mudguards, which would be better treated this way, in which case you will have to get these enamelled before painting the rest of the car in order to match the colours perfectly.

The body and its accessories are now ready for refitting to the chassis and great care should be taken while doing so. It is impossible to do the operation without a little touching up being required on a few places, so do this while your painting materials are to hand and you will then be ready to turn to the upholstering and trimming.

CHAPTER XVII

COACH TRIMMING

W<small>E</small> have now come to a part of the restoration which is probably the most difficult for the amateur to tackle, and one which very few will be able to carry out without professional help. For this reason we propose to describe in some detail the tasks which the majority can do on their own, and to refer briefly to those details which can be only of academic interest except to the few with the necessary skill and equipment. We have completely re-upholstered a Vintage car in leather without any professional help, but it must be admitted that we had a fair knowledge of some of the operations and, what is even more important, we had the use of the necessary heavy sewing machines. The domestic type of machine will not do for this work.

Upholstery

Determine first whether renovation or complete restoration is necessary, then examine the material used and find out if it is leather, or imitation leather such as "Rexine". If this is not obvious, examine the underside of the material; an easy place to do this is where the covering is finished off under the seats. Should the material be leather, the underside will be the flesh side, whereas if it is imitation leather, the underside will be woven fabric. The upholstery may also be of Bedford Cord and this will be obvious.

If the upholstery is washable leather, that is motor hide, and otherwise in good condition, it can easily be renovated. Motor hide has a doped finish which is impervious to water whereas furniture hide, which is always brown, is aniline-dyed with a natural grain showing and is highly absorbent to water. A test with a wet sponge will show the difference.

If your upholstery is motor hide, wash all the leatherwork thoroughly with warm water and non-caustic soap, or preferably with Connolly s Concentrated Cleaner according to the instructions. If necessary a small brush, such as a nail brush which is not too hard, can be used to remove dirt which has become ingrained in the cushions or the top and corners of the seat squab. Avoid flooding with water, the temperature of which should not exceed 105°F. Never use quick cleaners such as spirits. Such agents, whilst removing the dirt very effectively, may damage the surface finish of the leather.

After cleaning, one or two thin coats of Connolly's Clear Reviver should be applied to the leather. This reviver is a special varnish which seals and

147

protects the colour surface. It should be applied in accordance with the manufacturer's directions.

If the surface of the leather has been scratched or abraded, the affected parts should be treated with Connolly's Coloured Lacquer, which is available in all colours. In some cases it suffices to "touch in" the damaged parts with the lacquer, which can be applied by a suitable brush or swab. It may be necessary to treat the entire surface of a seat with the coloured lacquer, and to do this the lacquer, which is supplied ready for use, should be well stirred before application. Having made sure that the leather is thoroughly dry after washing, pour a small quantity of the lacquer into a shallow vessel and apply thinly and evenly with a stockinette swab. Do not rub. A second coat can be applied, if necessary, after the first is dry. In both cases of local or general use of the coloured lacquer, the operation should be completed by the application of a coat of Clear Reviver.

It will be appreciated that in the case of antique or two-tone leathers, the two-colour effect cannot be retained or reproduced when using the lacquer over a large area. Consequently, the lacquers are supplied to match the predominating colour.

Motor-cars are occasionally upholstered in brown furniture hide and, as this is aniline-stained, it will not stand washing but should be cleaned with Connolly's C.B. Hide Food which will also help to maintain the original suppleness; this dressing is also very good for the preservation of motor hide.

All these preparations are supplied by Connolly Bros. (Curriers) Ltd., who are also large manufacturers of upholstery hides. They will give advice on the treatment necessary to restore old upholstery and are also equipped to carry out the renovation but, in this case, all the leather work will have to be removed from the car and sent to them. They can also supply hides to match the original in most cases.

If the covering is Bedford Cord and it is in good condition but dirty, it can be cleaned up quite well. Use petrol or carbon tetrachloride for removing grease marks, then sponge over with soapsuds and warm water, afterwards sponging off the soap with cold water.

If the material is leathercloth, you must first ascertain the type of coating and, should it be P.V.C., it can only be cleaned as described in Chapter XV. If it is nitrocellulose and it is quite sound, then the surface can be reconditioned with "Nuagane" or "Leatherlac" according to the instructions on the tin. If you are re-upholstering using leathercloth, then we recommend a P.V.C.-coated cloth such as "Lionide" as it is more suitable than a nitrocellulose one for this purpose. Stitches should number about six to the inch.

If the upholstery is too far gone and you are not in a position to do the job yourself, then you will have to take it to a coach trimmer, but this can be rather expensive. It may be that the upholstery is in good condition except for one or more holes or tears so that only a small part will have to be renewed, and in this case you may be able to do it yourself. The covering will be either of the plain or pleated variety, and the latter is rather more easy to patch as it is only necessary to replace one or more pleats. The seams of the pleats are sewn to a backing cloth and the spaces formed are filled with wadding or a hair and fibre mixture. The covering will have to be removed, and this will be either hand-stitched or tacked in position.

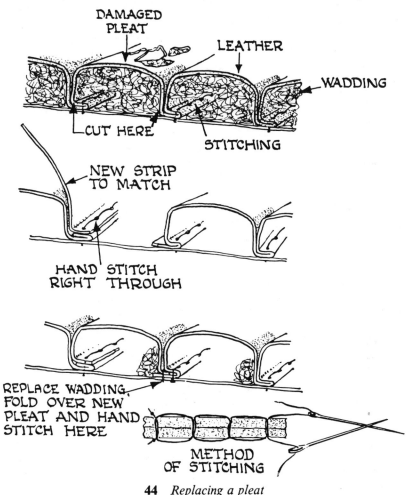

DAMAGED PLEAT

LEATHER

WADDING

CUT HERE

STITCHING

NEW STRIP TO MATCH

HAND STITCH RIGHT THROUGH

REPLACE WADDING, FOLD OVER NEW PLEAT AND HAND STITCH HERE

METHOD OF STITCHING

44 *Replacing a pleat*

Great care should be taken in this removal that no additional damage is done, and the procedure for replacement should be noted. When refitting the repaired covering, tack in one or two places and then check the alignment of the pleats with the remainder of the upholstery; the method of cutting out damaged pleats and fitting new ones is shown in fig. 44.

Hand stitching should be done with linen thread which has been waxed. Two needles are used, one on each end of a length of thread, as is also shown in fig. 44. When threading the needles, pass the point of each needle back through the thickness of the thread and pull tight so that the thread is firmly fixed in the eye of the needle. Wax the thread by pulling it across a block of beeswax. Holes for stitching should be made with an awl before attempting to push the needles through the leather.

If you do decide to carry out the upholstery yourself, the best advice we can give you is to study the way in which the work has been done as you carefully take it to pieces. Strip and recover one part at a time so that you do not forget the procedure for remaking. The leather panels, when they have been removed, will do as a guide but, as they will have stretched with use, they cannot be used as cutting patterns. New brown-paper patterns will have to be made before you commence cutting up the skins. For an average open four-seater body you will require $2\frac{1}{2}$ to 3 hides. If you are doing the work in leather, you will have to make your own piping, the string core for which can be obtained from the coachbuilders' supplier.

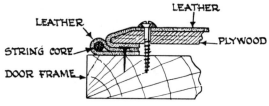

45 *Construction of door panel*

Should you be using leathercloth, and in this case we recommend "Vynide", you can obtain all the types of covered beading and piping, and also draught excluder, ready made-up to match your covering.

The door panels have usually been tacked in place and then finished off round the edge with some form of beading, also tacked in place, so that if it has to be removed to get at the lock, the panel is sure to be damaged. A better panel, and one that can readily be removed if necessary, is cut out of plywood 2–3 mm. thick and covered with leather. The leather is glued in place and turned over the edges. It can be glued all over, or to look and feel more luxurious it can be left loose on the surface and have a layer of thin wadding between it and the plywood, but in this case make sure that you pull the leather really tight. The edges of the plywood must be chamfered or they will look clumsy with the additional thickness of the leather. The completed panel can then be fitted to the bodywork with countersunk raised head screws and cup washers. The panel will look much more professional if it is finished off round the edges with single cord piping, which is tacked in place on the door before the panel is screwed home, as in fig. 45.

When the seat covering has been removed, examine the spring case, which usually consists of two wire frames with a series of coil springs sandwiched between them. The springs collapse in time but if only one or two are faulty it is quite easy to replace them. The springs are often kept in position by small metal clips holding the springs to each other and to the frame, and frequently the only trouble is that the clips have become dislodged. This trouble can be quite easily repaired, putting the clips back into position, closing them down and then soldering them. If the spring cases are beyond repair, new ones can be obtained from T. P. Colledge but you will have to send paper patterns.

Should you be unfortunate enough to have the pneumatic type of upholstery, this is the time to carry out some modifications, as this form of seating is never satisfactory. If the seat is deflated, a large pothole taken at speed is almost enough to produce the now-popular slipped disc, and if it is inflated you will roll about like a pea on a shovel. A spring case can be made to fit the covering and fitted without any great difficulty, or you might consider a filling of latex foam. This is obtainable from the Latex Cushion Co. Ltd., and again a paper template is required.

Head lining for Closed Cars

If the head lining is in sound condition it may be possible to clean it with petrol or carbon tetrachloride. Should it require replacement you can either take the car to an expert or have a go yourself; it is rather tricky but it can be done. Having removed the old cloth and bought the new, which should be large enough to allow for a cut off all round, first of all measure the position of the roof cross members. The position of these must be marked on the back of the cloth. Now cut some strips of linen or thin canvas of a length the same as the width of the head lining. The width of the strips should be about 3 in., but this will depend on the construction of the roof. In any case it does not matter if they are a little too wide as they will not show when the head lining is in place. These strips must now be stitched by one edge (about $\frac{1}{4}$ in. from the edge) across the head lining where you have put the marks, one strip to each mark. When this has been done you will have a series of narrow flaps down the back of the head lining, coinciding with the roof members. These are known as felling strips. The stitching can be done on the home machine, but you will have rather a lot of material to handle.

Having done all the preparation you now take the cloth inside the car, and tack the appropriate felling strip to the centre roof cross-member in such a way that when the whole job is finished the lining will be taut and true. Starting with the centre you will work outwards, completing each strip in turn until you reach the ends, now tack these and the sides and trim of the excess fabric. Finish off the edges with beading or double cord piping to match the roof lining or the upholstery.

Floor Covering

New floor mats can easily be made by the amateur from rubber-backed carpet, as this material when cut out does not require any binding. How-

151

ever, it never looks very good and it does not wear too well. Much better mats can be made from any type of plain woven carpet and we have found the hair-cord variety to be very satisfactory. All woven carpets will require binding with strips of leather or "Lionide" to match the upholstery, as shown in fig. 46. We show two ways of doing this binding; it should, however, be remembered that the stitching requires a fairly heavy machine.

Be careful when cutting the carpet that it is a good fit and not too skimpy, as not only is it required for the sake of appearance and for somewhere soft to rest one's feet but, if properly fitted, it will cut out draughts and deaden chassis noises. The shape can be drawn on the carpet with chalk but, if you are in any doubt, it will be better first to make a paper pattern and then cut the carpet from this. Stitch a rectangular piece of hide about 2 mm. thick on the carpet for the driver's heels. This will prevent what

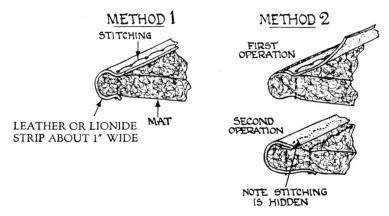

46 *Alternative methods of binding mat edges*

would otherwise be very rapid wear. You should be able to get this piece of hide from any saddlers.

Underfelt is well worthwhile using, as it not only makes the carpet feel more luxurious but it reduces wear and acts as a better sound deadener and draught excluder. An even better material than underfelt is $\frac{1}{4}$-in. Latex Foam sheeting.

The carpets should be well fixed in position with press fasteners and there are several types on the market which are suitable for this purpose.

Another type of floor covering for open cars is coconut matting; these mats wear well, are easily cleaned and are not damaged by wet. They can be made to measure by the Birmingham Workshops for the Blind, and paper patterns will have to be sent with the order. Care should be taken to make sure that there is sufficient pedal clearance. No fixing will be required with this type of carpet due to its greater weight and rigidity.

Hood Covering and Side Curtains

Hood covering is a most difficult job for the amateur to tackle and the work requires a fairly heavy sewing machine, so in most cases it will be more satisfactory to take it to a specialist. Hoods were usually covered with double texture material. This material consists of two plies of fabric with rubber in between. A better material is "Vynide Hoodcloth"; this material is, of course, non-Vintage, but it is more durable and has the great advantage that mud stains and oily finger marks are readily removable. "Vynide" is also suitable for the side curtains. It may be possible when re-covering the hood to tidy up the shape, especially if you are not using side curtains. Some original hoods were very untidy in appearance.

The material to be used for both the hood and side curtain windows is transparent plastic and we recommend "Vybak", as this is specially made for the purpose. You will require semi-rigid plastic for the side curtains and flexible plastic for the hood window. Make sure that all the fasteners are sound and replace any that are faulty. All types can be obtained from coachbuilders' suppliers.

Examine the fixing of the side curtains and be certain that they are rigid or they will flap about in a most irritating manner.

Have the window in the hood large enough, as one too small will necessitate an outside mirror and will make reversing very difficult. "Vybak" plastic is so strong that a very large window can be used.

For those rebuilders domiciled in the Midlands all types of hoods and side curtains can be re-covered by Auster Ltd.

Wood Panelling and Beading

Should the panels be damaged in any way they will have to be removed for renovation. If they are very badly scratched you will have to sandpaper them down smooth and then repolish. Broken panels can be repaired by glueing in new pieces of wood to match using "Cascamite Glue"; when this has set sandpaper the panel smooth. If the panel is in a very bad state it will probably pay you to make a new one and walnut is a very good wood for this purpose, but of course all the panels must match.

If the panels are veneered and if they are in a bad state you may be able to repair the veneers, but if not it will be better to remove the veneer and repolish in the plain state.

Dents can be removed by placing a damp cloth over the dent and then putting a hot iron on top, continue damping the cloth as it dries until the dent is filled up by the swelling of the wood. After it is dry the panel can be sanded smooth ready for the polishing.

All interior ornamental woodwork should be held in position by countersunk raised-head screws and cup washers.

CHAPTER XVIII

THE BONNET

W E have purposely left the treatment of the bonnet as a separate study in order to emphasise the point that, until the radiator and body are both in position on the chassis, it is impossible to tell whether the bonnet will fit snugly between the two. If the bonnet has been lost or is damaged and a new one has to be made, it is essential to leave the making until you have reached this juncture. Be extremely critical of the bonnet condition, especially along its upper surfaces. Small waves or dents in the metal will show to a much greater extent here than in any other part of the motor-car. They will also be a constant source of irritation to the driver.

Repairs to the Bonnet

Presuming the bonnet to be of the normal four-piece type the hinge-pins have already been removed at the dismantling stage. Examine the hinges for cracking and deformation. If it is apparent that new hinges will be necessary the old ones should be removed, which will also be the case if you wish to replate the hinges. Hinge removal requires great care if the bonnet is to be preserved and, with riveted-on hinges, the heads of the rivets should be chiselled off against the hinge and not along the outside of the bonnet. The rivets should be punched out, taking great care to support the sheet metal around the rivet head while doing so to avoid stretching the metal. New hinges of all types are available from coachbuilders' suppliers and it is best in each case to send a short sample length of the hinge required together with a measurement of the length needed. A hinge-pin of stainless steel or brass is far better than one of steel. Examine the bonnet edges for chafing where they have come into contact with the bonnet tape and if they are worn thin the edge must be trimmed off and a new strip welded on, the weld being filed off flush. This is best done by a competent sheet-metal worker. If the bonnet has louvred side panels it is worth going to some trouble to preserve the original sides, as making louvres in a new panel is a difficult job for anyone to tackle. If any work is needed on the bonnet it will be best to remove all the paint first, and this must be done with " Nitromors" and not a blowlamp which will buckle the sheet metal. Generally restore the shape of the bonnet paying particular attention to the top surface which, if it is wavy or dented, should be re-rolled by a sheet-metal worker.

If the hinges have been removed, replace them in a temporary manner when reassembling the bonnet, i.e. fit them with small nuts and bolts in the case of a riveted-on hinge or, with other types, clamp them in place and try the bonnet on the car. It will generally be found that the bonnet has changed shape due to stretching of the metal during repairs and the assembly should proceed in careful stages starting from the centre hinge and working towards either side, checking each stage actually on the car. See that the centre hinge is a good fit end-wise between the body and the radiator as this locates the position of the whole bonnet. If necessary fit a spacing washer to compensate for wear that may have taken place at this point. Check now to see that there is at least $\frac{1}{8}$ in. clearance at the edges of the bonnet to allow for chassis flexing. With less clearance the paint will be chipped off the bonnet edges and you may chafe the radiator through to the water.

Next inspect the bonnet fasteners, replacing them if worn or replating them if necessary. The best types of bonnet fasteners are those which hold the bonnet under spring tension and therefore allow it to give a little with chassis flexing. Any fastener which holds the bonnet rigidly should be discarded. Many types of fastener are available from coachbuilders' suppliers and it is quite possible that exact replicas of what are already fitted to your car can still be supplied from stock if yours are worn out.

It is well worth fitting four large button-headed bolts to the bonnet tops in such a way that each pair meet when the bonnet is opened to avoid damage to the paintwork and straining of the centre hinge. Many cars are already fitted with such bolts. These can be either plated or made from stainless steel.

Other bonnet fittings such as handles and locks should be repaired and replated if necessary and, finally, when you are quite sure that the bonnet is well fitted, it can be dismantled and painted.

Making a New Bonnet

If a new bonnet has to be made then use 16 S.W.G. half-hard aluminium. Start by putting the centre hinge in position on the car and then set about making the top panels. These will have to be rolled in a set of sheet metal rolls and are best left to the professional. If you do not want to take the car to him it is not very difficult to make a jig conforming to the shape of the scuttle and radiator, as shown in Fig. 47. Ask the sheet-metal worker to leave $\frac{1}{2}$ in. overhang on the fore-and-aft edges of the two panels for you to trim off actually on the car. In the case of a riveted-on hinge, as is generally found on Vintage cars, mark on the jig the distance apart of the top edges of the two panels to allow the hinge to project through the gap. With other types of hinges which require folding of the panel edges it will be best to take the hinges to the sheet-metal worker so that he can also do the necessary folding.

Having obtained the rolled panels for the top of the bonnet, offer them

155

up to the car. With a riveted-on hinge, put this in position on the car and hold one panel up to the hinge. Very carefully mark off the exact width of the final bonnet and trim the panel to this marking. Drill two $\frac{1}{8}$-in. rivet holes through panel and hinge, one at each end, and secure the two together with $\frac{1}{8}$-in. nuts and bolts. The panel and hinge can now be re-

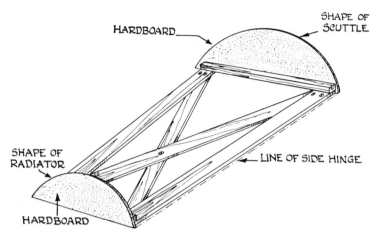

47   *Bonnet-forming jig*

moved, the remaining rivet holes drilled and the two riveted together. On long bonnets, it is advantageous to back up the hinge with a piece of 1-in. × 1-in. × $\frac{1}{8}$-in. angle duralumin to stiffen the whole assembly as shown in fig. 48. A great help to final painting is to anodise the panels and the rivets and if you can have this done the whole bonnet must be made up using nuts and bolts instead of rivets, dismantled, ano-dised and finally riveted up. Failing this treatment, rough emery cloth the panel before riveting to form a key for the paint. It is very difficult to roughen the metal round the rivet heads after rivet-ing.

48   *Stiffening hinge by means of angle*

We will now break off for a moment to give a few tips on riveting. Firstly, always use aluminium rivets of $\frac{1}{8}$-in. diameter with snap heads for bonnet work. These are obtainable in all lengths from C. F. Bridges and many other stockists. It is essential to have the two correct snaps or rivet sets to do the job properly, one to support the rivet head and the other to form the other end of the rivet. Hold one snap in the vice, thread the rivet through the holes, place the head in the snap and then tap the various pieces together with a tube punch. Cut the rivet to a length gauge, which you can make, the length of rivet required having been determined by experiment, and finally close the rivet over with the other snap. It is nearly always necessary to have a mate to hold the work and to keep it level, in order to stop the edge of the snap cutting into the panel. Snaps are available at many good tool stores and are specified by the diameter of rivet you are going to use. They can be made from best cast steel by turning a recess of approximately the right size in the end and hammering the snap on to a bearing ball of the right diameter. The snap is then hardened. The riveting procedure is shown in fig. 49.

Reverting to the bonnet, the side hinges can now be riveted on to the lower edges of the top panels and the whole assembly put back on the car. Measurements can now be made for the side panels and you will have to find out whether or not you will be able to louvre them. When cars were originally made with louvred bonnets they were cut with press tools which

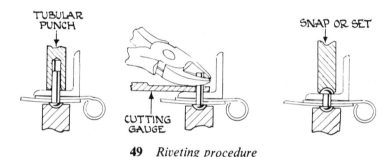

49 *Riveting procedure*

are now unobtainable by most of us. It is possible for a skilled panel beater to cut a row of louvres by hand, but it is likely to be an expensive job. However, there are one or two sheet-metal workers who have machines which can cut louvres very quickly, and if you can find such a firm your problem is solved. We were recently faced with this problem and, although we could not find a firm of sheet-metal workers owning the necessary equipment, we were lucky enough to find that a local firm of machine-tool dealers had the right machine in their showrooms. With some persuasion we were allowed to try our hand at using the machine and spent a happy afternoon producing a perfect pair of bonnet sides.

If you decide to have louvres cut, leave metal all round the edges of the panel for trimming after louvering. Finally the side panels can be riveted to the hinges and the bonnet catches and lifting handles fitted. It is very desirable to fit stiffeners on to the inside of the panel, from the bonnet fasteners up to the side hinges, to stop the panel bending under the pull of the catches.

The bonnet can now be dismantled and painted to match the rest of the car. A very professional touch is to line the edge of each louvre with another colour and to put one line down the side of the car at a suitable level. Although lining is a specialised trade, quite good results can be obtained by the amateur using a very fine brush and a piece of wood as a hand rest.

CHAPTER XIX

SPECIAL FINISHES

THROUGHOUT the preceding chapters we have made references to various finishes which can be applied to the components of a motor-car in order to relieve the monotony of having everything painted, and also to give protection to bare metals in cases where painting is impossible. We will now elaborate on the variety of finishes available and, in the case of work which can be done at home, give some indication as to the methods to be adopted.

Electro-plating

This is the most universally accepted method of metal protection and decoration. It is essential to find and become friendly with the local plating firm and, since platers generally are not very enthusiastic with regard to replating a few odd pieces, it is better not to start off on the wrong foot by sending them the work in a filthy condition. Do not send parts in a battered state; they should first be restored to their original shape by filing or machining and only the minimum of polishing left for the plater to do on the mop. This is the secret of restoring old parts so that when they are plated they will look like new. A good example of this is a Rudge Whitworth wheel-locking ring of the eared type, which are usually very bruised from hammering.

The deposits usually available are copper, brass, chrome, cadmium, zinc and silver. Any of these deposits can be used on any base metal found on a motor-car with the exception of aluminium, and while this metal can be plated it is rather a specialised process. Always use the same plating throughout the motor-car, e.g. do not mix nickel and chrome, and if you have an early model with polished brass parts remember that steel can be polished and brass-plated.

Cadmium plating is a very good finish for steel parts where a spanner is likely to be used at intervals, e.g. brake adjusters. Chromium or nickel plating can be either polished or dull and engine parts often look better in a dull or satin finish. Where mating pieces have to be a good mechanical fit, ask the plater to mask off the mating surfaces, and beware of chromium plating on fine threads, as the plating will often make the fit too tight, and it is very difficult to remove.

A very pleasant black finish for brass parts such as controls and dashboard fittings is to have them copper oxidised and lacquered; this is a nice contrast to the bright parts and should be kept clean with a wax polish.

159

Anodising

This finish can only be applied to aluminium or its alloys and is often done by electro-plating firms. For motor-car decoration it can be either self-colour or black, and again either polished or dull. It is a very pleasant finish and is proof against any corrosion, so to keep it clean it is only necessary to wash it. An anodised finish can be wax polished, but it must never be cleaned with metal polish. This finish also forms a very good key for paint. Do not attempt to anodise old castings as it is very doubtful that these will be in an anodising quality alloy and they may easily fall to pieces during the process.

Metal Spraying

This process has been mentioned in earlier chapters as a method of building up worn parts, but it can also be used as a rustproof finish and for embellishment. Practically any metal can be sprayed on to any other metal base, but the finish is very matt and it will therefore require careful polishing if it is used as a decorative finish. We have found that aluminium spraying is the best possible rustproof finish for exhaust systems. Brass spraying, well burnished, could be used as a very good substitute for the close plating which was used on such components as the brake lever on early motor-cars, as it is very difficult to find anyone who could do this work today and in any case it would be rather expensive. For those who have never encountered close plating, it is a finish for steel which consists of coating the component with thin sheet brass soldered in position. It is often found that the brass has worn right through or is peeling off due to rust forming underneath.

Chemical Blacking

This is a very attractive lustrous black finish for steel parts such as levers and control rods; it can be done by Tool Treatments Ltd. It is not a sufficiently rust-resisting finish for parts which are exposed to the weather, but it is excellent for engine parts and forms a good contrast to plating and polished aluminium. It should be polished with oil as for a gun. This finish does not increase the dimensions and it is therefore good for threads or working parts. The final finish will depend on the state of the parts when they are sent for treatment.

Stove Enamel

We have already recommended this finish as the most durable one for wheels; it is also useful for engine parts as it is proof against hot oil. To obtain a good finish the parts should be reasonably smooth before treatment. Stove enamel is used by Rolls-Royce for their cylinder-blocks and valve covers.

Vitreous Enamel

A very good and durable heat-resisting finish for cast-iron exhaust manifolds. This finish can be done by Hurst Hill Enamel Co. Ltd. in a number of colours, no preparation is necessary and this firm will take care of the mating surfaces. While this finish is quite tough, it is of course glass, and can be chipped if it is knocked about, particularly on sharp edges.

Mottling

This is a delightful finish for polished metal surfaces, and particularly for aluminium. It was the standard finish on some high-quality Vintage engines and was used on many show models (see Plate V). It has also been used on polished aluminium bodies.

The finish is produced with a circular felt mop and carborundum paste in a suitable rotary drive. The mop is made in the form of a steel cup into which a piece of hard felt is pressed, as shown in fig. 50. This cup has a small spindle for holding in the chuck of the drive, it will also be found advantageous to make up another cup with a longer spindle for getting into awkward places. The hard felt can be obtained from suppliers to the plating trade who use it for making polishing mops. The felt can be cut to shape very easily with a sharp knife. Use carborundum valve grinding paste No. 366 fine, which should be painted on the work in a very thin coat. The mop should be running fairly fast and not too much pressure used, or discoloration will take place due to the heat generated.

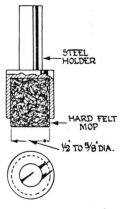

STEEL HOLDER

HARD FELT MOP

½ TO ⅝ DIA.

50 *Mottling tool*

Flat pieces of metal can be mottled in a drilling machine. If the work is an irregular shape, like a dashboard, screw it to a rectangular board so that the mottling will be in straight lines. Use a set edge on the machine table which can be moved half a diameter on completion of each row of circles. Work from one side to the other, the same way each time, and each circle should overlap the next by half a diameter. The first row should only be half circles so that all the surface will be covered, as in fig. 51.

Curved surfaces will have to be done with a hand tool, either a flexible drive, compressed-air drill or an electric drill, but the latter is rather difficult to handle owing to its weight. Practice will be needed to hold the mop steady on each circle, otherwise the procedure is the same as for flat surfaces. After a lot of work the mop will wear, more on the outside than in the centre, forming a tit which can be removed with a sharp knife. The metal need not be polished first, but it must be very smooth and free from any scratches. After mottling all the grinding paste must be carefully

161

removed by washing lightly with petrol, do not rub or you will spoil all your work.

Mottled parts for the body, such as the instrument panel, can be lacquered or anodised and they will then keep bright for a very long time. Lacquer with clear cellulose lacquer thinned to spraying consistency. The work must be absolutely clean and free from any grease.

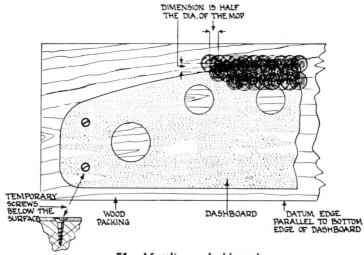

51 *Mottling a dashboard*

Do not lacquer engine parts as the hot oil will soon cause them to go brown. With the mottling unprotected great care must be taken when you are cleaning, as it is very easy to rub it all off in the case of aluminium, but if the work is in stainless steel the finish will of course be more durable.

As an alternative to lacquering on an aluminium instrument panel a more durable finish can be obtained by having it clear anodised by your local electro-plater after mottling. If you dislike a mottled finish, then a very pleasing appearance can be obtained by having the panel vapour blasted (not shot-blasted) followed by clear anodising. On no account attempt to anodise old aluminium castings as usually the alloy is not suitable for this treatment.

Cellulose Polishing of Wood

This is a far better finish for the wood panels in a motor-car than French polish, as moisture will not cause it to bloom.

The wood must be finished absolutely smooth with the finest grade of garnet paper before anything else can be done. If you are using a soft wood, it will have to be filled using a wood filler, a tin of which can be obtained from any good ironmonger. This filler must be rubbed in by hand up and down the grain of the wood, and then rubbed off with a piece of hessian across the grain; leave it to dry off according to the instructions on the tin. After the filler is dry, the wood can again be rubbed down, using well-worn garnet paper. The filling need not be done if you are using a hard close-grained wood such as walnut. If you wish to do any staining, it should be applied now, use "Colron" which can be obtained in twelve shades, or any other good naphtha stain, allowing this to dry thoroughly. The next procedure is to spray on one coat of cellulose sanding sealer; allow thirty minutes for drying and rub down with very fine worn garnet paper. Now spray on one coat of clear cellulose wood finish, which should be thinned, and the air pressure should be set as for the cellulose painting.

When this is thoroughly dry, spray on a second coat and leave it to dry for at least two days. Now rub down with 400-grade wet-and-dry paper using water with a spot of detergent, paying particular attention not to rub through any sharp places; when it is finished the surface should be matt all over. Polish with cutting paste, and when this is done to your satisfaction, finish with "Autobrite" car polish which will remove any trace of grease. If you have done the work meticulously you will have a superb finish like plate glass.

CHAPTER XX

THE GARAGE AND WORKSHOP

THE hobby of restoring interesting motor-cars is carried on by amateurs in all sorts of places ranging from the front garden to the most palatial of workshops imaginable. While it is by no means true to say that the best cars come out of the finest garages, we do feel that it will be helpful to some of our readers if we describe, in this last chapter, the bare necessities for working in comfort. We will follow this with a description of what would, in our opinion, constitute an ideal workshop and garage.

The garage itself must be large enough to house the motor-car and to allow of walking all round it. There must also be room for a bench. Circumstances will probably dictate the ultimate choice of shape in plan view, but, if alternatives are possible, then make the garage longer than necessary to house the motor-car and build the bench across the end furthest from the doors. It is desirable to have a window over the bench, as good light is essential to good work. It is surprising how well a job can look by artificial light which, when wheeled out into the full glare of a summer's day, looks rather second-rate. This fact is well understood by certain gentlemen in the second-hand-car trade.

Artificial lighting should be as powerful as possible; a coat of whitewash on all the walls and ceiling can save many a pound spent on electricity.

Reverting to the bench, remember that this is the primary and most essential piece of equipment in the workshop. It is in constant use while the job proceeds and it is worth making it exactly the right height to suit yourself. The normal height is 33 in. but this can be very tiring to work at for those above or below average height. Above all, the bench must be strong and rigid. The best construction is to have cast-iron legs with a 3-in. thick soft-wood top bolted to them. The whole bench must then either be anchored to the wall, or into the floor, to obtain the maximum rigidity.

The next essential is a fitter's vice. This vice should be made of steel—cast iron is useless—and any size over 4 in. will be suitable. Bolt the vice directly over one of the bench legs so that, when brute force has to be used, any downward blows are strongly resisted. Most vices are sold with serrated jaws, but it will be found that there is practically never an occasion when these are necessary. Therefore, to avoid leaving the indelible mark of the poor tradesman all over your work, remove the jaws and have the serrations ground off. The vice can then be used without recourse to loose, soft jaws, which are always a nuisance. A tip outside the scope of this

164

chapter can be included here, while talking of vices. Should a part ever have to be held extremely tightly in the now smooth-jawed vice and it shows signs of slipping, a strip of emery cloth wound tightly round it will generally give a perfect grip and leave no marks.

Essential Hand Tools

We now come to the necessary hand tools which will be needed for the rebuild. Before embarking upon this list, let it be said that, no matter how many tools one has, the best implement for some particular job will always be missing, but it is possible with a few primary tools and a lot of ingenuity to do very passable work. The restoration of a motor-car covers a multitude of specialist trades and it is almost impossible to have the tools that each tradesman would have to perform his portion of the whole. The amateur is lucky in that he often has no fixed ideas of how to perform a certain task but knows the result which he wants to obtain. Never be afraid to "have a go" at what is reputed to be a very skilled job, if you think that you stand a chance of succeeding. A joiner would frown at the thought of using a file on wood, but if you have no plane but have a file, do not hesitate to find out how good a result you can get.

As the first work on the motor-car will be to take it completely to pieces, obviously a set of spanners will be necessary. Open-ended chrome vanadium from $\frac{1}{8}$-in. to $\frac{9}{16}$-in. Whitworth will cover most needs. There will always be the unusually large nut which these sizes will not cover but the largest adjustable spanner that you can afford will cope with these. The American-type adjustable, with the jaws at only a small angle to the handle, will be found better than those with the jaws at a right angle. An adjustable spanner is never to be recommended where the correct size of set spanner can be borrowed, but as a life saver it is indispensable. A set of socket spanners of the same size as the open-ended ones is a very pleasant possession, but it is not truly indispensable. If a set of socket spanners is out of the question, then a set of tubular box spanners and a suitable tommy bar must be the substitute. If a bonus has just been paid, have both!

The next essential is a set of good screwdrivers. Three will cover most jobs: a small electrician's type, a medium size and the largest and longest which you can afford. The latter should preferably have some means of rotation other than by its own handle; some have a hexagonal portion to which a spanner can be fitted, and others have a hinged tommy-lever. Never use your screwdriver as a lever. A set of long tire levers of the old-fashioned type about 12–14 in. long, which used to be sold by Michelin, are well worth searching for and will be constantly used, even if you never remove a tire.

Hammers may be known as "Brummagem screwdrivers" but there must be at least two in every workshop. Choose a $\frac{1}{2}$-lb. ball peen and a 2-lb. model of the same type for jobs where brute force is the only possible

165

means to an end. A cold chisel makes a companion for the hammers for, say what you will, there is always the nut which just will not come undone despite all the penetrating oil and blowlamps. Another indispensable is the hack-saw. A 10-in size with carbon-steel blades having 22 teeth per inch is admirable. High-speed blades last longer with careful use but are very expensive and easily broken.

A pair of combination pliers can be very useful and the Mole wrench, which will give a phenomenal grip, had better be included. These two tools are only to be used on rough dismantling jobs or where nothing else will do, as, like the vice with serrated jaws, they always leave their mark.

Reverting to the hammer department, a rawhide or hard-wood mallet is essential for assembling the jobs which need the gentle tap fit, and can also save the thinner types of casting having to go to the welders before the work of restoring really begins.

Files are called by various queer names, one being very rude. You can never have a large enough variety of files, but as a start to a collection, this list will be a guide:

12 in.	Half-round medium cut
12 in.	Flat bastard
12 in.	$\frac{7}{16}$-in. round medium cut
10 in.	Flat Dreadnought
10 in.	Half-round Dreadnought
8 in.	Pillar smooth
6 in.	Rat-tail smooth
16 cm.	French three square No. 0 cut
16 cm.	French half-round No. 4 cut

The uses of most of the above will be apparent, but if any reader is not acquainted with the Dreadnought-type of file, let it be said that the way in which it will shift aluminium or wood needs to be experienced to be believed. An alternative to the Dreadnought is the "Surform", which is excellent for wood or aluminium but which must not be used on harder metals.

If any bearings are to be fitted, and they assuredly will have to be before the restoration is complete, then a half-round scraper will be wanted. This can either be bought as a new tool or made by softening an old half-round file, curving the end and shaping to a scraper, and finally re-hardening. A flat scraper is very useful for the final fettling of castings and can be made in a similar fashion from an old file.

The last essential hand tool is a breast drill of $\frac{1}{2}$-in. capacity and a set of high-speed drills. These can either be bought as and when each necessity arises, or as a set. The most useful single set is the range $\frac{1}{16}$ in. to $\frac{1}{2}$ in. in $\frac{1}{64}$-in. steps. Keep your drills in a stand so that it is immediately obvious if one is missing.

In passing, it will be as well to mention that keeping one's tools clean and in some sort of order makes life very much easier. It is not necessary to have every spanner hanging on its own hook with its silhouette painted on the wall behind, but at least keep all the spanners in a box together, the files in another and so on. Nothing is more annoying in the middle of a job then to have to search round under piles of motor-car for the spanner which was left where it was last used. A set of open-topped shallow boxes on the back of the bench forms admirable storage for the tools in constant use.

We must now enumerate a small number of pieces of equipment which are not hand tools but which will nevertheless be needed on the job. As the car will be wheel-less for a considerable period, it has to rest on something else. Jacking stands can be bought fairly cheaply and these should be of an adjustable nature, so that they can either support the chassis or be put under the axles. Failing these, four suitable stands can be made of wood, but make sure that they are adequately strong as it is easy to go on adding weight to the chassis, forgetting that it is still resting on the flimsy stands which were knocked up just to hold the bare frame. One jack of any type, providing it will lift one end of the motor-car in question, will now suffice.

While on the subject of lifting, a length of rope is very useful. This can, in turn, be used to lift out the engine and to tow the completed motor-car if it refuses to start; a 12-ft. length of 3-in. Manila will be found most universally helpful.

One of the early tasks will be a tedious amount of scrubbing with paraffin. Do not use the household scrubbing brush and bucket for this, for such actions tend to put the restoration on the wrong footing with the distaff side of the home. A stiff bristle brush, a steel wire brush and some suitable tray, or even an old oil drum cut down, will save many a rift in family life.

A refinement which may seem on first sight rather a luxury is a dust sheet. If the gradually-growing restoration is kept covered up while not being worked on, it will be found to keep its appearance, particularly so far as polished and plated surfaces are concerned, much better than if left uncovered. Research into this seems to show that, particularly in and around large cities, it is the dust that bears the chemicals that start the rot, and it is quite amazing how a piece of polished metal—which would have oxidised quickly if left uncovered—will keep its lustre if protected from the dust. Smaller assemblies should also be kept covered while in a partly dismantled condition, to prevent the ingress of foreign bodies. No engine goes better with Crown corks accidentally dropped into the crankcase when the inevitable visitor to the restoration was being entertained.

The last tool in the minimum list is a folding twelve-inch rule. Carried in the pocket it is in constant demand and also adds a certain professional appearance to the youngest beginner if produced at the right moment.

Summarising then, our list of basic essential equipment is as follows:

1 Bench	1 Rawhide or wood mallet
1 Fitter's vice	1 Set files, as listed
1 Set open-ended spanners	2 Scrapers, flat and half-round
1 Large adjustable spanner	1 Breast drill ½-in. capacity
(American type)	4 Jacking stands
1 Set socket or tubular spanners	12 ft. 3-in. Manila rope
3 Screwdrivers, large, medium	1 Paraffin tray
and small	1 Wire brush
2 Hammers, ball peen, ½lb. and 2lb.	1 Stiff bristle brush
1 10-in. Hack-saw and blades	1 Dust sheet
1 Pair combination pliers	1 12-in. steel rule
1 Mole wrench	

We have not, in this book, dealt in detail with the correct way in which to use the primary fitters' hand tools. There are many excellent workshop manuals already dealing with this subject and we have only mentioned special applications of their use which have been found applicable to certain jobs. This remark also applies to the use of the more extensive equipment which we shall now describe as being ideally available when restoring a motor-car.

The Ideal Workshop

In fig. 52 will be found a plan of the ideal workshop and garage, which very few people will ever be lucky enough to attain. However, it is always as well to have a target in mind and it may well be that, if you are about to embark on the erection of a workshop, you will be able to benefit at least in part by studying this plan.

The garage and workshop form one building, but there is a partition between the two, preferably mostly of glass, so that the workshop may be sealed off completely from the garage. The reasons for this are threefold. First, as most of the work will be done in the workshop, it is desirable to keep this reasonably warm in winter for comfort and to prevent rust on machines and tools. It is possible to economise greatly on fuel by only keeping the chill off the garage, but keeping the workshop at a reasonable temperature. Second, as there is plenty of room in the garage, all the major assemblies can be kept in there and only that which is being worked upon brought into the workshop. A definite partition is the only way of keeping to this rule, which in turn helps you to keep the workshop tidy and therefore pleasant to work in. Third, when the motor-car is complete the engine will probably have to be run for considerable periods within the garage, and exhaust gases tend to rust the bright surfaces of machine tools; this possibility is eliminated by the partition. While talking of running the engine in the garage, we should like to advise that a piece of flexible pipe

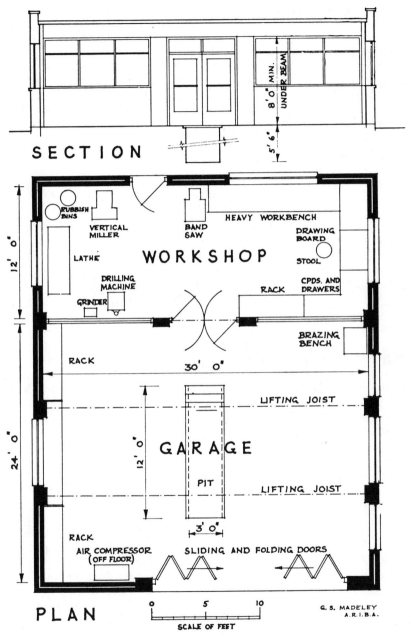

SECTION

8' 0" MIN. UNDER BEAM

5' 6"

RUBBISH BINS

VERTICAL MILLER

BAND SAW

HEAVY WORKBENCH

DRAWING BOARD

LATHE

WORKSHOP

STOOL

DRILLING MACHINE

CPDS. AND DRAWERS

GRINDER

RACK

RACK

12' 0"

BRAZING BENCH

RACK

30' 0"

LIFTING JOIST

24' 0"

GARAGE

12' 0"

PIT

LIFTING JOIST

3' 0"

RACK

AIR COMPRESSOR (OFF FLOOR)

SLIDING AND FOLDING DOORS

PLAN

0   5   10
SCALE OF FEET

G. S. MADELEY
A.R.I.B.A.

52 *Plan of garage and workshop*

169

for connecting to the car's exhaust be kept for the purpose of taking the exhaust gases right outside the garage; this is an obvious safety precaution. A 6-ft. communicating opening from workshop to garage is closed by two swing doors which will allow the largest component to pass through.

The building should be of brick which is by far the most lasting and heat-insulating material. The walls will also be strong enough to support equipment and will carry the heavy joists which span the garage, on which engines and other heavy components can be suspended when being removed from the chassis. The building can either have a flat roof or, better still, a pitched roof with a floor above the garage, which can be the store place for all the precious junk which is so dear to the heart of every keen collector.

The garage has been made large enough to hold three of the largest cars, side by side. The general plan of using this space is that the chassis will occupy the centre position on the floor. On one side of it the body will stand, and both units will have plenty of room to walk and work all round them. The remaining portion of the garage will be taken up by the dismantled components of the motor-car in the first stages, and latterly, will be needed for a large trestle table, on which the cutting and marking out of materials for bodywork can be executed. There will also be permanent steel racks and pigeon holes on this side for the storage of the innumerable stocks of nuts, bolts, rivets, washers, piping and rubber which are accumulated over the years and need to be kept in some sort of order.

A pit occupies the centre of the floor which is not essential during the restoration, although very useful, but, if no access to a hoist is available, is very necessary for maintenance when the motor-car is in use. The most desirable size of pit is 12 ft. × 3 ft. × 5 ft. 6 in. deep, which will give access to the lower vitals of the largest car. The top should be covered by 2-in × 9-in. pine boards, which will stand the load of a jack working off the centre.

The floor should be as level as possible, as measurements have to be taken from it to various points on the car. A wood floor is very desirable from a comfort point of view but is expensive compared with concrete. The wood floor has another advantage over concrete in that it does not generate its own dust. Sweeping a concrete floor always tends to cover all the equipment with a layer of fine dust which is abrasive and also rust-provoking to iron and steel.

Regarding services to this building, the more the merrier. Water, gas, electricity and even the telephone if it is a long way from the house. The latter will be very popular with the rest of the household, as fetching you on a wet night to answer the telephone again does not help true family harmony. The electricity supply is the better for being three-phase as the machine tools can then be more easily reversed. Plenty of single-phase, 5-amp power plugs should be sited round the walls of both garage and workshop for supplying electric tools and inspection lamps. It is desirable in the interest of safety to instal a transformer which will provide a 12-volt supply for low-voltage inspection lamps. This also enables a very small lamp to be used for illuminating such places as cylinder bores. If gas is not available for soldering and brazing, then Calor gas is an excellent substitute.

The method of heating the building must be an individual choice and must depend upon balancing convenience against expense. The most economical system is some type of solid-fuel burner which may be the straightforward coke stove or a boiler connected to heating pipes. If the latter is chosen, then the heat distribution can be adjusted to give the workshop a higher temperature than the garage, as most of your time will be spent in the workshop. At the other end of the scale, a system which is now coming into more general use is the electrically-heated floor. This consists of an element set in the floor, which is thermostatically controlled and gives perfect heat distribution. It is completely inconspicuous and trouble-free but, at the same time, it is fairly expensive to run.

Have as many windows as you can, as daylight is far better than artificial light. Here again, whitewash the walls to keep the general lighting at a maximum.

Having got this far in the description of our ideal, lest the reader may think the whole proposition rather overdone, let it be said that both the Authors have garage and workshop buildings which approach fairly near to this ideal and which they built largely by themselves. Bricklaying can be very good fun and not nearly so expensive as one would imagine at first thought.

We now come to the equipment to be installed into the workshop. So far as hand tools are concerned it is quite impossible to list all those that can be used or that it would be nice to have. As the work proceeds, so the need for tools will arise, and the individual must make up his mind whether he will have sufficient future uses to warrant buying such a tool or whether he can borrow that which he will only use once or twice in a lifetime.

Machine Tools

There are certain fundamental machine tools without which the life of a motor-car restorer can be made rather troublesome. The first of these is a lathe. Maid-of-all-work and most useful instrument in the workshop, the centre lathe, once owned, is indispensable. The best size for our purpose is a 6-in. screw cutter of robust construction. This will not handle the very largest jobs, such as skimming a flywheel, but if you have a lathe large enough to cope with anything, it is then clumsy for the average work. If possible, fit the lathe with a means of reversing, as this can be very useful at times. The lathe will, of course, have to have a certain amount of equipment, the minimum being the following:

1   5-in. 3-jaw self-centering chuck
1   6-in. 4-jaw chuck
1   10-in. faceplate

171

1 Tailstock centre
1 Headstock centre
1 Drive plate and carrier
1 Tailstock drill chuck 0–$\frac{1}{2}$ in.
1 Slocum centre drill
1 Tool holder into which various H.S. bits can be fitted
1 Parting tool

Other equipment for the lathe can be accumulated as time goes by.

The next machine tool in order of usefulness is the drilling machine. This can be either pedestal- or bench-mounted and should be able to accommodate drills up to $\frac{1}{2}$-in. diameter. There are many excellent models on the market and, if a choice can be made, it is recommended that one with back gearing is chosen, as this type will run very slowly and can be used for tapping after drilling. This will result in a far truer thread than can usually be obtained by hand tapping. Once again, have a reverse on your drilling machine in order to wind the tap out again. A drilling-machine vice is a necessity, also a nice flat block of wood to save the drilling-machine table from becoming pock-marked.

Having installed these two machines it is now necessary to have a bench grinder, in order to sharpen the lathe tools and the drills. A double-ended model, designed to carry 8-in. stones, is about the size and it is not a bad idea to use only one stone of a fairly fine grit, using the other end of the spindle to carry a rotary wire mop for rust removal on small parts.

Probably the next most useful machine is the vertical milling machine. A good size is one having a table 9 in. × 17 in., but a few inches either side of these measurements will be just as useful. The uses to which a vertical miller can be put are legion, but many jobs can be done on the lathe, although not so conveniently, by putting the milling cutter in the chuck of the lathe and holding the workpiece on the cross slide. It is not recommended that a horizontal miller is considered in place of a vertical type as, in the particular case with which we are dealing, its application is not so universal.

The final multi-purpose machine for the workshop is the band-saw. The correct type should have back gearing so that a large range of speeds is available. This will enable metals or wood to be cut, and if extensive re-making of timbers for the bodywork or long cuts of sheet metal are to be indulged in, this is the tool to use. A circular saw can be useful, but its occasional use on restoration work hardly warrants its installation in our ideal workshop. It may be said that the ownership of a band-saw and a circular saw is the sign of true opulence. If, however, you do decide to have a circular saw, it is essential that it be mounted on a retractable under-carriage which enables the saw to live in some remote corner and only be brought out into the middle of the shop when required to give enough room for the sawing of planks.

There always seem to be a lot of holes to drill when rebuilding a motor-car. An electric brace takes the hard work out of this operation. The two most useful sizes are 0–$\frac{1}{4}$ in. and 0–$\frac{1}{2}$ in. The slower the large one runs the better but also, generally, the more expensive. The "Rolls-Royce" in this line is the Desoutter 0–$\frac{1}{2}$ in., which has two speeds, the higher for putting a small drill through first and the lower for use in opening out with a large drill. Another useful electric tool is the motor-driven flexible drive, which can power rotary wire brushes and rotary files. These are excellent for fettling rough castings, removing rust and port polishing.

In these days of labour saving, it is very desirable to have a source of compressed air in the workshop. This can either take the form of a static compressor and receiver, with the air piped round to various convenient take-off points where a snap-in coupling forms the connection, or a portable compressor on wheels which can be pushed to where it is needed. Compressed air in the workshop is primarily used for blowing away swarf or dirt, working a paraffin spray for cleaning purposes, spray painting and blowing up tires.

Further Workshop Equipment

The remarks made earlier in this chapter apply to the workbench. However, as we are discussing the ideal, a wood-working vice can now be added and also a planing stop let into the top of the bench.

A very necessary part of the workshop equipment is a soldering and brazing bench. This can be made of wood, with a fireclay top about 2 in. thick and a back plate of $\frac{1}{4}$-in. steel sheet. A drawing of a suitable bench appears in fig. 53. There should be two sources of heat for use with this. First, a small gas soldering-iron muffle, and secondly a brazing torch. An excellent make for home-use in this connection is the Bullfinch blowpipe, which can be supplied for use with either town gas or Calor gas and which, without an external source of compressed air, will raise a sufficient amount of heat to silver solder moderate-sized jobs. It is not at all a good thing to have soldering carried out in the workshop proper. The fumes from soldering flux are very corrosive and will quickly rust any ferrous metals with which they come into contact. It is better, therefore, to instal the soldering and brazing bench in the garage or, even better, in some other building if this be possible. Likewise, it is always as well to wash your hands after using soldering flux, otherwise rusty finger prints will appear on all the bright steel parts you may touch.

It would be very pleasant also to have oxy-acetylene welding equipment but, with the very occasional use which it would get on the type of car which this book covers, it will probably be more economical to take the few parts needing this treatment to an outside expert.

The storage of nuts and bolts has been mentioned earlier on and here it can be said that a very easy and convenient way of storing these, and similar stocks of small parts, can be made by acquiring all the 1-lb. jam

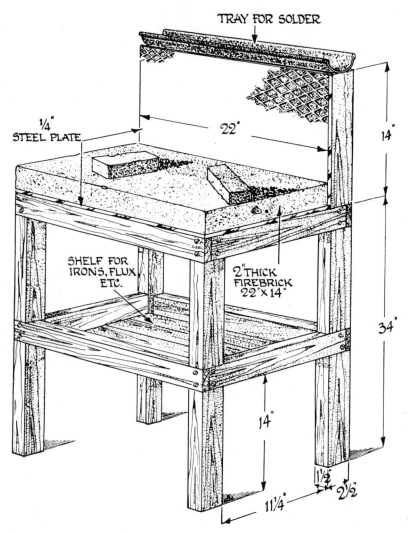

TRAY FOR SOLDER

1/4" STEEL PLATE

22"

14"

SHELF FOR IRONS, FLUX ETC.

2" THICK FIREBRICK 22" × 14"

34"

14"

1 1/4"

2 1/2"

11 1/4"

53 *Soldering and brazing bench*

jars that you can lay your hands on. These are arranged on shelves which are just wide enough and far enough apart, one above the other, to accommodate the jars. The various articles are stored in the jars and a visible check on stock is always available; this method eliminates labelling. By having the shelves only just the right size, one is never tempted to put other articles in front of the stock jars or on top of them. Another admirable arrangement is the use of steel binnage in the form of pigeon holes.

Talking of storage brings us to another point. In the workshop have a multi-tiered steel or timber rack, which can be used to lay out all the individual components of the sub-assembly which is being worked on. This keeps the bench clear and makes the parts easier to find than if they are put into boxes. If mounted on wheels it can be moved out into the garage and is particularly convenient when you are making up an assembly direct on to the car.

Another useful tip while on the subject of storage is this: household guttering, if fixed to the wall in lengths of about 4–6 ft. one above the other, forms a very good storage for rodding, angle and tubing and keeps it off the floor.

A low and very sturdy bench about 18 in. high and 3 ft. × 2 ft., on which to dismantle the heavier assemblies such as the gear-box and axles, can be very useful. This should be movable and can be stowed away in the garage when not in use in the workshop. The trestle table mentioned before for use on bodywork should be 6 ft. × 4 ft. and have folding legs so that it will go flat against the wall when not in use.

It would be easy to go on and on with a list of desirable workshop equipment, but from here the reader will be left to find out his own requirements as the work proceeds. Before the chapter ends, however, we would like to mention the use of the drawing board and drawing instruments. If the reader is not familiar with the use of these, then let us hasten to explain that there is no need to be a competent draughtsman in order to benefit from them. It is so much easier to think out a design on paper, and iron out all the snags before embarking on the much longer task of making the piece under consideration, than to make a mistake and have to start all over again. Rubbing out mistakes on a drawing is a moment's work which may save hours of hard work later.

Having very briefly described the place in which we hope that you will spend many happy hours, we must now get back to work on our own Vintage and Thoroughbred restorations.

"Whatever is rightly done, however humble, is noble."—HENRY ROYCE.

APPENDIX I

Names and Addresses of Recommended Firms

Name	Address	Service or Product
Abingdon, King Dick, Ltd.	Abingdon Works, Kings Road, Birmingham, 11.	Spanners.
Amal Ltd.	Holford Road, Witton, Birmingham, 6.	Control joints.
George Angus Ltd.	Oil Seals Division, Coast Road, Wallsend-on-Tyne, Northumberland.	Oil seals.
Associated Engineering (Sales) Ltd.	Highgate Road, Birmingham, 12.	Pistons, rings, gudgeon-pins, circlips, liners.
Automotive Products Ltd.	Tachbrook Road, Leamington Spa, Warwickshire.	Hydraulic brakes and clutches.
Bailey and Mackey Ltd.	7 Baltimore Road, Birmingham, 22.	Pressure gauges.
Basset Down Farms Ltd. (Engineering).	Basset Down, Nr. Swindon, Wilts.	Complete restorations.
G. Becktel Ltd.	35 Carver Street, Birmingham, B1 3AT	Screws, nuts, washers, bolts, spring washers, split pins.
A. H. Bedford and Son Ltd.	The Corn Exchange, Team Street, Tenbury Wells, Worcestershire.	Dial painting.
Richard Berry & Co. Ltd.	Birmingham Road, West Bromwich, Staffs.	Road springs.
Birmingham Safety Glass Co. Ltd.	Lower Essex Street, Birmingham 5.	Plate and safety glass.
Borg-Warner Ltd.	Letchworth, Herts.	Inverted tooth silent chain and roller chain.
Bosch Ltd.	P.O. Box 166, Rhodes Way, Watford, Herts.	Electrical equipment.
Brammer Transmissions Ltd.	Hudson Road, Leeds, LS9 7DF	Whittle belting.
Brireten Engineering Ltd.	Brireten Street, Walsall, Staffs.	Machined parts, hardening, grinding, gear cutting.
Britachrome Ltd.	Cope Street, Birmingham, 18.	Hard chrome plating.
B.B.A. Group Ltd.	Cleckheaton, Yorks.	Brake and clutch linings.
British Piston Ring Co. Ltd.	Holbrook Lane, Coventry.	Cast-iron bar.
Brown and Cook Ltd.	37 Ludgate Hill, Birmingham, 3.	Upholstery supplies.
Brylite Batteries Ltd.	Facet Road, Birmingham, 20.	Wood-cased batteries.
W. H. M. Burgess Ltd.	Brunel Road, Old Oak Common Lane, East Acton, London, W.3.	S.U. carburetters, post-1930.
W. Canning and Co. Ltd.	Great Hampton Street, Birmingham, 18.	Skalene descaler.
Chas. Cantrill Ltd.	69 Carver Street, Birmingham, 1.	Cork clutch relining, cork washers.
Central Pneumatic Supplies Ltd.	120 Elkington Street, Birmingham, B6 4SJ	Pipe fittings, drain plugs, filler caps.
Central Wheel Co. Ltd.	Lichfield Road, Water Orton, Warwickshire.	Wire wheel rebuilding.
City of Birmingham Workshop for the Blind.	62 Woodville Road, Birmingham, 17.	Coconut mats.

Name	Address	Service or Product
Clayton, Dewandre Co. Ltd.	Titanic Works, Lincoln.	Vacuum servo motors.
Commercial Ignition Co. Ltd.	Longfield Works, Denham, Middlesex.	Bosch magneto and electrical equipment overhauls.
Commercial X-Rays Ltd.	Foundry Lane, Birmingham, 40.	X-ray and crack detecting.
Complete Automobilist Ltd.	39 Main Street, Baston, Nr. Peterborough.	Vintage bodywork and electrical accessories.
Connolly Bros. (Curriers) Ltd.	Chalton Street, London, N.W.1.	Leatherwork renovation.
Cooper & Co. Ltd.	Brynmawr, Breconshire.	Felt washers.
T. D. Cross and Sons Ltd.	Shady Lane, Birmingham, 22b.	Sprockets.
Joseph Dixon Tool Co. Ltd.	Bott Lane, Walsall, Staffs.	Bone folders.
Dunbar and Cook Ltd.	107 New John Street, Birmingham, 6.	Balancing.
Charles Eades Ltd.	New Summer Street, Birmingham, 19.	Engraving.
W. G. Eaton.	18 Freeman Street, Birmingham, 5.	Leather clutch linings, belting and straps.
Electric Service Co. (B'ham) Ltd.	32 Lower Essex Street, Birmingham, 5.	Electrical repairs and supplies.
Enfield Auto Electrical Ltd.	61 Main Avenue, Bush Hill Park, Enfield, Middlesex.	Magneto and electrical equipment overhaul.
Exceloid Ltd.	Greenhoughs Row, Lichfield, Staffs.	Steering-wheel covering.
Fergus Engineering Ltd.	Dorrington, Spalding, Lincs.	Complete restorations.
William Gabb Ltd.	127 Barr Street, Birmingham, 19.	Non-ferrous metals.
Hallam, Sleigh & Cheston Ltd.	Widney Works, Bagot Street, Birmingham, 4.	Coachbuilders' suppliers.
Hardy Spicer Ltd.	Chester Road, Birmingham, 24.	Propeller-shafts.
Heat Treatments Ltd.	Holford Road, Birmingham, 6.	Heat treatment.
Heaven Dowsett and Co. Ltd.	197 Shady Lane, Birmingham, 22a.	Tufnol, ebonite and plastics.
J. A. Hemming Ltd.	Pelsall Road, Brownhills, Staffs.	Shim steel.
H. M. Hobson Ltd.	Fordhouses, Wolverhampton.	Telegauge repairs.
Hofmann and Burton Ltd.	Fairfield Works, Reading Road, Henley-on-Thames, Oxon.	Engine and complete car overhaul, resplining of hubs.
Hopton & Sons Ltd.	Union Works, Market Harborough, Leics.	Bent ash hoodsticks.
Hurst Hill Enamel Co. Ltd.	Biddings Lane, Deepfields, Nr. Bilston, Staffs.	Vitreous enamel.
Industrial Bearings (Wellington) Ltd.	Orleton Lane, Wellington, Telford, Shropshire	Ball, roller and taper roller bearings. Oil seals. Roller chain and sprockets. Obsolete brake linings.
Albert Jagger Ltd.	Green Lane, Walsall, Staffs.	Coachbuilders' supplies.
W. G. James Ltd.	Starts Hill Avenue, Farnborough, Orpington, Kent.	Valves.
Jenolite Ltd.	Boundary House, Boston Road, London, W.7.	Jenolite.
Johnson Matthey and Co. Ltd.	65 Vittoria Street, Birmingham, 1.	Silver solder.

Name	Address	Service or Product
Kayser, Ellison and Co. Ltd.	Carlisle Steel Works, Sheffield, 5.	Alloy steels.
A. J. Lander & Co. Ltd.	55 Stanhope St., Birmingham, 12.	Metal spinnings.
Latex Cushion Co. Ltd.	830 Kingsbury Road, Birmingham, 24.	Latex foam cushions.
Laystall Engineering Co. Ltd.	53 Great Suffolk Street, London, S.E.1.	Brake-drum lining and crank balancing.
Lewthwaite Miller Ltd.	Middlemore Lane West, Aldridge, Staffs, WS9 8DS	Inverted tooth silent chain, roller chain, sprockets, ball and roller bearings.
Lifford Engineering Co. Ltd.	47B Factory Centre, Kings Norton, Birmingham, 30.	Engine and complete car overhaul. Reboring, crank grinding. Polishing, plating, stove enamelling.
Marples and Beasley Ltd.	5 South Road, Birmingham, 19.	Enamelled badge repairs.
Metal Treatments Ltd.	86 Heathmill Lane, Birmingham, 9.	Stove enamelling.
Metallisation Ltd.	Pear Tree Lane, Dudley, Staffs.	Metal spraying.
Metalock (Britain) Ltd.	Grand Buildings, Trafalgar Square, London, W.C.2.	Metalock casting repair.
Miller-Bridges Ltd.	Humpage Road, Bordesley Green, Birmingham, 9.	Nuts, screws, washers and bolts, spring washers and split pins.
Joseph Nichols and Sons, Ltd.	Cheapside Works, Birmingham, 12.	Wire stone guards.
Northampton Auto-rads Ltd.	39 Regent Square, Northampton.	Radiator and petrol tank repairs.
R. H. Nuttall Ltd.	97 St. Clements Road, Birmingham, 7.	Leather and fibre washers.
E. Perkins and Co. Ltd.	19 Selborne Street, Walsall, Staffs.	Plastic knobs.
E. Potterton & Son Ltd.	Laurel Road, Birmingham, 21.	Pipe manipulators in non-ferrous and stainless steel.
Arthur Price Ltd.	Vevo Works, Park Lane, Birmingham, 6.	Windscreens.
Quality Springs and Productions Ltd.	St. Georges Road, Redditch.	Springs other than road springs.
Ram Research Ltd.	Susan Wood, Chislehurst, Kent, BR7 5RD.	Hot paint.
Renold Ltd.	Renold Works, Didsbury, Manchester.	Roller chains.
Thomas Richfield and Son Ltd.	Broadstone Place, Blandford Street, London, W.1.	Bowden cables.
Henry Righton & Co. Ltd.	Brookvale Road, Birmingham, 6 and Depots in all large cities	Non-ferrous metals and stainless steel stockholders.
Ripaults Ltd.	Southbury Road, Enfield, Middx.	Armoured electrical cable.
Rocol Ltd.	Rocol House, Swillington, Nr. Leeds.	Heavy gear oil, anti-scuffing paste.
Rubery Owen and Co. Ltd.	Chassis Repair Section, Meeting Street, Wednesbury, Staffs.	Chassis frame repairs.
Rudders & Paynes Ltd.	Hollies Avenue, Cannock, Staffs.	Timber supplies and bent ash hoodsticks.
Llewellyn Ryland Ltd.	Balsall Heath, Birmingham, 12.	Paint and varnish.

Name	Address	Service or Product
George Salter and Co. Ltd.	High Street, West Bromwich, Staffs.	Flexible roller bearings.
Schofield and Samson Ltd.	Spencer Works, Roger Street, London, W.C.1.	Gear wheels.
Scraggs, Whatley & Co. Ltd.	212 New Kings Road, London, S.W.6.	Ball and roller bearing reconditioning
Seager (Bearings) Ltd.	52 Goldsmith Road, Birmingham, 11.	Ball and roller bearings.
Silentbloc Ltd.	Manor Royal, Crawley, Sussex.	Silentbloc flexible bearings.
C. E. Smith Ltd.	82 Franchise Street, Birmingham, 22b.	Reboring, crank grinding, balancing.
J. E. Smith.	24 Lyndon Croft, Marston Green, Birmingham.	Magneto repairs.
Sorber Accessories Ltd.	16a Osten Mews, South Kensington, London, S.W.7.	Reconditioning of Hartford shock absorbers.
Speedometer Supply Co. Ltd.	34 Shelton Street, London, W.C.2.	Speedometer and tachometer repairs.
Springfield Wheel Co. Ltd.	14 Medina Road, Birmingham, 11.	Wire wheel rebuilding.
S.U. Carburetter Co. Ltd.	Wood Lane, Birmingham, 24.	Pre-1930 S.U. carburetter repairs.
Herbert Terry and Sons Ltd.	Redditch, Worcester.	Valve springs.
F. W. Thornton & Sons Ltd.	57 Wyle Cop, Shrewsbury, Shropshire	Pistons, rings, liners, valves and springs.
Tool Treatments (Chemical) Ltd.	Colliery Road, Birmingham Road, West Bromwich, Staffordshire.	Chemical black.
G. H. Turner & Co. Ltd.	Pountney Street, Wolverhampton.	Gear cutting.
Venesta (Veneers) Ltd.	Hayseech Road, Halesowen, Staffs.	Hardwood veneers.
Vintage Racing Cars Ltd.	Derby Road Garage, Northampton.	Autovac repairs and spares.
Vintage Tyre Supplies Ltd.	Jackman Mews, Neasden, London, N.W.10.	Beaded edge and Vintage sizes of tire.
James Walker and Co. Ltd.	Depots throughout the world.	Copper and asbestos gaskets, Gaskoid and Nebar jointing materials.
Walker Spencer Components Ltd.	5 High Street, Birmingham, 14.	Nuts, screws, washers and bolts.
Walsall Locks and Cart Gear Ltd.	Neale Street, Walsall, Staffs.	Door locks.
A. P. Warren Ltd.	37 Sheen Road, Richmond, Surrey.	Stud extractor.
West London Repair Co. Ltd.	5 Lancaster Road, Wimbledon, London, S.W.19.	Wheel rebuilding and road spring reconditioning.
Wilcot (Parent) Co. Ltd.	Fishponds, Bristol.	Leather gaiters.
I. Wilkinson and Son Ltd.	Stafford Street, Derby.	Coachwork restoration.
F. B. Willmott Ltd.	36 River Street, Birmingham, 5.	Starter rings.
Jonas Woodhead Ltd.	Kirkstall Road, Leeds.	Road springs.
Jonas Woodhead and Son (Scotland) Ltd.	Chapelhall, Lanarkshire.	Hartford shock-absorber repairs.
Woodstock Weaving Co. Ltd.	Seale Street, Mansfield Road, Derby.	Bonnet tape.
Zenith Carburetter Co. Ltd.	Honeypot Lane, Stanmore, Middx.	Zenith and Solex carburetters.

Clubs and Registers Specialising in Vintage and Thoroughbred Motor-Cars

Club or Register	Address of Secretary
A.C. Owners Club	28 Downsview Road, Upper Norwood, London, S.E.19.
Aston Martin Owners Club Ltd.	22 The Mall, East Sheen, London, S.W.14.
Alvis Owners Club	31 Pennington Drive, Oatlands Chase, Weybridge, Surrey.
The Alvis Register	'Lawnview', Towpath, Shepperton, Middlesex.
Auburn Cord Duesenberg Club	830 Miranda Green, Palo Alto, Ca. 94306. Maple Rise, Oakhanger-Bordon, Hants, England.
Bentley Drivers Club Ltd.	76a High St., Long Crendon, Aylesbury, Bucks.
B.M.W. Car Club	3 The Avenue, Chinnor, Oxford OX9 4PA.
Bugatti Owners Club	40 Bartholomew St., Newbury, Berks.
Bullnose Morris Club	3 Glebe Lane, Great Shelford, Cambridge.
Citroen Car Club	32 Lower Road, Fetcham, Leatherhead, Surrey.
Delage Owners Club and Register	6 Hillbrow Road, Withdean, Brighton, Sussex.
Fiat Car Club of Great Britain	The Mount, Willingham Road, Lea, Gainsborough, Lincs.
Fiat Motor Club (G.B.)	3 Woodfield Road, Ashtead, Surrey.
Fiat Register	Dickenson and Norris Ltd., Melton Mowbray, Leicestershire.
Frazer-Nash Car Club	Shellingford House, Nr. Faringdon, Berks.
20 Ghost Club	Aldwick Hundred, Aldwick, Sussex.
Les Hommes a L'Hispano	37 St. James Place, London. S.W.1.
Humber Register (1900–1930)	108 Barnett Wood Lane, Ashtead, Surrey.
Lagonda Club	35 Cobbold Ave., Eastbourne, Sussex.
Lancia Motor Club	10 Arthur Road, Motspur Road, New Malden, Surrey.
Lea-Francis Owners Club	105 Boxley Drive, West Bridgford, Nottingham, NG2 7GN
Mercedes-Benz Club	Hollyhurst House, Barton-under-Needwood, Staffs.
M.G. Car Club	c/o The M.G. Car Co. Ltd., Abingdon-on-Thames, Berks.
Rapier Register	7 Gray's Walk, Druids Green, Cowbridge, Glam.
Renault Owners Club	15 Lowshoe Lane, Romford, Essex.
Riley Motor Club	Riley Motors Ltd., Abingdon-on-Thames, Oxon.
Riley Register	162 Leicester Road, Glenhills, Leicester.
Rover Sports Register	11 Woodhall Drive, Pinner, Middlesex.
British Salmson Owners Club	14 Rowhill Crescent, Aldershot, Hants.
French Salmson Register	Apple Tree Cottage, Rectory Close, Ashtead, Surrey.
Singer Owners Club	31 Rivershill, Watton-at-Stone, Hertford.
Sunbeam S.T.D. Register	5 Wood Lodge, Wimbledon, London, S.W.19.
Sunbeam-Talbot Owners Club	Ladbroke Hall, Barlby Road, London, W.10.
Vintage Sports Car Club Ltd.	Bone Lane, Newbury, Berks.

Manufacturers and Stockists able to supply certain items of new spares for Vintage and Thoroughbred Motor-cars

Make of Car	*Manufacturer or Stockist*
Alfa-Romeo	Alfa-Romeo, Via Marco Ulpio Traiano 33, Milano, Italy. Thomson and Taylor Ltd., Canada Road, Oyster Lane, Byfleet, Weybridge, Surrey.
Alvis	Red Triangle Auto Services, Common Lane, Kenilworth, Warwickshire.
Aston-Martin	Friary Motors Ltd., Straight Road, Old Windsor, Bucks. Winter Gardens Garages, 139 The Arches, Shepherds Bush, London, W.14.
Auburn Cord Duesenberg Durant Franklin Graham Hupmobile Star Stern's Knight Tucker	Auburn Cord Duesenberg Co., Auburn, Indiana, U.S.A.
Bentley (Pre-1932)	Hofmann and Burton Ltd., Fairfield Works, Reading Road, Henley-on-Thames, Oxon. Elmdown Vintage Automobiles Ltd., Elmdown, Ramsbury, Wiltshire.
Bentley (Post-1932)	Rippon Bros. Ltd., Viaduct Street, Huddersfield, Yorks.
Bugatti	Automobiles E. Bugatti, 10 Rue de la Commanderie, Molsheim, Bas-Rhin, France. H. H. Posner, 28 Hayward Road, Oxford. A. F. Loyens, 32 Rue de la Montague, Hamm, Luxemburg. J. Lemon Burton, Edgware Road, Cricklewood, London, N.W.2.
Delage Delahaye Hotchkiss	Société Hotchkiss-Delahaye, 239 Bd. Anatole-France, Saint Denis, France.
French makes	Depanato & Cie., 1 Rue Giroust, Nogent-le-Rotrou, (E et L), France.
Ford	The Ford Motor Co. Ltd., Dagenham, Essex.
Jowett	Jowett Cars Ltd., Howden Clough, Birstall, Batley, Yorks.
Lagonda	Maurice Leo Ltd., Gregories Road Garage, Beaconsfield, Bucks.
Lancia	Lancia (England) Ltd., Lancia Works, Alperton, Wembley, Middlesex. Lancia & C., Torino, Italy.
Lea-Francis	A. B. Price Ltd., Hardwick House, Castle Road, Studley, Worcs.
Morgan	Morgan Motor Co., Malvern Link, Worcestershire.
Mercedes-Benz	Daimler Benz A.G., Stuttgart, Germany.
Mercer	Vincent Galloni, Lincoln Garage, Chambers Street, Trenton, New Jersey, U.S.A.

Make of Car	*Manufacturer or Stockist*
M.G.	M.G. Car Co. Ltd., Abingdon-on-Thames, Oxon.
Oldsmobile	Lex Garages Ltd., 2 Lexington Street, London, W.1.
Peugeot	Société Peugeot, 102 Rue Danton, Levallois-Perret, Seine, France.
Renault	Welhams Ltd., 7 Surbiton Hill Road, Surbiton, Surrey.
Rolls-Royce	Rolls-Royce Ltd., Spares Dept., Pym's Lane, Crewe, Cheshire.
Stutz	A. K. Miller, West Topsham, Vermont, U.S.A.
Sunbeam	R. C. Carter, Ninefields Nursery, St. Albans, Herts.
Talbot (English)	J. Bland, 27 Southfields Road, London, S.W.18.

INDEX

INDEX

The numerals in **heavy type** refer to the *figure numbers* of drawings in the text

185

Recommended Suppliers of Parts and Services in U.S.A.

Name	Address	Service or Product
The Acme Garage	16848 Alisal Ct., San Lorenzo, CA 94580	Complete restoration.
Adams Custom Engines, Inc.	806 Glendale Ave., Sparks, NV 89431	Complete restoration.
Amchem Products, Inc.	Brookside Ave., Ambler, PA 19002	Pre-paint chemicals for corrosion resistance and paint adhesion.
American Crankshaft Co.	4150 Yancey Rd., P.O. Box 1498, Charlotte, NC 28232	Remanufacture of steel crankshafts.
Antique Auto House, Inc.	P.O. Box 685 3329 No. Garfield, Loveland, CO 80537	Restorer.
Antique Auto Shop, Inc.	R.D. #2, Pleasantville, NJ 08232	Restorer.
Paul Beechy	Winesburg, OH 44690	Restorer.
Belote's Bayshore Garage	949 Broadway, Dunedin, FL 33528	Mechanical restoration.
Bill's Metal Polishing, Inc.	David Rd. & Camden Ave., Magnolia, NJ 08049	Metal plating.
Al T. Boatz	980 Carr St., Denver, CO 80215	Oil lamps.
William A. Borba	908 9th St., Turlock, CA 95380	Restorer.
Ron Brown Top Sockets	P.O. Box 1516, Auburn, CA 95603	Top sockets, hood formers.
Burchill Antique Auto Parts	4150 24th Ave., U.S. 25 North, Port Huron, MI 48060	Parts.
Carter's Cut & Cover Shop	P.O. Box 80, 800 East 6th St., Beardstown, IL 62618	Ford top and upholstery kits.
James F. Cecil	906 Forest, Morristown, TN 37814	Wood graining.
Chelsea Auto Parts Co.	22 N. Cameron St., Harrisburg, PA 17101	Parts.
Clark-Patton, Inc.	4775 Curtis, Plymouth, MI 48170	Complete restoration.
Cloyes Gear Co.	17214 Roseland Rd., Cleveland, OH 44112	Timing chain sprockets.
Coker Tire Co., Inc.	5100 Brainerd Rd., Chattanooga, TN 37411	Tires.
Custom Auto Service	302 French St., Santa Ana, CA 92701	Restoration.
Del's Auto Body	Glen St., Glen Cove, NY 11542	Chassis restoration.
Dick's Autobody	Marshfield, WI 54449	Restorer.
Leif Drexler	P.O. Box 128, Sickerville, NJ 08081	Upholstery and topping.
E.I.du Pont de Nemours & Co., Inc.	Refinish Sales, Room B-5376, Wilmington, DE 19898	Spray paint materials.
Durland Edwards	350 Slocum St., Swoyersville, PA 18704	Restorer.
Fleet Supply Co.	2896 Central Ave., Detroit, MI 48209	Complete restoration.
Franklin Service Co.	1405 E. Kleindale Rd., Tucson, AZ 85719	Complete restoration.
General Chain & Belt Co.	2120 Jericho Turnpike, Garden City Park, NY 11040	Renold & Coventry roller chains.
James Gullihur	Miller Lane, Fernley, NV 89408	Complete restoration.
The Gwilliam Company	Crosby St., Danbury, CT 06810	Ball and roller bearings.

Name	Address	Service or Product
Head Gasket Company	164 So. Park, San Francisco, CA 94107	Custom made gaskets.
Heiges Bros. Wheel Service	633 N. Cameron St., Harrisburg, PA 17101	Wire wheels.
Henry's Antique Car Shop	174 Somers Landing Rd., Oceanville, NJ 08231	Restorer.
Hercules Welding & Machine Co.	762 N. Uber St., Philadelphia, PA 17030	Metal spraying, rebabbitting, machining.
Hibernia Auto Restorations, Inc.	Maple Terrace, Hibernia, NJ 07842	Complete restoration.
J. B. Hildreth	7305 Lakehurst, Dallas, TX 75230	Restorer.
Hoe Sportcar	446 Newtown Turnpike, Weston, CT 06880	Mechanical-chassis repair and restoration.
Horseless Carriage Shop (Josey, Inc.)	P.O. Drawer 898, 1881 Main St., Dunedin, FL 33528	Complete restoration.
Andy Hotton Associates	510 Savage Rd., Belleville, MI 48111	Restorer.
E. F. Houghton & Co.	301 W. Lehigh Ave., Philadelphia, PA 17133	Steamer oil.
Houpert Machine Co.	Atlantic Ave. Berlin, NJ 08009	Complete machine shop.
J & J Chrom Plating	1000 Orange Ave., West Haven, CT 06516	Chrome plating.
Jahns Quality Pistons, Inc.	2662 Lacy St., Los Angeles, CA 90031	Alluminium alloy pistons.
Johnson Iron & Machine Co.	P.O. Box 435 East Grand Forks, MN 56721	Mechanical restoration.
George Kella	411 N. Parma, Parma, MI 49269	Upholstery and top refurbishing.
Klein Kars, Inc.	2650 Columbia Ave., Lancaster, PA 17603	Parts.
Kline, Savidge Co. Inc.	163 No. 3rd St., Philadelphia, PA 19106	Custom leather straps.
Kling Machine & Tool	2101 Calumet St., Clearwater, FL 33515	Machining.
Lackawanna Leather Co.	Richard Mine Rd., Wharton, NJ 07885	Leather.
Lancaster County Motors	420 N. Prince St., Lancaster, PA 17603	Restorer.
Lancaster Glass Corp.	220 W. Main St., Lancaster, OH 43130	Mangin mirrors, Model A tail and cowl lenses.
LeBaron Bonney Co.	14 Washington St., Amesbury, MA 01913	Upholstery and tops.
Philip Lebzelter & Son	Old Manheim Pike, Lancaster, PA 17603	Top bows.
Lester Tire Co.	26881 Cannon Rd., Bedford Heights, OH 44146	Tires, brass moldings, magnetos.
Lonsdale & Young	2323 W. Fairview Ave., Montgomery, AL 36108	Complete restoration only.
The Lunkenheimer Company	Beekman, Waverly & Tremont, Cincinnati, OH 45214	Gauges, pipe fittings, and supplies.
McCord Corp.	2850 E. Grand Blvd., Detroit, MI 48202	Gaskets.
Chet McLean Automobile Upholstery	1307 Portia St., Los Angeles, CA 90026	Upholstery and tops.
Joseph R. McNutt	4228 State Rd., Akron, OH 44110	Restorer.
Merit Auto Service	1 Way St., Woodridge, NJ 07075	Restoration, appraisals, magneto and carb. rebuilding.

Name	Address	Service or Product
Metlab Company	1000 E. Mermaid Lane, Philadelphia, PA 19118	Heat treatment, magnafluxing, X-raying of metal.
Middletown Leather Co.	200 Valentine St., Hackettstown, NJ 07840	Upholstery hides.
Morse Chain Div., Borg-Warner Corp.	So. Aurora St., Ithaca, NY 14850	Timing chains.
G. H. Mos Co.	731 Sansom St., Philadelphia, PA 19106	Enameling of emblems and name plates.
Motor Parts Depot, Inc.	211 E. College, Louisville, KY 40203	Restorer.
Narragusett Restoration Co., Inc.	P.O. Box 36, Kingston, RI 02881	Authentic wiring harness reproduction.
Nelkco Bearing & Machine	2101 Allport Ave., Santa Fe Springs, CA 90670	Engine boring and align boring.
Nisonger	35 Bartels Place, New Rochelle, NY 10801	Rebuilding and restoration of instruments.
Oakrest Machine Shop	2110 Boda St., Springfield, OH 45503	Custom wood wheels, wire wheels, and metal hardware.
Oaks Bows	122 Ramsey Ave., Chambersburg, PA 17201	Top bows.
Edgar O. Oeters	162 Lippincott St., Philadelphia, PA	Fabricated/molded plastics; fibre; bakelite parts.
Page's Model A Garage	Main St., Haverhill, NH 03765	Ford restorer, manufacturer of replacement top wood.
Pearson & Marzian, Inc.	501 E. St. Catherine St., Louisville, KY 40203	Restorer.
Pearson Restorations	1511 So. 25th St., Kansas City, KS 66106	Restorer.
R. O. Peters Garage	Bethlehem, PA 18016	Restorer.
Philadelphia Auto Radiator	2120 Fairmont Ave., Philadelphia, PA 19123	Radiator repairs.
Philadelphia Gear Corp.	So. Gulph Rd., King of Prussia, PA 19406	Gears.
Tommy Protsman	2542 Young Rd., Atlanta, GA 30317	Restoration of brass horns and lamps.
Pulfer & Williams	5059 Washburn Ave. So., Minneapolis, MN 55410	Radiator scripts, enamel emblems, hub cap inserts, plates, badges, motometers.
Raybestos-Manhattan, Inc.	Stiegel St., Manheim, PA 17545	Brake and clutch linings.
The Restoration Shop	Cranberry Rd., Jamesburg, NJ 08831	Restorer.
Richard's Auto Restoration	P.O. Box 83, Wyoming, PA 18664	Restorer.
C.A. Rosencrans	406 Princeton Rd., Haddonfield, NJ 08033	Custom brass parts, copperelectro-forms.
Schaeffer & Long, Inc.	210 Davis Rd., Magnolia, NJ 08049	Restorer and body builder.
J.M. Seasholtz & Sons	100 First Ave., West Reading, PA 19602	Porcelain enameling for exhaust manifolds.
Snyder Brothers	R.D. #2, Mount Joy, PA 17552	Restorers.
Ken Sorensen	38 No. Hill Ave., Pasadena, CA 91106	Model T Ford top kits.
Sports and Vintage Motors	901 Walnut St., Boulder, CO 80302	Mechanical restoration.

Name	Address	Service or Product
Steering Wheel Exchange	14214 Rosecrans Ave., La Mirada, CA 90638	Refinishing rubber steering wheels.
Stitts Mfg. & Supply Co.	2771 Brunswick Pike, Trenton, NJ 08608	Upholstery and top materials.
Stuard's Foreign Motorcar	122 Ramsey Ave., Chambersburg, PA 17201	Mechanical restoration.
Wm. E. Swigart, Jr.	Swigart Museum, Museum Park, Huntingdon, PA 16652	License plates and automobile name plates.
J.C. Taylor	55 Long Lane, Upper Darby, PA 19082	Insurance.
Top Brass, Inc.	637 Baxter Ave., Louisville, KY 40204	Restorations, rebuilds Bosch magnetos.
Universal Tire Co.	2650 Columbia Ave., Lancaster, PA 17603	Tires, brass stemmed tubes, technical information.
Vetco New England Inc.	East St., Northfield, MA 01360	Body repairs, painting, upholstery, tops.
Vintage Auto Restorations, Inc.	P.O. Box 83, Ridgefield, CT 06877	Chassis and mechanical restoration.
Vintage Auto Shop	430 Mill St., Cincinnati, OH 45215	Complete restoration.
James F. Wild, Inc.	P.O. Box 1584, 345 Queen St., Lancaster, PA 17603	Paint supplies (Ditzler).
Wiley Metalspinning Specialties & Co.	237 Jacksonville Rd., Hatboro, PA 19040	Metal spinning.
Wilkinson & Sharp	233 Philmont Ave., Feasterville, PA 19047	Restoration.

APPENDIX V

American Clubs Specializing in Antique and Classic Automobiles

Club	Address
AC Owners Club, American Centre	44 Barrett St., Needham, MA 02192
Antique Automobile Club of America	501 W. Governor Rd., Hershey, PA 17033
Aston Martin Owners Club	195 Mt. Paran Rd., N.W., Atlanta, GA 30327
Auburn-Cord-Duesenberg Club	P.O. Box 11635, Palo Alto, CA 94306
The American Bugatti Club	8724 E. Garvey Ave., Rosemead, CA 91770
Buick Collectors Club of America	4730 Centre Ave., Pittsburg, PA 15213
Cadillac-La Salle Club	3340 Poplar Dr., Warren, MI 48091
Classic Car Club of America	P.O. Box 443, Madison, NJ 07940
DeSoto Club of America	P.O. Box 4912, Columbus, OH 43202
Early Ford V8 Club of America	P.O. Box 2122, San Leandro, CA 94577
Model A Ford Club of America	P.O. Box 2564, Pomona, CA 91766
Model A Restorers Club	P.O. Box 1930 A, Dearborn, MI 48121
Model T Ford Club International	P.O. Box 11253, Chicago, IL 60611
Penn-Ohio "A" Ford Club	R.D. #1, Stewart Dr., Rittman, OH 44270
The H. H. Franklin Club	P.O. Box 66, Syracuse, NY 13215
Horseless Carriage Club of America	9031 E. Florence Ave., Downey, CA 90240
Hupmobile-Graham Club of America	P.O. Box 215, Glenview, IL 60025
Isotta-Fraschini Owner's Association	9704 Illinois St., Hebron, IL 60034
The Lagonda Club	10 Crestwood Trail, Sparta, NJ 07871
Lincoln Continental Owners Club	P.O. Box 549, Nogales, AZ 85621
Marmon Owners Club	5364 Stuart Ave., S.E., Grand Rapids, MI 49508
The Mercedes-Benz Club of America, Inc.	P.O. Box 66, Glenview, Ill 60025
Milestone Car Society	2422 Inglewood North, Minneapolis, MN 55404
Oldsmobile Club of America	3104 No. Inglewood St., Arlington, VA 22207
Packard Automobile Classics	P.O. Box 2808, Oakland, CA 94618
Packard International Motor Car	P.O. Box 1347, Costa Mesa, CA 92626
Pierce-Arrow Society	c/o Aldrich Iverson, West Concord, MN 55985
Rolls-Royce Owners Club	1822 N. Second St., Harrisburg, PA 17102
Steam Automobile Club of America	333 N. Michigan Ave., Chicago, IL 60601
Veteran Motor Car Club of America	105 Elm St., Andover, MA 01810
The Vintage Chevrolet Club of America	P.O. Box 1135, Bellflower, CA 90706
Vintage Sports Car Club of America	53 Rockledge Rd., Bronxville, NY 10708
The Wills Club	705 S. Clyde Ave., Kissimmee, FL 32741

APPENDIX VI

American Sources of Replacement Parts for Antique
and Classic Automobiles

Make of Car	*Name*	*Address*
Auburn	Auburn-Cord-Dusenberg Co.	P.O. Box 15520, Tulsa, OK 74115
Bentley	Antiques, Inc.	P.O. Box 1887, Muskogee, OK 74401
Bentley	Klein Kars	2650 Columbia Ave., Lancaster, PA 17603
Cadillac	Jeff Schneider	19 So. Union St., Bay Shore, NY 11706
Chevrolet	Obsolete Chevrolet Parts Co.	506 West Marion St., P.O. Box 497, Nashville, GA 31639
Cord	Auburn-Cord-Duesenberg Co.	P.O. Box 15520, Tulsa, OK 74115
Duesenberg	Auburn-Cord-Duesenberg Co.	P.O. Box 15520, Tulsa, OK 74115
Durant	Auburn-Cord-Duesenberg Co.	P.O. Box 15520, Tulsa, OK 74115
Ford	Antique Auto Parts	173 Hotchkiss St., Jamestown, NY 14701
Ford	Continental Motors Corp.	205 Market St., Muskegon, MI 49482
Ford	"Tin Lizzie" Antique Auto Parts	5259 North Rose St., Rosemont, IL 60018
Ford	Mark Auto Company	Layton, NJ 07851
Ford	Snyder's Antique Auto Parts	12925 Woodworth Rd., New Springfield, OH 44443
Ford	Rick's Antique Auto	P.O. Box 662, Shawnee Mission, KS 66201
Ford	Page's Model A Garage	Haverhill, NH 03765
Ford	Maupin Auto Salvage, Inc.	315 W. 3rd, P.O. Box 463, Hutchinson, KS 67501
Ford	Antique Auto Service & Supply	P.O. Box 6072, Lincoln, NE 68506
Ford	Gaslight Auto Parts, Inc.	P.O. Box 291, Urbana, OH 43078
Ford	Tom Donahue, Jr.	Scottsbluff, NE 69361
Franklin	Auburn-Cord-Duesenberg Co.	P.O. Box 15520, Tulsa, OK 74115
Graham	Auburn-Cord-Duesenberg Co.	P.O. Box 15520, Tulsa, OK 74115
Hupmobile	Auburn-Cord-Duesenberg Co.	P.O. Box 15520, Tulsa, OK 74115
Lincoln	Continental Service	P.O. Box 355, Blue Bell, PA 19422
Lincoln	Atlantic Auto Parts	19020 Anelo St., Gardena, CA 90247
MG	Abingdon Spares, Ltd.	1329 Highland Ave., Needham, MA 02192
Oldsmobile	Jack Miller	P.O. Box 159, Buchanan, TN 38222
Oldsmobile	Duane Steele	12442 Topaz St., Garden Grove, CA 92845
Oldsmobile	Carlo Cola	39 Jasper St., Valley Stream, NY 11580
Oldsmobile	Max Hineman	13020 Turner, DeWitt, MI 48820
Pierce-Arrow	Irvin Blonder	1119 W. Orange Grove, Burbank, CA 91506
Packard	Lancaster County Motors	420 N. Prince St., Lancaster, PA 17603
Packard	Klein Kars	2650 Columbia Ave., Lancaster, PA 17603
Packard	Classic Cars, Inc.	P.O. Box 56M, Morristown, NJ 07960
Packard	Packard Parts Unlimited	Groveland, MA 01834

Make of Car	Name	Address
Rolls-Royce	Klein Kars	2650 Columbia Ave., Lancaster, PA 17603
Rolls-Royce	Antiques, Inc.	P.O. Box 1887, Muskogee, OK 74401
Star	Auburn-Cord-Duesenberg Co.	P.O. Box 15520, Tulsa, OK 74115
Stern's Knight	Auburn-Cord-Duesenberg Co.	P.O. Box 15520, Tulsa, OK 74115
Stutz	A. K. Miller	West Topsham, VT 05086
Tucker	Auburn-Cord-Duesenberg Co.	P.O. Box 15520, Tulsa, OK 74115